THE SELF SUFFICIENCY MANUAL

BLOOMSBURY

ALISON CANDLIN

Contents

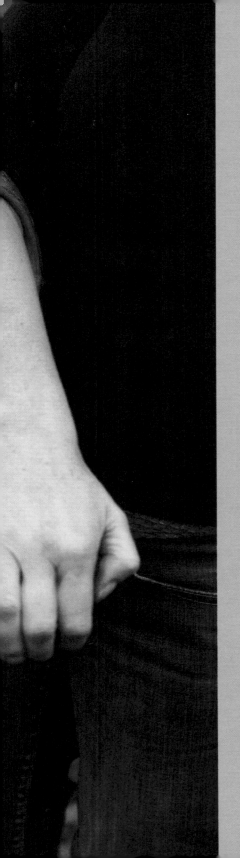

FOREWORD

This book is for those who wish to approach the 'good life' gently and gradually. Perhaps you want to try your hand at growing some fruit and vegetables, producing your own honey or eating your own eggs, drinking milk or eating cheese from your goats, or rearing your own pigs so you can enjoy home-produced meat. It is for those people, too, who would like to make more use of the free produce that may be found in the countryside – in the hedgerows, woodlands and rivers or by the seashore.

In time, you may want to turn the hobby into a way of life and aim to become fully self-sufficient, but it is wise to start slowly and get a feel for whether this is the life for you. Do not try to grow all your own fruit and vegetables, and keep all the animals discussed in this book in your first year of operation. Instead, tackle it little by little, finding what you most enjoy doing, and giving yourself time to learn from your mistakes.

THE LAND YOU OWN

You need very little land to produce at least some of your own food. A tiny backyard – even a terrace or a patio – can yield a surprising amount of produce if you use it efficiently.

However big your plot, always try to put back into your land what you take out of it. No ground will go on producing crops or supporting livestock of any type unless it is well maintained. This is not as daunting as it may sound and this book will help you to understand the needs of the soil and the effects of growing various crops so that you can ensure a good balance.

NEIGHBOURS AND OFFICIALS

The relationships you establish with those who live close by can make a surprising difference to the success of your operation.

People who have lived in the area for some time often have valuable hints and advice on what does and does not grow well, and knowing this can save you a great deal of time, money and exasperation. In return, be mindful of your neighbours when deciding where to keep your livestock. Few people will thank you for shattering their early morning peace with a crowing cockerel, but a little polite consultation and the odd box of produce will go a long way towards building a harmonious relationship.

If you intend to start a smallholding with livestock and a quite large cultivated area, you will often find the local farmers will be willing to offer advice and help – and maybe even share machinery.

Essential rules and regulations

Before you start, contact the government organisations that exist to offer advice to smallholders. Start with Defra (the Department for Environment, Food and Rural Affairs) and find out who your local government officials are. They will be able to guide you in planning, getting the appropriate licences for keeping livestock and give you information about pests and diseases that could be a problem. There are rules and regulations governing to the keeping of all farm-type livestock, and in some areas you are not allowed to keep such animals at all.

STORAGE SPACE AND OUTBUILDINGS

The amount of storage space and outbuildings you will need will depend on the scale and scope of your home production plans.

Even if your plot is confined to your back garden you are unlikely to be able to eat all the vegetables and fruit you grow as you harvest them. And, in any case, the whole point of self-sufficiency is to be able to enjoy your produce all year round.

Root vegetables can be stored in their natural state (see pages 207–208), but for this you either need to allocate them a patch of ground (for clamping), or some sort of weather and rodent-proof shed.

Keeping preserves and other food

You will need ample shelf space in a cool, well-ventilated, but shady place for storing chutney, pickles, sauces, jams and other preserved foods. And a deep freezer is another essential – invest in a chest freezer that can be kept as close as possible to the kitchen.

Making space for livestock

You will find out what you need to house livestock in the pages of this book devoted to each type of animal (see pages 152–177), but again there are further space considerations. If you intend to keep goats, you should give some thought to the milking conditions and whether you can accommodate some sort of dairy (goats should not be milked in the shed in which they are kept, because conditions are not hygienic enough).

You will also need room to keep eggs as they come in, storing them in such a way that they can be used in strict rotation. Egg trays or boxes can take up quite a lot of room on a shelf or in a larder, yet they must be kept somewhere cool, where there is no danger of the eggs being smashed.

Storing animal feed

It is most economical to buy in bulk food to be fed to the animals, but you must weigh up the savings against the storage room you will need. Hay and straw are bulky and must be kept in a weather-proof shed. Other more concentrated foodstuffs must be kept in rodent-proof containers, and these too should be housed in a shed or outbuilding of some sort. Anything rodent-proof must be made of galvanized metal, ideally, with a lid that fits right over the container. Failing this, a heavy, thick wooden barrel will keep the rats out for some time but plastic presents no challenge at all.

The closer your storage buildings are to the house or to the animals' quarters, the more convenient you will find them, but always make use of any old shed or outbuilding that is already there on your property before spending money on new buildings. If you are lucky enough to live in a house with an attic or a cellar, make full use of this added storage space, erecting a system of shelves if there is enough room.

CONSERVATION

Conservation of energy and the environment are often high on the list of priorities for people striving for self-sufficiency. These concerns go hand in hand with a wish to minimise food miles, grow and produce food in organic or ethically sound ways and to move away from a wasteful, throw-away lifestyle.

Being aware of ways to reduce energy and water consumption and doing all you can to collect and recycle water around the garden and your fruit and vegetable plots all help to conserve the environment. On top of this, technology is improving all the time and making it more and more feasible to generate your own energy with solar panels, wind turbines or water turbines if you are lucky enough to have a stream. You may even be able to sell some excess power back to the National Grid (*see* page 246).

Generating and conserving energy
In the temperate climate of the United Kingdom, solar power is still more effective for heating water than generating electricity, and these kinds of solar systems are likely to pay for themselves in savings within a couple of years. Many local authorities offer grants to help towards the installation of energy-generating systems, as well as energy conservation measures, such as upgrading household insulation. Contact your utility supply companies and your local council to see whether you qualify for a grant.

Sustainable energy sources
If you have a good supply of sustainable wood on your property, wood-burning systems are a good option for heating your home and hot water, but – for the sake of future generations – you should always replant trees to replace any that you fell and take great care not to cut down and burn all the mature trees in an area.

KEEPING ACCOUNTS

If you are growing your own fruit and vegetables and keeping the odd chicken and a hive of bees more as a hobby than a money-saver, there is no real need to keep any sort of specific accounts.

If, however, you are running the operation on a larger scale, it is a good idea to follow some accounting routine, or else it is quite possible to delude yourself about how much money you are saving.

Balancing the books
The cost of animal food, fertiliser, fuel, equipment, machinery and the like must all be noted and balanced against the cost of the food you produce, should you have had to buy it in a shop. By keeping detailed accounts like these, you will be able to pinpoint those areas which are really not economically viable, and either abandon them or alter them in some way.

It is important to remember that the first year or two often involve much greater outlay and some inevitable failed projects, so do not expect a huge profit from the start. Finances are just one of the rewards of this kind of lifestyle and you will need to be prepared for a slow start, balanced out by fresh enthusiasm for your new working routine.

Quality and savings
You may well find that keeping livestock saves you very little money and may even cost you more than your old life of supermarket shopping. You will not be producing free food by any means, although your eggs, milk and meat should cost you less than if you were buying them. What you have to remember is that you are producing food of infinitely better quality than it is possible to buy. The eggs are richer, the milk fresher and the meat more tasty. Add to this the satisfaction you are getting from looking after the animals and watching them flourish in your care.

Understanding the rhythm of life
It is a good idea to keep records of how many eggs you get each day, the numbers of young in a litter or brood, the date they were born and so on. It might help, too, if you keep similar records of the fruit and vegetable production so that you can see what does particularly well, and notice when certain fruit trees or bushes start to become less productive and need replacing.

Diaries and records like this make fascinating and illuminating reading to help you to understand your land and crops by noting patterns of planting times and places, the effects of weather in different years, successes and failures that you can learn from for future years. It is this sort of observation and practice that could ultimately make the difference between an operation that is relatively cost-effective and one that is little more than a money-waster.

STARTING OUT

Planning the Plot

Whatever sized area of land you have available for your home production of food, careful planning and judicious use of the space can make a great deal of difference to its productivity.

Even a comparatively small garden, well-planned and worked, could prove more productive than a larger amount of land where things are just allowed to happen at random. Think carefully at the outset about the positioning of everything you want to include, even if you are not planning to do it all straight away. Many features of the plan – the vegetable garden, fruit patch, pig sty and goat shed, for example – are likely to be

in one permanent site, so be sure you have chosen the best possible place, both in terms of convenience to you and best conditions for them.

The following guidelines will help you to decide where to site each productive element of your plot, but remember that they are only that – guidelines. Your vegetable garden, for example, can be as large or as small as you want or are able to make it. It is possible to provide a family of four with fresh vegetables each week of the year from a plot that measures only 3 x 4m (10 x 12ft): a space that can be found in most suburban back gardens by sacrificing some ornamental flower beds or part of the lawn.

If you have a larger space you will need to decide what proportion of it to devote to each type of cultivation

and to livestock. Think about which fruit and vegetables you and your family most enjoy eating, which ones will store best to see you through the winter and allocate space accordingly to try to avoid a surplus of a crop that no-one really likes or that will spoil before it can be eaten.

Making space for livestock
How much space you need for keeping chickens depends on whether they are to be kept in a permanent run or whether you are able to move them around (*see* page 166). Remember that you

Planning and organisation are essential. Regular-sized plots like these make it easy to measure out rows and rotate crops from year to year, while good paths give access for tending and harvesting your produce.

will need to go to and from the hen house regularly to feed and water the birds and collect their eggs and consider how close and convenient you want them to the house against the disadvantages of noise and disruption of having them nearby.

Similarly with goats – are you going to take them out during the day and tether them on nearby wasteland, if this is possible, or on an area of uncultivated land at the edge of your property, or are they to stay permanently on one patch of ground? If kept in one place, they will need more space and supplementary feeding.

Start your planning on paper
Make a list of all the crops you want to grow and the livestock you want to keep. Note down sowing and harvesting times, how much space each crop requires and any information about good companion plants that will help you to plan your plot. Then draw a scale plan of your land and sketch out areas for planting, storage, livestock and any new buildings. Don't forget to think about paths for easy access, making use of any existing features and hardstandings if you can before planning new building works.

Once you have a rough plan, pace it out on the ground itself. Try to envisage how each element will work together and how practical the space will be to use on a daily basis. Only when you are happy that you have it right should you start digging, fencing and putting in permanent structures that will be difficult to relocate later on.

Providing you use your common sense in the early stages, you will find that you can bend nearly all the following rules about planning your plot to suit your particular needs.

THE VEGETABLE GARDEN

The plot you choose for growing vegetables should not be overhung or heavily shaded by large trees. Vegetables grow best if they are exposed to the maximum amount of sun possible; few will really flourish in shady conditions.

Shelter from strong winds, in particular those from the north or north-east in the UK, will make your vegetable plot a much easier place to cultivate successfully. This is best provided by a solid fence or a low hedge. A hedge should have a path sited between it and the edge of the vegetable plot, and all protruding roots from the hedge must be cut through each year when you dig over the plot, or else they will rob the vegetables of essential nutrients from the soil.

The size and shape of the plot will of course depend on the space

Think about everything you would like to grow and keep, including livestock like hens, and whether they will be free-range or kept in an enclosure.

you have available, as well as to how much time you are willing to devote to working it, but a rectangular shape is generally the easiest to subdivide. Working will be cleaner and easier if the patch is surrounded by solid paths, ideally constructed from hard material such as brick, concrete or paving slabs, rather than compounded earth, which is bound to get muddy during winter. Paths should be wide enough to take a wheelbarrow. If the patch is very large, similar paths sited at intervals across it would be a good idea, too.

Where you decide to site the vegetable garden in relation to the house is not usually a major consideration; some people like to have it close by, others favour a spot away from the house to which they can retire. In some cases, there may be only one suitable spot. However, bear in mind that it is probably better to have the vegetable garden nearer the house than the pig sty or the chicken run. Position the greenhouse and cold frames close to the vegetable plot for convenience when planting out seedlings. Remember that the sloping side of any cold frames should face south. If you can, allocate space next to the cold frames, for seed beds.

The compost heap should also be sited within easy access, although it is perhaps best placed at the furthest corner from the house, as it can attract flies and may smell a little in hot weather. It does not have to be within the vegetable garden at all of course, but you will find it inconvenient if it is too far away.

Subdividing the plot

If your vegetable garden is on an irregular-shaped plot of land, try to divide it so there is a rectangular patch within it. This is the most convenient shape to divide for a crop rotation plan (*see* page 40). The remaining patches of land could be used for perennial crops, such as asparagus and globe artichokes.

There are advantages and disadvantages to planting rows running east/west or north/south and you must choose for yourself which way to orientate yours. Rows that run north/south get the maximum amount of sun, catching it on one side in the morning and on the other in the afternoon. Rows that run east/west tend to be shaded by those on either side for part of the day, but they are better for crops that are going to be grown through the winter under cloches. If the plot is on a slope, it is better to plant rows across the slope, than up and down it.

THE FRUIT GARDEN

Different considerations apply to the fruit garden and to the two types of fruit – soft and tree fruits. Although it is possible to dot soft fruit bushes around the garden wherever there is space, you will find it much more convenient to keep them together.

When working in the plot or harvesting your fruit, your time will be used more efficiently if all the bushes are close together; it is also far quicker and easier to provide netting protection from birds over a large clump of bushes, than to cover each bush individually, and this is an unavoidable task if you want a decent crop of anything. If you are growing a lot of soft fruit of this type, consider growing it in a fruit cage, which allows you easy access, whilst keeping the birds off the fruit.

If the spot chosen for the soft fruit is close to the vegetable garden, try to site it so that it will not cast shade over the growing vegetables. Some soft fruits, such as blackberries, loganberries and raspberries, are, themselves, shade-tolerant, so they

Fruit trees can be grouped in an orchard or dotted around wherever you have room. Don't try to grow crops beneath them, as the shade will be too deep.

can occupy shadier parts of the patch, leaving the sunny areas for plants that will benefit most.

Remember that soft fruit bushes last for several years, so don't plant any in a place that you might want to change in a year or two's time.

Orchards of fruit trees

Tree fruits should not be planted close to the soft fruits, as they will soon overshadow them and rob them of important soil nutrients. Instead, incorporate fruit trees into an overall garden plan or allocate a large area to be a dedicated orchard. Fruit trees can be placed either where there is room for them or in a spot where you want to introduce some shade. They can be planted too, to improve the view from the house, perhaps by hiding or screening some unattractive feature.

Remember to choose tree fruits carefully, making sure they have been grown on the rooting stock that will give you the size of tree you want (*see* page 113); otherwise you could end up with a giant that overshadows everything in the plot.

The more delicate tree fruits – apricots, peaches and nectarines – together with vines, should be sited against a south-facing wall for the best results. Walls can also be used for growing cordon or espalier trees of apples and pears, or for some of the soft fruits that need training and supporting as they grow.

THE HERB GARDEN

Herbs might not seem critical to becoming self-sufficient, but a herb garden will not only allow you to add flavour to your food, but introduces delightful scents to your garden and will attract myriad beneficial insects to your plot, which will help to keep plant pests under control without the use of chemical insecticides.

Because herbs are an additional bonus rather than an essential part of your plan, the herb garden usually takes up the smallest amount of space. Herbs can be grown anywhere that is convenient, but are best sited close to the kitchen, so that they are readily to hand when you want them as you are cooking. Grow them in a small plot, so you can reach them all easily, and one with lots of sun – few herbs will do well in a shady spot with heavy, damp soil. If space is at a premium, you can grow herbs within a flower border or in pots or window boxes wherever there is room.

A herb bed can be as ornamental as it is useful. Here, the feathery fronds of a row of dill plants and their bright umbrella flowers are as pretty as any herbaceous border – and edible, too.

DRAW UP A PLAN

Before you begin to plant anything on your land, you must decide how it can be used to its best advantage.

A small plot for the bare essentials
If you don't have much room (below), it is wise to devote your land almost entirely to growing vegetables and fruit. You may have room for

some chickens to supply fresh eggs and meat, but probably not enough room to let the birds live free range.

More scope on a bigger plot
A larger plot of land (opposite) allows for more features, such as a permanent pig sty and a movable hen house within an orchard, so that the chickens can scratch around. The extra land means that you can

grow a bigger variety and larger harvest of fruit and vegetables.

A smallholding on a large plot
This large plot (bottom) not only has space for pigs and chickens, but for goats, bees and even a horse. The extra land allows for a system of crop rotation where there will always be one plot lying fallow, which can be used for grazing livestock.

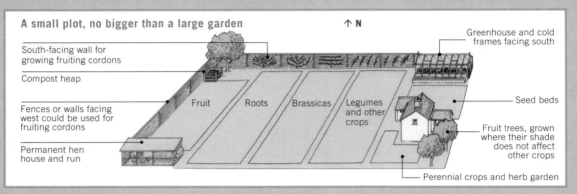

A small plot, no bigger than a large garden ↑ N

- South-facing wall for growing fruiting cordons
- Compost heap
- Fences or walls facing west could be used for fruiting cordons
- Permanent hen house and run
- Fruit
- Roots
- Brassicas
- Legumes and other crops
- Greenhouse and cold frames facing south
- Seed beds
- Fruit trees, grown where their shade does not affect other crops
- Perennial crops and herb garden

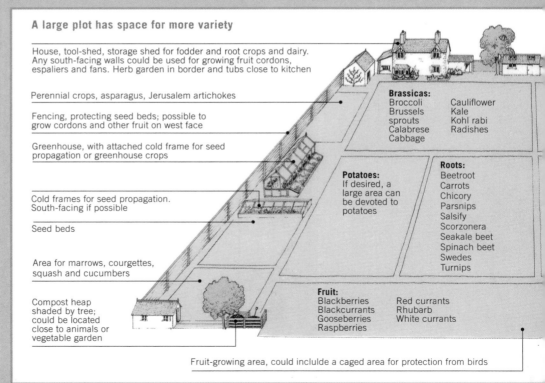

A large plot has space for more variety

- House, tool-shed, storage shed for fodder and root crops and dairy. Any south-facing walls could be used for growing fruit cordons, espaliers and fans. Herb garden in border and tubs close to kitchen
- Perennial crops, asparagus, Jerusalem artichokes
- Fencing, protecting seed beds; possible to grow cordons and other fruit on west face
- Greenhouse, with attached cold frame for seed propagation or greenhouse crops
- Cold frames for seed propagation. South-facing if possible
- Seed beds
- Area for marrows, courgettes, squash and cucumbers
- Compost heap shaded by tree; could be located close to animals or vegetable garden

Brassicas:
Broccoli
Brussels sprouts
Calabrese
Cabbage
Cauliflower
Kale
Kohl rabi
Radishes

Potatoes:
If desired, a large area can be devoted to potatoes

Roots:
Beetroot
Carrots
Chicory
Parsnips
Salsify
Scorzonera
Seakale beet
Spinach beet
Swedes
Turnips

Fruit:
Blackberries
Blackcurrants
Gooseberries
Raspberries
Red currants
Rhubarb
White currants

Fruit-growing area, could include a caged area for protection from birds

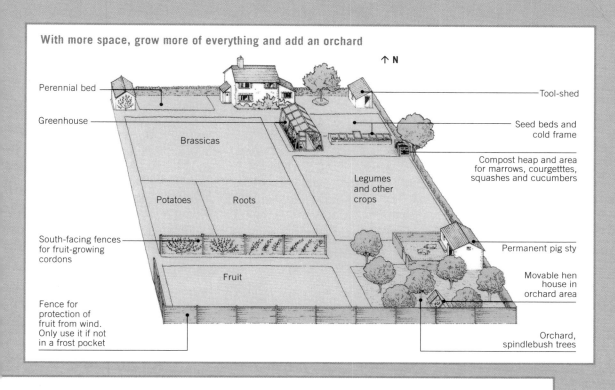

With more space, grow more of everything and add an orchard

↑ N

Perennial bed

Greenhouse

Brassicas

Potatoes

Roots

South-facing fences for fruit-growing cordons

Fruit

Fence for protection of fruit from wind. Only use it if not in a frost pocket

Tool-shed

Seed beds and cold frame

Compost heap and area for marrows, courgetttes, squashes and cucumbers

Legumes and other crops

Permanent pig sty

Movable hen house in orchard area

Orchard, spindlebush trees

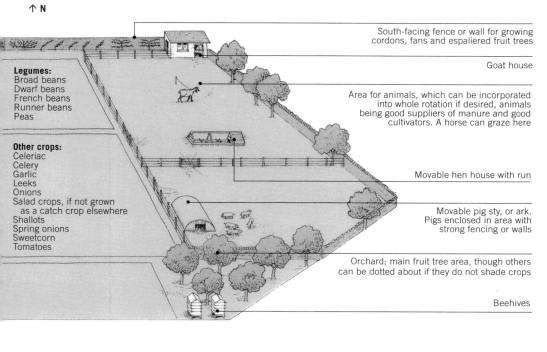

↑ N

Legumes:
Broad beans
Dwarf beans
French beans
Runner beans
Peas

Other crops:
Celeriac
Celery
Garlic
Leeks
Onions
Salad crops, if not grown as a catch crop elsewhere
Shallots
Spring onions
Sweetcorn
Tomatoes

South-facing fence or wall for growing cordons, fans and espaliered fruit trees

Goat house

Area for animals, which can be incorporated into whole rotation if desired, animals being good suppliers of manure and good cultivators. A horse can graze here

Movable hen house with run

Movable pig sty, or ark. Pigs enclosed in area with strong fencing or walls

Orchard; main fruit tree area, though others can be dotted about if they do not shade crops

Beehives

CHICKENS

Where you site your chickens in the overall plan will depend as much as anything on which method you choose to keep them. Free-range chickens need only a permanent house and this can be sited anywhere. If there is a building suitable for a hen house already installed on the property when you take it over, then this is undoubtedly the best place to choose.

If you intend to keep your chickens in a permanent run (as opposed to free-range), it might be advisable to site this a little way from the house as it is not likely to be the most attractive of all your garden features.

The size of it is really up to you; allocate as much space as you feel you can spare. Common-sense will tell you whether the chickens have enough room. In fact, they do not need a great deal of space in the run, although they will peck over as much land as you give them; it is far more important to ensure that you provide 10–15cm (4–6in) per bird

around the feeding trough or hopper, and about 20cm (8in) per bird roosting space in the hen house (*see* page 166).

If you can allocate two patches of ground to the chickens, there is more chance of keeping both of them in better condition than if you have only one, as they can be rested in turn. Think of siting these two plots side by side; if there are two entrances to the hen house, this can be used for both runs and the fence dividing them would provide a boundary for both patches.

OTHER POULTRY

Although chickens are the most common choice for keeping poultry, ducks, geese and even turkeys are also popular and productive. The considerations for keeping them and allowing them sufficient space follow the same common sense factors as for chickens, above.

A gaggle of geese looks appealing, but be warned that geese are exceptionally noisy, so take care where you keep them.

As all poultry must be shut up by night and let out by day, it may be more convenient to site them close to one another. It could make feeding a quicker operation, too.

If you want your geese to act as watchdogs, and make the loudest of all possible noises whenever anyone enters your property, put them near the gate; if you want a more peaceful plot, put them further away.

Ducks, of course, need a pond, though this need not be large. They need a house, too, but very little additional ground space, and are usually happy to share space with your chickens.

Never keep chickens and turkeys together as this can spread blackhead disease, which is fatal.

GOATS

A goat or two can make a worthwhile addition to your land. It may not be practical to keep a cow, but a goat is a far easier proposition and will provide you with milk that you can drink or turn into cheese. They are appealing creatures, too, and are not hard to accommodate, even on a relatively small plot.

If you intend to run the goat shed on a deep litter system – that is, to keep adding more and more bedding to the floor and then mucking it out when it gets too deep (*see* page 162) – it is probably best to site the goats some way from the house where any smell it creates will be less of a problem.

There is no essential reason for the goats' living quarters to be near to the dairy, if this is a separate unit, although you will need to milk the goats twice daily, so the closer the two are, the less tiresome the job will be – particularly in bad weather.

Regulations and Licences

To keep pigs, goats or sheep – even just one animal – you must register your property as an agricultural holding and apply for a livestock licence. When you buy an animal, you will need to complete various official forms, register and tag it and keep records throughout your ownership. There are also legal restrictions on moving livestock, with which you must comply. Contact Defra, visit its website or check with your local authority for more information.

Most smallholders can keep chickens and other poultry without restrictions. As long as you have fewer than 50 birds you do not need to notify Defra.

There are no particular size requirements for a goat run, even if this is to be their permanent home, although it must be very strongly fenced if they are to be turned loose within it as goats are determined escapees. Goats are infinitely adaptable and will live happily in most circumstances and conditions.

Making enough space

Having given them room to graze without bumping into one another all the time, the only consideration regarding the size of your goat run is how much you want to supplement their feeding. The smaller the grazing area, the more additional feed you will need to supply. Also, if the area is to remain as grass and not be stripped bare, it will need resting from time to time – just as

with chicken runs – which means you must either allocate another patch of land, similarly fenced, to the goats, or you must have access to wasteland or thickets where you can take them out and tether them during the day.

If you tether goats, they should be moved twice a day as they will not eat greenstuff that they have fouled, and you should not place them too close to bushes or long patches of tough grass, in which the rope could

The most important thing when preparing a space for keeping goats is to make sure that the fences are really strong.

become entangled. If this happens there is a risk that the goats could strangle themselves.

In winter, it is best to keep goats on a piece of land that has been concreted (again it does not have to be very big) if the ground is liable to become very muddy, as this could lead to various feet disorders.

PIGS

It is a myth that pigs are dirty, smelly creatures, but nonetheless, their food (which is usually root vegetables and fruit) is liable to smell. In addition, their run needs to include a muddy puddle and they are undoubtedly noisy, so they are best kept at a distance from the house.

If you are keeping pigs to help you cultivate a very rough area of land, you will move them and their movable sty around as necessary. They will soon clear the land of scrubby undergrowth, weeds and brambles. It is more likely, though, that you will want to keep them in a sty with a permanent yard.

Pigs do not need much room if they are not relying on the land for their food. All they need is space to rootle around and to make a nice, deep dust or mud hole.

This doesn't apply if you are planning to let your sow have a litter. She is likely to have about ten piglets and these have to be weaned when

Pigs are happy without a lot of space as long as they have a muddy spot to wallow in. Always offer them shelter from the sun.

they are between five and eight weeks old. At this point, they will need separate accommodation from her, and depending on how long you mean to keep the young pigs, it may be necessary to split them up still further as they grow. Ten healthy, squealing piglets is a large number to keep in one fairly small yard, and overcrowding can lead to health problems and fighting.

BEES

These are the livestock that take up the least amount of ground of all. Their only housing or space requirement from you is the provision of a hive.

There are some points to bear in mind when you are considering where to position your beehives, and these are discussed on page 176. Most people choose to put their hives at some distance from the house, so that regularly-used paths from the house to various parts of the garden do not clash with the bees' most usual flight path to and from the hives.

Think about neighbouring gardens, too, to try to avoid your bees flying regularly through your neighbour's patio or other seating area, where they would cause a nuisance.

Position beehives where the flight paths of the bees will not pass through your own most-used areas of the garden.

Clearing Overgrown Land

If the land you want to cultivate is a tangle of bushy undergrowth, it has first to be cleared. Pigs and goats are renowned as excellent ground-clearers, but in most cases this is an arduous task best tackled with some mechanical help. The sweat and toil of digging and clearing by hand will be hard but satisfying work.

The basic and most useful tools and equipment for clearing and turning over your land are discussed below. If you intend to keep goats, it may be worth getting them now, because they will do most of the work for you, eating their way through the undergrowth, even stripping the bark off trees and killing them, if you let them, although it will, of course, take a while. Pigs will also clear the land.

Clearing and felling

For tackling overgrown land by hand, you will need a fork, spade, scythe, pickaxe, mattock, shovel, axe, sickle, crowbar and possibly a chainsaw. Always wear tough boots to protect your feet and sturdy gloves.

Attack brambles, thin-stemmed bushy clumps and young saplings with a scythe – either a traditional hand tool or a power scythe. Use the shorter-handled sickle in awkward places and on tougher stalks and stems. Remove all the fallen branches and other pieces of wood, chop them into manageable sizes and store them for use as firewood.

Having cleared the ground of the undergrowth, decide if you want to remove any trees. This is probably a job for an expert, although

instructions for felling a tree are given on page 203. Remember that you must also remove the stump from the ground and doing this is a major job in itself. Stumps can be dynamited out, pulled out with a special winch or ground out of the earth with a large drill-like tool (again, all jobs for an expert). If you opt for grinding the stump, make sure that you ask the tree surgeon to grind it deep enough. That's 20–25cm (8–10in) for laying turf, and for cultivated ground you will

If you have a large area to clear and prepare for growing, a rotavator makes fast work of the job. Try to hire or borrow one, since you will not use it often.

need to go at least 30cm (12in) below the surface.

If you decide to remove a stump yourself, the best DIY approach is to dig it out with a mattock and a spade, but this is a long job. Alternatively, stumps can be treated with a chemical to speed up their rotting. Use a specialist stump killer

Use a pick axe and spade to dig out roots and stumps of shrubs and to break up well-compacted soil. Hard work now means better crops later.

THE SELF-SUFFICIENCY MANUAL

treatment and make sure to wear protective clothing and follow the manufacturer's instructions carefully.

Rotavating to break up the soil
Neglected land is best broken up for initial cultivation by a rotavator. Before you can do this, all large stones, boulders, builders' rubble, bits of brick and wire or binder twine must be removed, or these will damage the blades of the machine. Large boulders may have to be levered up out of the ground (above right) and you will need help for this. Remember to lift all heavy items carefully: bend your knees and lift with your back straight, rather than stooping over the object and straining your back muscles. Very heavy boulders could be hauled away by towing them with a tractor or a car with a tow bar attachment.

MOVING A BOULDER

It may be possible to work the position of a large, deeply set boulder into your plan, but if it is in the way of a proposed path or building, or if it lies in one of your planned planting areas, it will need to be moved. Dig around it to establish its full size and see how best to tackle it. You may be able to pull a boulder out of a shallow dip with a rope, but well-buried stones must be levered out.

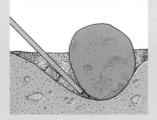

1 Using a strong pole, work it under the boulder. Put a brick under the pole, and use it for leverage.

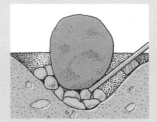

2 Still holding the pole, begin to place large stones under the boulder to raise it from the bottom of the hole.

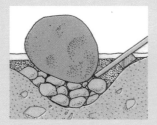

3 Having raised the boulder, lever it in the same way from the other side. Continue adding stones to raise it.

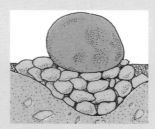

4 Finally the stones will bring the boulder up to the level of the ground, at which point it can be rolled away.

Do not necessarily dispose of all the debris you have picked off the ground. Bricks and large stones or slates can be very useful in building paths, raising all sorts of structures slightly off the ground, and many other jobs around the plot. Stack anything that might become useful later in an out-of-the-way place.

Once the ground is cleared, rotavate the areas you want to cultivate or dig them over thoroughly by hand (*see* page 28). Again, goats allowed to graze the area for a week or so will remove many harmful weeds – at least disposing of seeds, if not the deep-seated roots. If the weed growth is very heavy, you can work over the entire area a few times with a flamegun – but only if you know how to use one properly, and the weeds are really persistent. This will destroy weed seeds, but also the natural organic matter that will help to improve the ground.

Various types of rotavator are available, both powered and driven by hand, but their basic purpose is the same – to turn over the ground. Do not try to rush the machine over the surface area, as it will not reach deeply enough into the ground.

Improving the Soil

The soil on any plot of land is made up of a series of layers. The top layer, or topsoil, is the one that most affects the successful growth of fruit and vegetables.

Topsoil can be categorised into five main groups, although these could be endlessly further subdivided, as few soils fall so neatly into one simple category. In general, most soils are sandy, loam, clay, chalky or peat. One method of assessing your plot's soil type is to mix a handful with water, shake it well and leave it in a jam jar overnight (right).

Another technique is to identify the various plants that are growing on the land and then check in a gardening encyclopaedia to see what kind of soil they require to flourish.

THE JAM JAR TEST FOR SOIL TYPE

Before drawing up your planting plan, you must discover what sort of topsoil you have, because some vegetables and fruit will only grow well on particular types of soil. There is no point in wasting time and money in growing produce on soil to which it is not suited.

Shake a small quantity of your garden soil in a jam jar of water and leave it to settle overnight. Gravel and coarse sand will sink to the bottom and will be topped by a layer of gritty material. Above this will be the clay. If the gravel and sand makes the largest layer, the soil is sandy. The middle layer indicates the amount of loam present; if it makes up about 40 per cent in all, the soil is a good loam. If the top layer of clay is equal in depth to the other two layers together, you have a clay soil.

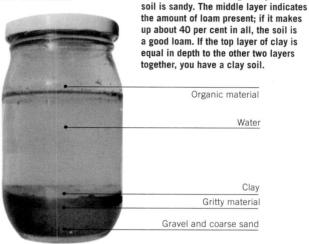

Organic material

Water

Clay

Gritty material

Gravel and coarse sand

Sandy soil

This is light and easy to dig over. The soil offers little resistance to a spade or fork and is not heavy or sticky to lift. Pick up a handful; it should feel gritty and slip easily through your fingers. In windy weather, the surface of sandy soil is easily blown away and water drains through so quickly that it can soon become very dry. In addition, vital nutrients are washed away. The lost nutrients should be replaced and the ground made more water-retentive by digging in large quantities of well-rotted compost or farmyard manure.

Loam

This is the ideal soil for all types of cultivation. It is darker than sandy soil (owing to its humus content) and crumbly rather than gritty. A handful rubbed between the fingers will feel smooth; moisten it slightly and it should not feel gritty, nor should it stick in lumps.

Clay

Clay soils are heavy to work, sticking to the spade and your boots. A handful pressed between your fingers will stick together in a lump and after a heavy rainfall, puddles will remain on the surface of the ground for a considerable time. In a long, dry spell, clay soils can become very hard.

These soils can be improved by being dug thoroughly in the autumn, leaving large lumps on the surface which will break up in the winter frosts. Dig in large quantities of any available organic material – such as well-rotted compost, farmyard manure or leaf mould – to break down over winter.

When the soil has dried out in the spring, it can be forked down and raked to a fairly fine tilth.

Chalky

Chalky soil is best identified by its grey-white surface – particularly noticeable during a dry spell. If the surrounding area is chalky, then your land probably is, too. Water generally drains quickly through chalk, but this can be improved by digging in lots of organic material.

Peat

Such soil is found in relatively few areas and is the result of centuries of growth and decomposition of certain types of plants. It is generally highly organic and, provided it drains well, it will be easy to work and extremely fertile. In areas where peat has formed over non-porous subsoil, the soil will become easily waterlogged and is usually acid.

TESTING THE SOIL PH

In addition to their type, soils are either alkaline, neutral or acid and this, too, will affect the growing of crops. You can assess your soil's acidity by using a soil-testing kit, available from any garden centre.

The soil tested will register a number on the pH scale. A neutral soil has a pH of 7; above this the soil is alkaline and below it, it is acid.

Most vegetables grow best in a slightly acid soil with a pH reading of 6.5. Brassicas prefer a pH of 7 to 7.5, whilst marrows, potatoes and tomatoes like a pH of 5 to 5.5. Most fruit will be most likely to thrive in a neutral or slightly acid soil.

As a broad generalisation, most soils tend to be acid, rather than highly alkaline, the exceptions being chalky soils and some clay ones. Over-acid soils can be corrected by adding quantities of lime. It should be sprinkled over the soil as long as possible before growing the crops, but after the ground has been dug in the autumn or winter. It can then be left to be washed through the ground by the winter rains. Most soils should be limed every three years to rebalance their levels.

A good soil is rich and crumbly, with plenty of organic matter. It should feel smooth, not gritty.

USING A PH AND NUTRIENT TESTING KIT

As well as discovering the type of soil you have, you can find its pH and nutrient levels using a soil-testing kit. Take small amounts of soil from different parts of your land and place them in test tubes. By adding different solutions, you can discover the pH and the level of the three main nutrients required for healthy plant growth: nitrogen, phosphorus and potash. Using the charts in the kit, you can work out whether any lime should be added to correct the pH balance and decide which fertiliser to use to boost any nutrient deficiencies.

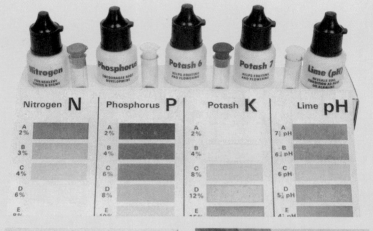

1 Take samples of soil from different parts of your land, allow them to dry, remove any foreign bodies and crumble the soils. Quarter-fill each test tube with different soils and label.

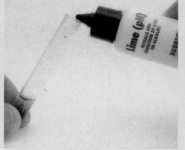

2 Holding each test tube carefully, add a few drops of solution, according to the chemical for which you are testing. Shake the mixture for 30 seconds and then leave for 10 minutes.

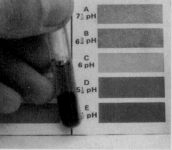

3 When the soil has settled to the bottom of the test tube, match the colour of the solution to the appropriate chart. The result gives the pH level of the soil or the percentage of each chemical nutrient.

Composting and Manure

As they grow, all plants take nutrients from the soil. Unless these are replaced, subsequent crops will fail. Whenever possible, soil should be revitalised and its stocks of plant food replenished using organic manures and fertilisers – and home-made compost.

Inorganic or chemical fertilisers generally produce more immediate results than compost or manure, but in some cases they can cause lasting damage to the soil. It is usually possible to keep the soil consistently healthy by adding little more than an annual application of well-rotted farmyard manure and garden-made compost, usually dug in during the

autumn. Mulches of these materials – a layer spread over the soil – help to prevent the ground from drying out in hot or windy weather.

GARDEN-MADE COMPOST

This is produced by compacting together all manner of organic waste – dead plants and flower heads, vegetable peelings and remains, fruit skins, crushed egg shells, hedge and grass cuttings, and so on.

Compost ingredients should be layered in a suitable container interspersed occasionally with an activator, which helps to speed the decomposing process by feeding the bacteria. The chemical that helps with this is nitrogen, which can be supplied organically with a layer of poultry or other animal manure, fish

meal, dried blood or sewage sludge. You can also buy compost activators in garden centres and add these to your heap from time to time.

What to add to the heap
Begin the compost heap with a layer of coarse twigs or stems to allow the air to circulate from the bottom (air is essential for the decomposing process), then add organic waste in even layers as it is available. Press the layers down and dampen them if they are very dry.

Do not compost perennial weeds or annuals that are full of seeds, any diseased materials (such as the infected roots of a cabbage, for example) or scraps of food that are greasy – the seeds will grow and the infections spread. Anything that is very thick or woody should be chopped or squashed first. Lawn mowings should be mixed with

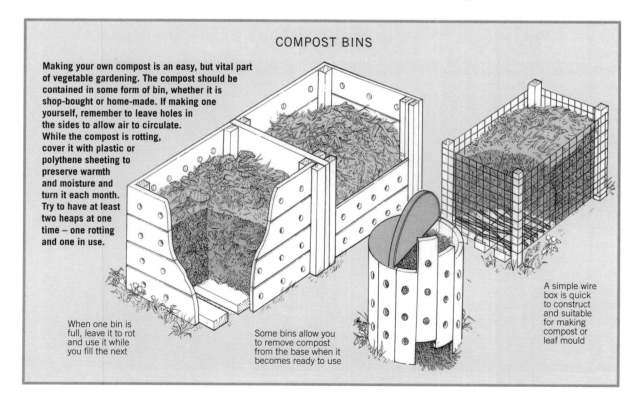

COMPOST BINS

Making your own compost is an easy, but vital part of vegetable gardening. The compost should be contained in some form of bin, whether it is shop-bought or home-made. If making one yourself, remember to leave holes in the sides to allow air to circulate. While the compost is rotting, cover it with plastic or polythene sheeting to preserve warmth and moisture and turn it each month. Try to have at least two heaps at one time – one rotting and one in use.

When one bin is full, leave it to rot and use it while you fill the next

Some bins allow you to remove compost from the base when it becomes ready to use

A simple wire box is quick to construct and suitable for making compost or leaf mould

other materials rather than spread in a solid layer as this will form an effective air-excluding barrier, and prevent the bacteria from working.

Water a compost heap in hot, dry weather to keep it moist and cover it with a plastic sheet or offcut of old carpet to insulate it and help it to retain moisture.

Waiting for it to be 'cooked'

A compost heap is most successful if built quickly, preferably in the spring and summer when the warmer atmosphere speeds up the decomposing process. At this time of year it will be ready in a month or two, at which point it will be brown, moist and crumbly, with a uniform appearance and texture throughout. It will take at least twice as long to rot down in winter.

You can make your compost in a loose heap in an out-of-the-way corner, in home-made bins (*see* page 25) or shop-bought plastic bins or cones. Plastic composters are often the quickest method – they are usually black, to retain heat effectively – but they do not hold large quantities and you are likely to need several of them. Because they

An open compost heap in a wooden frame will hold much more than a plastic bin, but take longer to decompose.

work fast, you do not need to turn the contents as they rot, as you must with an open heap. Many bins have a hatch at the base, allowing you to scrape out ready-to-use compost at the bottom. What is left drops down inside the bin, creating space for new material to be added at the top.

FARMYARD MANURE

This is most likely to be horse, cow, pig or poultry manure, mixed with the original bedding of straw or wood shavings, and may be used to add valuable humus to the soil.

Manure is very valuable to the fruit and vegetable gardener, although it is seldom as rich as well-made compost. This is particularly true if the manure has been stacked out in the open, as the rain will have washed away many of the soluble nutrients. Poultry manure is usually best added to a compost heap, rather than straight to the soil, as it tends to be rather dry.

OTHER ORGANIC ADDITIVES

You can also enrich your soil by digging in one of the natural additives listed below, either made in your garden or shop-bought.

Leafmould

This is produced by composting dead leaves and adds valuable humus to the soil. If you do not have enough leaves to warrant composting them on their own, add them to the general compost heap. If you have a lot of leaves, layer them in a heap, press them down well and dampen them if they are very dry. Do not make a pile more than 1m (3ft) high and turn it three or four times a year. It will take around 18 months to decompose, by which time it will have shrunk to half its size.

Seaweed

If you live in a coastal area, you could collect seaweed, which is an excellent source of plant nutrients. Leave it outside for one or two rainfalls to wash away the salt then dig into the soil in autumn or winter.

Peat

Dark brown or black-coloured peats are useful for enriching the humus content of the soil and, therefore its drainage, but contain little in the way of plant food. Lighter-coloured peat is not so well decomposed and will be less rich in nutrients.

Bonemeal

Dried blood, fish meal and hoof and bone are all used as a top dressing to soil, or added at the bottom of a planting hole to enrich the soil at planting time. They are valuable, but expensive and add no bulk or humus to the soil, but enrich its content.

Draining Waterlogged Soil

Soil with poor drainage can often be improved by regular digging and incorporating lots of organic material.

If you have improved the humus content of your soil and the ground still appears to be waterlogged, or if puddles hang about for days on the surface, try raising the level of the plot, by still more digging and adding bulky organic matter.

Better drainage can sometimes be achieved by draining the ground above the plot. Dig a ditch at the end of this area, sloping it down into a sump (a deep hole, the bottom of which should be beneath the level of the water table) filled with rubble. Mark the position of the sump in some way, as it will probably need periodic cleaning out to remove silt and other rubbish.

Draining with a sump

A drain-trench can be dug in the subsoil, sloping from the highest to the lowest point and leading to a sump. It must be as deep as it is wide and have a layer of rubble in the bottom, with smaller pieces of clinker on top. The sub- and topsoil are then replaced.

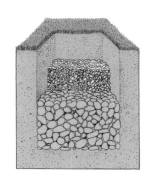

Draining with a pipe

To make a sump drainage system more effective, lay a pipe in the trench before filling it up with rubble and clinker. Use a stone pipe or a plastic one that has had slits cut into it along its length. The water soaks through the porous stone pipe or through the slits cut in the plastic one and away into the sump.

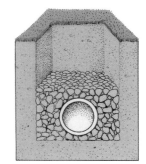

The herringbone system

You can make your drainage system more sophisticated by laying proper drains in the trench, arranging them in a herringbone pattern (left) of smaller pipes leading into a main pipe and, from there, into a nearby stream or piece of land where drainage is not a problem.

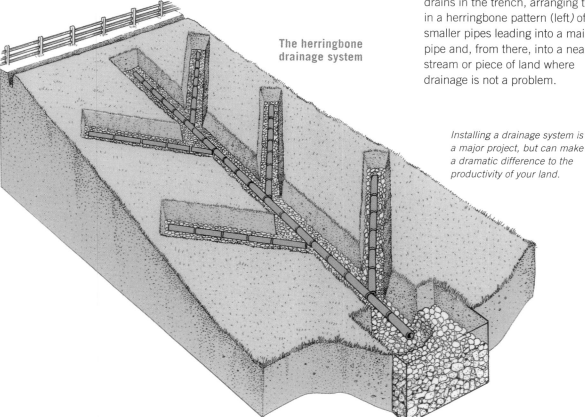

The herringbone drainage system

Installing a drainage system is a major project, but can make a dramatic difference to the productivity of your land.

STARTING OUT · DRAINING SOIL

Before you start digging a large area, choose a spade that is the right height and has a comfortable handle. Wear thick-soled boots to cushion your feet.

Digging

Turning the soil is an essential part of annual cultivation. It improves the soil's condition by aerating it and making drainage more efficient, while also making it easier for moisture to reach and be absorbed by the plant roots. It also provides an opportunity to clear the soil of old plant roots and weeds, and to incorporate organic material into the growing area to replenish lost nutrients.

Heavy clay soils should be dug in the autumn; not only will they be harder to dig later in the year, but they will not reap the benefit of the winter frosts in breaking up clumps of sod. Don't knock back the soil as you

dig, but leave it in large lumps on the surface to expose the maximum surface area to the coming frosts.

If you miss the opportunity to dig in autumn, wait until the spring winds have dried out the soil. Lighter soils can be dug later in the year.

Single or double digging?

A plot intended for growing fruit and vegetables may be single or double dug (*see* below and opposite). You will find either method strenuous and tiring, particularly if you tackle it incorrectly. Follow the method shown in the diagrams and always lift less on the spade than you think you can manage. Stand upright, stretching your spine at frequent intervals, and tackle the job slowly, especially if you are not used to regular digging.

Single digging is the more usual method of digging, and is quite adequate for most purposes.

Double digging is usually done on long-neglected ground. Heavy clay can benefit from double digging, as it will help to improve drainage. A new vegetable plot will yield better crops straightaway if it is double-dug at the outset.

As you dig, remove the roots of any perennial weeds. Annual weeds can be dug into the soil to add to the humus as they rot down.

SINGLE DIGGING

Work methodically and do not attempt to cover too large an area at any one time, particularly if you are not used to digging.

Mark the plot into two rectangular strips with garden twine. Dig out a trench on one strip, the depth of the spade and a little wider than its width. Put the soil in a wheelbarrow or just beyond the top of the next

Single digging

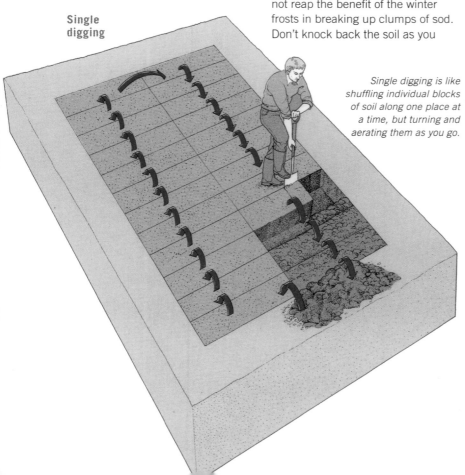

Single digging is like shuffling individual blocks of soil along one place at a time, but turning and aerating them as you go.

strip until you need it, at the very end of the job.

Dig narrow rows across the first strip, working backwards so as to avoid stepping on newly dug ground. Mark a line across the width each time with the edge of the spade, making each row 10–15cm (4–6in) wide – it is important to keep the trenches equal in size. Throw the soil forward into the previously dug trench, tilting the spade to the side to turn the soil as you go.

When you reach the end of the first strip, fill the remaining trench with soil taken from a trench at the same end of the adjoining strip. Work back down the other side of the plot in the same way, but the opposite direction, filling the final trench with the soil taken from the first trench you dug.

DOUBLE DIGGING

When you need to improve the basic structure or nutrient content of neglected soil, double digging is the best technique to use. It is hard work, but you will be rewarded in much better yields than if you had not done the job.

Use twine to mark out the plot into two rectangular strips, as you would for single digging. Dig the first strip the depth of the spade, but twice the width. Take out the soil.

Dig over the soil in the bottom of the trench, without removing it, then add an even layer of organic matter. Dig the next row, making it the depth and width of one spade, throwing soil forwards to fill the first trench. Dig out two rows of topsoil to form a new trench, two spades' width, and continue to work your way along the bed, digging in organic matter at the bottom of each trench as you go.

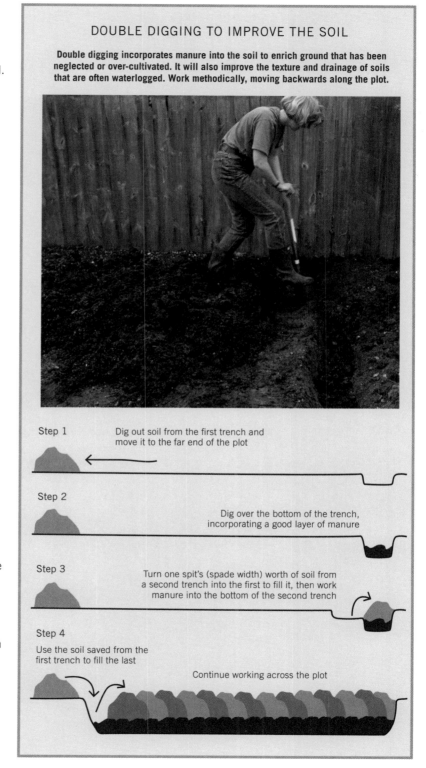

DOUBLE DIGGING TO IMPROVE THE SOIL

Double digging incorporates manure into the soil to enrich ground that has been neglected or over-cultivated. It will also improve the texture and drainage of soils that are often waterlogged. Work methodically, moving backwards along the plot.

Step 1 — Dig out soil from the first trench and move it to the far end of the plot

Step 2 — Dig over the bottom of the trench, incorporating a good layer of manure

Step 3 — Turn one spit's (spade width) worth of soil from a second trench into the first to fill it, then work manure into the bottom of the second trench

Step 4 — Use the soil saved from the first trench to fill the last

Continue working across the plot

STARTING OUT · DIGGING

Fences and Other Boundaries

Even the smallest patch of land will need fences – if only to mark its boundaries. If you're lucky you may already have sturdy walls or fences around your plot, but if not, choose wisely and take care to erect them correctly and your boundaries will be trouble-free for many years.

Fences have all sorts of other uses beyond being simple boundary markers. They can act as windbreaks to protect delicate fruit bushes or vegetables; they can form a screen which would hide untidy areas of the garden, such as the compost heap, or to keep bees, perhaps, away from certain areas; they are essential for containing livestock such as chickens, goats or pigs in a specific area, and they can act as supports for canes, vines or other climbers.

There are many different types of fencing. Some of the most common utilitarian options are illustrated overleaf, but there are others you might like to consider, including the common solid fence panels sold in standard sizes in most garden centres and DIY stores.

The cheapest of these panels may not stand up well to high winds and will present little challenge to a determined goat with a view to escape, but they make adequate boundaries for areas that are not exposed to rough weather and are both quick and easy to erect. Nail them to strong wooden posts set

Post and rail fences are strong enough to contain boisterous livestock, but will not keep hungry rabbits away from your vegetables.

in concrete footings or slide into securely bedded grooved concrete posts for a stronger fixing.

Think about form and function

Consider what function you want the fence to serve before selecting the type of fencing to use. This way you can choose the most suitable solution for the job. Of course, cost is a consideration, but do not necessarily choose the cheapest option. If it is not long-lasting, it will ultimately cost you more by having to replace it sooner than you would have done with a better initial fence.

Remember that boundary fences often have to keep pets and children in, as well as other people's livestock and destructive wild pests, such as rabbits, out. A post and rail fence makes an excellent barrier for containing livestock, but will do nothing to keep rabbits out of a vegetable patch.

Bear in mind, too, that solid fencing will block out all light from the area it casts into shadow, putting nearby fruit and vegetable plants into deep shade. Above all, any fence you erect is always only as good as its weakest point, so make sure that it is well erected, using solid posts.

Hedges and walls

A hedge is one of the most attractive of all boundaries and can form an effective barrier, too. Quickthorn and holly make good thick fences, quickthorn being one of the fastest to grow. But you must protect young hedges from animals such as goats, who will destroy them before they have chance to establish themselves.

As a hedge grows, it can be 'laid' to weave it into a more solid barrier by cutting into the base of growing stems and bending them over. In some cases, you can do this without any additional support; in others, separate upright stakes are driven into the ground and the living branches woven between them.

High walls are unbeatable for keeping pets, livestock and children in, and unwanted intruders out, but they can present a rather stark appearance. Attaching a wooden trellis, or stringing strong wire between vine eyes hammered or screwed into the wall makes it easier to grow climbing plants or espaliered fruit trees to soften the appearance of the bricks.

A south-facing wall is particularly useful for growing fruit, such as peaches, apricots and figs.

ELECTRIC FENCING

An electric fence can be useful for keeping pigs and goats in a contained area and it is easy to move from place to place if you vary your animals' grazing area.

Fences used to contain livestock must always have some sort of gate incorporated into them to give you access to feed, clean and inspect the animals. This is easy to incorporate into an electric fence. Drive two strong posts into the ground far enough apart for your access, then cut the wire between them and slide a plastic handle onto one end. Twist the final piece of this wire into a hook and twist the wire on the adjoining post into a loop. When you hook these together, the circuit will be reconnected.

Pigs will need a two-stranded electric fence to contain them securely; goats will need three, but the bottom wire does not have to be live. Position the live wire at around the nose height of the animals it is containing. They will very quickly learn to stay away, rather than getting repeatedly shocked by the wire. Make sure to clear any long grass around the site of the wire, as if it touches the electric fence it will allow some of the electricity to 'drain' into the ground.

An electric fence is an effective way of keeping livestock in their allocated space. Always erect a visible warning notice if a public right of way crosses your land.

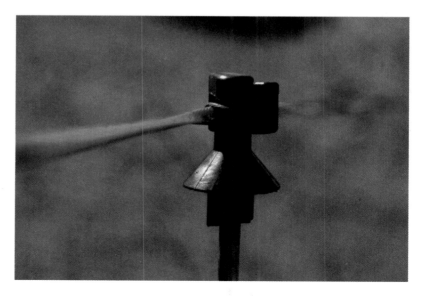

POST AND RAIL FENCING

There are many variations on the traditional style of post and rail fencing. They are one of the most attractive forms of fencing and form an extremely secure barrier, but once erected, they are permanently positioned, so you cannot easily move them to adjust the use of the land they contain. They are also an expensive choice.

All post and rail fences are constructed by nailing cross rails to sturdy vertical posts. Flat wooden boards can be used instead of chunky rails and these can be attached alternately to opposite sides of the vertical posts to give a different effect.

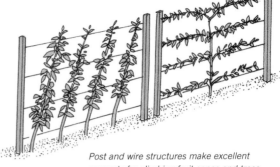

Post and wire structures make excellent supports for climbing fruit canes and trees. Use them together to make a productive and attractive boundary.

TYPES OF FENCES AND BOUNDARIES

The practicalities of fences and walls are important, but your boundaries should also blend in with your plot's surroundings.

A dry stone wall would look out of place in a suburban setting, just as barbed wire is an unattractive choice for a garden plot.

Dry stone walls

No cement is used in the construction. They are attractive and very stable if properly built. Semi-dry stone walls, in which cement is used in the centre, where it is hidden from view, are stronger, while retaining the dry stone effect.

Wattle hurdles

Can be purchased as panels or you can make them yourself by weaving split hazel branches between vertical posts. They provide a more solid-looking fence than ordinary hurdles (below), but are used in the same circumstances.

Post and rail fence

Quite crudely constructed, although a neater appearance can be achieved by cutting the ends of the horizontal rails at a 45° angle and splicing these together to form a continuous rail. In some fencing, mortise joints are used to join the horizontals to the verticals.

Wire netting fences

Often used for containing stock quickly and cheaply. Widely spaced pig wire is very strong; closer mesh wire, often called chicken wire, is easier to handle and perfectly adequate for poultry.

Hurdles

Very useful in making quick, temporary fencing to contain young livestock, for example. When not needed, hurdles can be neatly stacked against the wall of a shed or garage, where they will not take up much room.

Barbed wire fencing

There is rarely a good reason to choose barbed wire. It looks unattractive and can inflict very unpleasant injuries on livestock. In most circumstances, ordinary wire fencing will provide just as effective a barrier.

Tools and Equipment

The following selection of tools are those you are likely to find most useful in fruit and vegetable production. Start with a few core essentials and spend as much as you can afford, then add to your tool-shed bit by bit or if you need a particular tool for a job.

When buying gardening tools, it is usually true that you get what you pay for. In other words, the more expensive ones will generally be made of better, stronger material, and will not only last longer, but will also do their allotted job more efficiently. As with all garden tools, it is false economy to buy poorly made tools that will break much sooner than their more expensive, but better produced counterparts.

Do not make the mistake, though, of buying sophisticated equipment when much simpler tools will do the job equally well. Examine tools carefully before you buy, feeling to make sure the grip or handle is comfortable to hold and that they are the right weight for you.

Having bought good equipment, make sure you keep it in good condition. Scrape off all clinging soil before putting the tools away, and store them neatly, preferably by suspending them from hooks on the tool shed wall. Keep metal hinges oiled and greased, and sharpen all blades at least once a year.

Basic tool kit

These tools will form the basis of your arsenal of equipment. Use this as your 'start-up shopping list' and add to your shed as your experience grows.

- Spade and shovel
- Garden fork
- Rake
- Cultivators
- Dutch hoe
- Draw hoe
- Hand trowel and fork
- Broom
- Flower pots
- Garden twine and stakes
- Dibber
- Sprayer
- Watering can
- Hosepipe
- Secateurs
- Loppers
- Log saw
- Pruning saw
- Pickaxe
- Wheelbarrow
- Buckets

The Greenhouse

A greenhouse is by no means an essential item of equipment for growing your own garden produce but it can lengthen your growing season and widen the choice of crops that you can cultivate.

If you don't already have a greenhouse, the cost of buying and heating one (if you choose to do so) should be carefully weighed against the value of the crops you will produce. A greenhouse has two main functions: it enables you to produce a variety of crops (lettuces and dwarf beans, for example) outside the usual growing season, or to produce some of the rather more delicate crops that grow less successfully outdoors.

There are three main types of greenhouse and your choice may

Metal-framed greenhouses are light and the frames are slender, allowing the maximum possible area of glazing.

well be guided by the site you have available for it, but conventional ridge-roofed greenhouses are still considered by many to be the best shape of all. Buy the largest you can afford or accommodate – you are unlikely to wish you had less space.

Span or ridge roof
This is the most popular and useful greenhouse choice for vegetable production. The walls can be made completely of glass, or can be solid for the lower 1m (3ft) or so – perhaps brick or solid wood or metal, depending on the construction of the rest of the greenhouse.

Lean-to
A simpler structure, with the advantage that if it is built against a brick wall, the wall absorbs heat during the day and releases it into the greenhouse at night.

A lean-to can also be built alongside a potting shed, to keep tools and equipment close by. A disadvantage of a lean-to design is that it has light coming from only one side, so it must be constructed

against a south-facing wall. This sort of greenhouse is ideal for growing tree fruits, such as peaches or nectarines, and also for grapes.

Dutch-light
The sloping sides are constructed of large panes of glass and attract the maximum amount of light.

Variations on the basic designs
Even among these three basic shapes there are many different designs, and it is also possible to get circular or hexagonal-shaped greenhouses. These look attractive and are extremely practical in many ways, including the admission of as much light as possible, but they are generally not as good for vegetable and fruit production as the more conventional types as their size is usually limited.

The basic frame of a greenhouse may be constructed of wood or metal – galvanised iron, steel or

Polytunnels offer lots of space for growing. They may not look attractive, but if you have a suitable place they make an excellent choice.

aluminium, for example. Wooden frames look attractive, but the wood must be of good quality or it will warp or rot. It must also be treated or painted fairly regularly to keep it in good condition.

Metal greenhouses generally need very little maintenance and are easier to construct, but the material retains less warmth than wood.

Although the glazing in a greenhouse is traditionally glass, it is possible to use plastic or special polythene sheeting instead. This is cheaper than glass, but although it does not break, it scratches easily and heavily and needs renewing at regular intervals. Polytunnel greenhouses (opposite) are usually made of polythene sheeting stretched over a hooped frame.

The floor of the greenhouse can consist of soil borders for growing or may be paved or gravel throughout. Whichever you choose, the greenhouse walls must be erected on a solid foundation.

STAGING

If your greenhouse does not come equipped with staging, you will need to install some to make the most of your space. Benches positioned along one wall at roughly waist height provide a working platform and a second level for growing, if you also use the floor or a low-level row of staging, too.

Staging can be made from slatted wood or metal or grilles that also allow for drainage. Some staging can be turned over within a frame, with one solid side to act as a flat bench and one side with lips to make it a tray that will retain water for watering plants left standing in it. Some such trays are even deep enough to be used as a seed tray.

Removable panels make the staging versatile, allowing you to grow tall crops on the floor or lower level, lifting out the upper staging to give the crops more room.

Staging provides a comfortable working platform and leaves room beneath for storage, dormant plants or more young seedlings.

POSITIONING THE GREENHOUSE

In most cases the greenhouse has to go wherever there is room for it, but it must be in a sunny position and not heavily overshadowed by trees.

It is generally most convenient if the greenhouse is positioned fairly close to the house and it should have solid paths leading to it if possible, to make it easier to reach with wheelbarrows and in wet weather. Some gardeners think that it is best to site a greenhouse with the roof ridge running east-west; others will argue that a north-south orientation is better. East-west allows for more evenly distributed light to reach the whole greenhouse; north-south gives one warmer and one cooler side. Choose the orientation that best suits your site and your plans for growing.

Automatic window openers will help to prevent overheating in the greenhouse, so that tender plants do not 'cook' on very hot days.

HEATING AND VENTILATION

All the greenhouse crops described in this book can be grown in a cold greenhouse. The only heat they will need is to encourage germination from seed, and this can be supplied by a propagator (*see* page 60). If you want to grow crops out of season in the UK, you will need to install some sort of heating.

For most commonly grown crops, greenhouse heating does not have to be the sophisticated equipment needed for growing orchids, for example. Simple heaters readily available in garden centres and DIY stores will do the job perfectly well.

Choose the right fuel

Heating may be provided by gas, paraffin or electricity. Domestic gas heaters are simple and efficient, but if they are to be run off the mains supply, the greenhouse must be close to the house, or the installation costs will be prohibitive. Paraffin heaters are stand-alone devices and work well for little cost, providing

you burn high-grade fuel. Those with a temperature control are the best. Electricity is probably the most efficient form of heating and there are various types of heaters – fan, convector, tubular pipes or strips. Electric cables can also be buried in the soil to give it warmth, but they will not help much to raise the overall temperature.

Allow air to circulate

Good ventilation is crucial to prevent mould developing and diseases thriving. At least two panes in the roof should be hinged so they can be opened and ideally there should be one or two along the sides of the greenhouse as well. Louvred panels allow you to provide slight ventilation, by just opening them a fraction.

Some greenhouses are equipped with automatic openers which will open or close the panes according to the temperature inside. You can set your preferred opening and closing temperatures and leave them to monitor the greenhouse for you.

During summer, keep the windows open during the day and then close them at night before the outside temperature drops too low.

GREENHOUSE SHADING

Although greenhouses are designed to be warm, providing shading on very hot, sunny days is essential to prevent young plants, in particular, from getting burnt.

Shading can be provided by some sort of roller blind fitted in or outside the glass. A much cheaper alternative is to paint the glass with special shading paint, which can be washed off with soapy water when it is no longer required. Some modern

shading paints turn opaque in sunlight and fade back to being clear in overcast weather.

Another option is to drape horticultural fleece or mesh shade netting over the outside of the glass, but this is hard to secure from blustery winds.

COLD FRAMES

Cold frames are invaluable for hardening off seedlings that have been raised indoors and would find the shock of going straight outdoors too great.

If the cold frame has a base of good soil, it may be used as a protected seed bed or to bring on an early crop of lettuces or cabbages, for example. Less hardy crops, like cucumbers or melons, can be grown in a cold frame from sowing to harvesting.

Cold frames come in just about as many different designs and sizes as greenhouses; they can be permanent structures attached to the side of the lower solid wall of a greenhouse (in which case they get heat from it), or they may be portable so you can put them virtually anywhere convenient.

Consider building your own

The basic cold frame design is a square or rectangular box about 15cm (6in) higher at the back than the front, with sloping sides. The frame itself may be constructed of wood, brick or some sort of metal with glass or plastic sides, but the top must be glazed to allow light to penetrate. Ideally, the lid should be hinged at the back so it can be propped open on sunny days.

Many people make their own cold frames using an old window for the top and building sides to fit so that they have the right sized cold frame to suit their plot. Anyone with a little basic woodworking experience should be able to build a simple frame to hold glass or perspex for the top.

A window casement stay can be used to hold the lid open, or you could buy a special adjustable catch or just use a length of wood batten at varying angles to adjust the opening.

Site cold frames so that the sloping top is facing south, and keep the glass or plastic surface clean. Water plants sparingly so the atmosphere in the frame does not become too moist. You can keep the temperature stable by opening the top to varying degrees according to the weather. Use the cold frame to harden off crops raised in a greenhouse by gradually exposing them to longer periods of the cooler outside temperature before transplanting them into the vegetable bed.

Just as with a greenhouse, the size of the cold frame will depend on how much space you have available and how much you expect to use it. As a rule, aim for a minimum size of 1.2m x 1m (4ft x 3ft).

You can use cold frames to acclimatise young plants to outdoor temperatures, so they are not shocked by a sudden move from the warm.

Greenhouse Management

A greenhouse provides an excellent growing environment for your crops, but it is also a fertile breeding ground for bacteria and diseases, and plants can easily fail as quickly as they first grew.

Hygiene and good maintenance are crucial to keep your greenhouse crops and young plants in good health. One of the simplest and most important preventive measures is to avoid overcrowding. When plants are kept too close together, moist, stagnant air collects and this will encourage disease. Keep an eye on seedlings as they grow and make sure that you thin them out promptly if they are growing in a propagator or seed tray, or spread them out if they are in individual pots. Pinch off any unnecessary foliage on established plants, such as some tomato leaves, to reduce the bulk of larger plants and allow air to circulate more freely.

SPOTTING SIGNS OF DISEASE

Open doors and windows in fine weather to allow fresh air into the greenhouse and check all the plants in the greenhouse as you water them daily so that you are always vigilant for the first signs of disease.

Be scrupulous about removing diseased plants or leaves and taking them out of the greenhouse to dispose of them. If you spot signs of disease, treat it promptly and keep checking for indications that it is spreading. If necessary, be ruthless and get rid of any plants that look unhealthy – sacrificing one crop is better than losing all the plants growing in the greenhouse.

Don't allow dead leaves, rubbish or spilled compost to linger in the greenhouse. A paved floor is a good choice because it is so easy to sweep clean. If you have soil borders within the greenhouse, weed them regularly and pick out fallen leaves or other bits of plant debris left on the surface.

WATERING AND DAMPING DOWN

Although watering is vital, it is easy to overdo it and leave plants waterlogged. A little and often is far better than days of drought followed by a drenching. Water daily during the growing season and preferably twice on the hottest days.

Always use the rose on the spout of your watering can to give a shower of water to seedlings and young plants and avoid damaging them with a deluge.

Another way to get much-needed moisture to your plants in the heat of summer is to increase the humidity in the greenhouse. You can do this easily by spraying the leaves of your crops with a plant mister, rather than only watering at the roots with a watering can.

In addition, you can use the rose of a watering can to 'damp down' the greenhouse floor, if it is paved. The heat of the stones and of the sun will make the water evaporate.

AUTUMN AND SPRING CLEANING

Some diseases will inevitably find their way into your greenhouse and spores and bacteria can lie dormant in the fabric of the building from season to season, ready to attack your crops next year.

In autumn, when the summer crops have finished and you are no longer raising seedlings, give the greenhouse a really thorough clean. Choose a mild day so that you can move any plants that are ready to overwinter under glass outside while you work. Scrub the outside of any planted pots that will go back into the greenhouse later, taking care not to damage the plants in them.

Clear the greenhouse of all empty pots, potting equipment, labels and tools. Clean them all thoroughly, paying attention to the rims of pots and any corners, cleaning off algae and scraps of compost. Dry and store them neatly, ready for next year. Scrub wooden seed trays with disinfectant and allow them to dry thoroughly before storing.

Next, sweep the floor and brush the frame, staging and glass to get rid of any cobwebs, dust or debris. Make a note of any damaged panes

of glass or parts of the framework that need attention and fix them as soon as possible.

Wash the glass inside and out using a soft cloth and a bucket of warm water mixed with washing-up liquid and garden disinfectant.

Scrub the frame and staging with a stiff brush and clean algae from between overlapping panes of glass by sliding a thin plant label or piece of plastic between the panes and moving it up and down. Remove the panes of glass to clean them thoroughly if necessary.

Rinse everything with a hosepipe or pressure washer to remove any soapy residue. Remember to include the floor and any gravel in the trays of the staging. Shut the door and windows at the end of the day and fumigate the greenhouse with a smoke cone to finish the job.

It may seem laborious, but cleaning the greenhouse thoroughly will save you a good deal of time and effort next growing season in tackling pests and diseases on your crops.

Cloches

You can speed up plant growth by creating warmer, more humid conditions, and cloches are the simplest way of doing this. Use them to raise the temperature of the soil before sowing seed and to protect vulnerable seedlings.

Cloches have evolved from a sort of glass dome that was placed over one or more plants. They are now most commonly used as tunnel structures to cover a row of germinating seeds, young seedlings or even mature plants such as strawberries, to bring them on quicker. They are also useful when placed over the soil in spring to warm it prior to sowing.

The tunnels may be made of glass, moulded or corrugated plastic, or polythene sheeting. Polythene cloches are probably the cheapest and are easily constructed at home, just stretching a sheet of clear plastic over a row of hoops pushed into the soil or even a length of chicken wire bent into a tunnel shape and bedded into the soil. Cover the surface of the polythene with netting to protect it from damage by birds.

Provide some fresh air inside

Glass cloches are still regarded by many to be the best; they let in the maximum amount of light and do not cause condensation (as polythene does), but they are expensive, breakable and often difficult to get hold of in garden centres.

Whatever type of cloche you use, it must be closed at the ends if it is to be fully effective. But when plants are growing, closed cloches can get stale and condensation build up inside. Some plastic cloches now come with ventilation holes that can

be opened and closed as required to reduce the condensation.

If your cloches are open-ended (this makes them useful for joining together to cover a long row) close the ends with a pane of glass or sheet of plastic held in place with a brick, otherwise all the warm air under the cover will escape through the open ends. You can tie the ends of sheets of polythene to close them then stake them into the ground.

Keep an eye on the plants

Remember to check under your cloches regularly. The plants inside may need watering more frequently than those in the open soil, as the warm ground will dry out faster. And weeds will thrive under the protection of the cloche, just as well as your crops will.

If you are using cloches to protect tender plants, such as strawberries, remember to lift or open them to allow insects access to the plants when they need pollinating. You can do this by removing one rigid cloche and spacing the others out to leave gaps in between or by lifting one side of the plastic sheeting.

Tunnel cloches cover whole rows of seedlings. They are efficient and economical, whether made from polythene sheeting or hard plastic.

Traditional glass 'bell' cloches (front) or larger, square lantern cloches (behind) are an attractive way of protecting tender young plants in the vegetable garden, but they are only suitable for individual plants, so are of limited use to the self-sufficient grower.

Rotation of Vegetables

The first principle of growing vegetables is that the crops in each plant group should be grown in a different part of the vegetable garden each year, if possible.

This programme of crop rotation is important for two main reasons: the first is that different crops like different soil conditions. Peas and beans, for example, like ground that is rich in freshly added, well-rotted manure, whereas if roots, such as carrots and parsnips, are grown in the same soil, the result is a crop of twisted, forked, divided vegetables which have gone on a search for the organic matter within the soil.

The second reason is that the pests and diseases that plague individual groups of vegetables will remain in the ground, ready to attack again. They do not, however, affect vegetables in the other groups.

The most usual crop rotation operates on a three-year plan, although if you can divide the plot up into four patches and operate the four-year plan, so much the better.

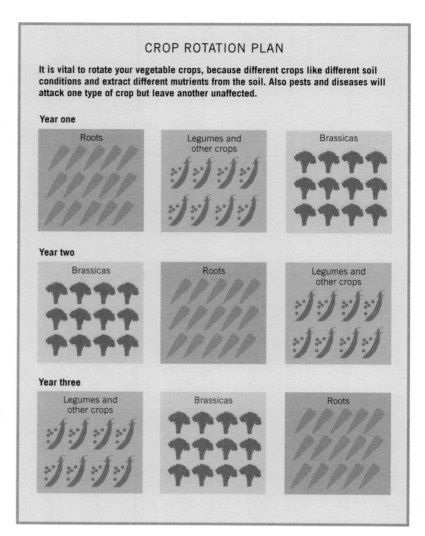

CROP ROTATION PLAN

It is vital to rotate your vegetable crops, because different crops like different soil conditions and extract different mutrients from the soil. Also pests and diseases will attack one type of crop but leave another unaffected.

Year one

Roots | Legumes and other crops | Brassicas

Year two

Brassicas | Roots | Legumes and other crops

Year three

Legumes and other crops | Brassicas | Roots

DEVISING YOUR CROP ROTATION PLAN

Following the three-year rotation plan, you must divide your plot into three areas and your crops into the three principal groups. These are the root crops (*see* page 66, but also including potatoes and chicory), brassicas (*see* page 62, plus radishes), and a combination of the legumes and other outdoor crops which, besides beans and peas, include celery, celeriac, leeks, onions, sweetcorn and tomatoes.

The salad crops not mentioned in these groups can be grown as catch crops – that is, as a quick crop to utilise the land after it has been cleared of a major crop and before the next one is sown – grown between rows of longer-maturing vegetables, or as successional crops.

Marrows, courgettes (large and small zucchini) and pumpkins can be included in the legume and other outdoor crop section, but if you have a patch of spare land or a space on a compost heap, they are best grown here, for they can take up much

valuable space in the vegetable garden proper.

The perennial crops, such as globe artichokes and asparagus, have to be allotted a permanent space as they will crop in the same site for a number of years. Jerusalem artichokes can be included in the roots group, but they are so pervasive that they are really best grown on a small patch of otherwise useless ground, perhaps in front of the garden shed or positioned to hide the compost heap and other work areas from view.

If you intend to operate a three-year rotation plan, and have divided the main part of the vegetable garden into three roughly equal-sized plots, allocate the first plot to the root crops, the second plot to the legumes and other outdoor crops and the third plot to the brassicas. The following year move the vegetables down the line, so that the first plot has the brassicas, the second has the root crops and the third the legumes and other outdoor crops. In the final year of the plan, the first plot will have the legumes, the second will have the brassicas and the third will have the roots.

Feeding the soil

You will get even better crops if you follow a system of digging lots of well-rotted manure or compost into the ground before planting the legumes, applying general fertiliser to the ground before planting the roots and applying both fertiliser and lime before planting the brassicas.

The roots will benefit from the manure dug in for the legumes, because by the time they are planted it will have become well-rotted and incorporated into the ground, thus making the soil moisture-retentive, rather than very rich. Potatoes, which can react very badly to lime, are not planted until two years after the lime was applied to the ground, but the brassicas, which thrive in alkaline conditions, have had full benefit from it.

A four-year rotation plan

If you are able to operate a four-year plan you can either separate out the peas and beans from the legumes and other outdoor crops, or you can treat potatoes as a separate group, perhaps using that plot also for marrows and courgettes and some

of the spinach crops. Divide your land into four equal areas and move crops one plot along each year.

GOLDEN RULES FOR SUCCESS

The most important things to remember in any rotation plan are to ensure that brassicas and potatoes never follow themselves in the same sites in successive years (and preferably not more than once every three years) and to plant quick-growing, successional crops after harvesting a major crop whenever possible.

If brassicas follow brassicas, you could easily get a build-up of the disease club root (*see* page 148) in the soil and once there, it will remain for several years, making it impossible to grow brassicas at all.

Constructing equal-sized raised beds is a good way to mark out zones for a crop rotation plan. Grow one whole bed of brassicas, another of roots and a third of legumes.

Likewise with potatoes, you could encourage the pest eelworm (*see* page 148) in the soil, and this too will remain for some time.

Remember, too, that some crops which take time to reach full maturity can be regarded as quick-growing when grown as successional crops. Carrots and beetroots, for example, which would take perhaps four months to reach full size, can nevertheless be harvested much quicker as young and delicious baby vegetables. In some instances you will find that there is time to grow a quick-maturing crop after harvesting the previous one, and before planting the next one outlined in the rotation scheme.

Watering and Conservation

Even in rainy Britain there will be periods of hot dry weather every year, when your crops will need to be watered if they are to thrive or even survive. There are ways to minimise the amount of watering you need to do, and to conserve supplies of clean, treated tap water.

Watering with a hosepipe is quick and easy – with a sprinkler attached to a hosepipe it's even easier – and it is tempting to do this when you have a large area to water and so many other jobs calling for your attention. But a hosepipe will use 17 litres (3.7 gallons) a minute, so that running a sprinkler for an hour takes 1000 litres (220 gallons) of water.

As our climate changes, water is becoming more scarce and a more valuable commodity at the same time as it becomes more essential

within the garden and the vegetable plot. You can do a lot to conserve water in the choices you make about how you use it, which plants and varieties you choose to grow and how you design and maintain your plot.

Follow the advice on these pages to cut down the amount of tap water you use and you will save yourself a considerable amount of money (if your water supply is metered), as well as helping to conserve precious supplies of water and the energy used to treat it and deliver it.

WHEN AND HOW TO WATER

Make the most of the water you give to your plants by targeting it well and watering at the right time of day. Always try to avoid watering plants at the hottest part of the day. The water will evaporate fast in the heat and much of it will be wasted.

Instead, water at the beginning or end of the day. Water at the base of each plant so that the water goes directly to the roots. With sprawling crops, such as pumpkins, it is a good idea to push a stake into the ground where the stalk emerges to help you to direct your water to the right spot.

Particularly thirsty crops – again, pumpkins are a good example – can benefit from a watering well. Build up a raised lip of soil around the stem at a diameter of around 50cm (18in); this will retain a well of water that will seep slowly into the soil, giving the plant a really good soaking that will last it for a couple of days in mild weather.

Direct water carefully to the base of each plant to make the most of each drop; widespread sprinkling is wasteful and ineffective.

Use a watering can with a rose on to water your crops, using this essential job as an opportunity to check plants for signs of pests or disease as you go. Twist the rose to point upwards when watering young seedlings, as this gives a more gentle spray.

If you need to use a hose, fit a trigger-operated spray nozzle that will deliver water just when and where you need it, rather than running continuously, even when you are moving from one area to another.

One golden rule of watering is not to water plants unnecessarily. In the open ground, where plants have access to reserves of water stored in the soil, you may only need to water every couple of days in average temperatures, particularly in spring and early summer. Be alert for signs

How soil holds water

If your soil is heavy and prone to waterlogging, you will see puddles sitting on the surface after heavy rain. You can dig in gypsum to improve it or install a drainage system (*see* page 27). Light sandy soil will drain very quickly, sometimes before plants can benefit from the water you give them, but this is harder to identify. To gauge how well your soil retains water, dig a large hole and fill it with water, then monitor how long it takes for the water to drain away. If the hole empties within an hour plants are unlikely to thrive in the soil; if the water is all gone within four hours, the soil would benefit from more organic matter. Dig in plenty of well-rotted compost and you should find that you need to water less and less often.

of drought – wilting foliage and leaves that are starting to look crisp and sunburned – and increase your watering regime for a while until the weather cools again.

AUTOMATIC WATERING SYSTEMS

If you have a large fruit and vegetable plot (making it impractical to water all the plants by hand on a daily basis), a micro-bore automatic system can be a good compromise and a less wasteful alternative to widespread sprinkling.

While much water from a broadcast sprinkler will inevitably fall on bare earth, paths and other areas that do not actually require watering, automatic watering systems are more

precise. Setting up requires a lot of work, as you must run narrow-bore hoses from the tap supplying the water throughout the plot, branching off to all the different areas and fixing outlet nozzles wherever they are needed. The result, though, delivers water directly to each plant or to a small area at a time.

Electronic timers and valves control how long the water runs for and when it is switched on, and the more sophisticated systems allow you to tailor the watering to different parts of your plot, giving more water where it is needed and a light sprinkling to less thirsty crops.

Soaker hoses can also be used in this way, rather than pipes with spray or drip nozzles attached. When the water is turned on, it seeps slowly through the fabric of the hose along

Commercial irrigation systems like this can be useful in a very large plot, where watering by hand is not practical. Install a programmable timer to make efficient use of the water.

its whole length, giving a gentle, slow watering to a strip of land.

COLLECTING AND USING RAINWATER

The very best water to use for your plants is rainwater. It is free, kept at the same temperature as the air – rather than the chill of tap water – and contains none of the chemical impurities of treated domestic water.

Position water butts or tanks around your property wherever you have downpipes or any pitched roofs (*see* page 247). You could be surprised at how quickly a water butt will fill up, even if it is only draining off a small shed. If you have room, you can join several water butts together to collect even more water. Even if you don't have any suitable buildings in one area of your property you could stand an open tank in an unused space and collect water that falls into it. Make sure that you cover the top with a grill of strong mesh, preferably fixed securely in place, to prevent animals or children falling in and drowning.

You can use your water butts to fill watering cans, or attach your garden hose to a submersible electric pump lowered into the butt that will allow you to water the plot more quickly. Gravity-fed rainwater systems are also available, which take water from the butt through a network of pipes to jets, similar to those found on other automatic watering systems.

PLANNING A WATER-WISE PLOT

You can help to protect your plants from heat and drought in the design of your plot and by choosing drought-resistant varieties if you live in an area that regularly suffers from long, dry spells and hot weather.

One of the most important things you can do before you start planting anything is to check the water-retaining quality of your soil (*see* page 42). If there is insufficient humus mixed in with the soil particles, water will drain through too freely and much of it will be wasted.

Trees and hedges are greedy and thirsty plants, and will suck up large quantities of water and nutrients in the soil, so if you position your vegetable plot too close you will

Rainwater collected and stored in water butts is perfect for plants: it does not contain chemical additives and is not delivered at high pressure and low temperature, as tap water is.

increase your plants' need for extra feed and water – making more work for yourself as well as extra demands on your water supply.

Protect against sun and wind
Overhanging trees will also cast shade over your plot, as will a hedge, fence or any other solid boundary unless it is to the north of the bed. While some shade can help to reduce wilting in very hot sun, in the British climate it is likely to make it more difficult for your plants to thrive and, again, you will need to work harder to achieve success than in a bright, sunny situation. Choose a site that gets at least six hours of sun a day – preferably in the morning, rather than the afternoon and evening sun.

In regions that often have periods of hot, dry, sunny weather, consider erecting a simple pergola

over an area of crops that might be susceptible to drought, such as a strawberry bed. The wooden framework will provide a little light shade without blocking out much-needed light at other times of year and can be draped with some horticultural fleece or other shading fabric on days when you need to add more protection.

Persistent wind will reduce the water-retention of your soil, so if you cannot avoid planning your garden in an exposed site that you know will be subject to high winds, work windbreaks into your plan. These could be trellis panels that can help to minimise the effects of the wind without blocking out too much sun, or could be living windbreaks, such as a row of raspberry canes planted along one edge of a plot.

When you plant your plot, try to avoid leaving large areas of bare earth close to planted sections, as water will evaporate from the bare ground in the sun or be stripped away by winds, and this will take valuable moisture away from the plants that are growing nearby. Use a mulch of compost or chipped tree and shrub prunings between rows and on empty patches of your plot to prevent this. A generous mulch of compost will also help and will rot down into the soil, feeding it at the same time.

Green manures
If you have a large area of ground that is lying fallow, consider planting a green manure. These are fast-growing crops, often rye grass, vetch or peas, which will cover the ground for a season. When they have died down, you should dig the foliage into the soil, where it will enrich it with nutrients as it rots. Garden centres and catalogues supply a range of

Green manures will cover an area of bare soil, helping to retain moisture. They will feed the soil, too, when you dig them in later.

green manure crops, many of them tailored to the particular needs of different types of soil.

Test your soil (*see* page 24) to find out more about its structure and nutrient levels then choose an appropriate manure crop.

CHOOSING THE RIGHT PLANTS

Plant breeders are all aware of the need to use less water and are constantly working to develop new varieties that are increasingly drought tolerant. Look for types of vegetables and some specific varieties that are better able to withstand hot, dry conditions.

Root crops, such as carrots, are generally more tolerant of drought than plants with swelling fruits, such as courgettes and tomatoes. Root crops can penetrate deep into the soil to reach moisture locked below the surface. Leeks also survive well in dry conditions; earthing up (a process of scraping soil around the stems to blanch them), also helps to lock in moisture. Leafy crops are less forgiving of drought, but spinach beet often does well.

Onions and lettuces are prone to bolting, or running to seed, in hot, dry weather, so look for drought-resistant varieties. In general, try to choose plants that grow in naturally hot regions if your own area is often affected by high temperatures. Okra and sweet potatoes, for example, which once would not have grown in the UK, are now widely available and make interesting options for the climate-change garden.

CALENDAR
OF SEASONAL
JOBS

The Year in the Garden
Spring
Summer
Autumn
Winter

The Year in the Garden

The calendar of work outlined on the following pages is meant only as a general guide to the principal tasks of sowing, planting and harvesting. Pick out the advice that relates to your crops – it is very unlikely that anyone will find themselves doing all the jobs listed here.

The climate where you live will dictate the actual timing for doing these jobs, and this will vary from year to year. This calendar follows the seasons rather than months, since you could safely start planting out in the warm regions of the south a good month before or even more than in the very north of the country, where temperatures are lower and winters usually harder and longer.

Be guided by the weather conditions and signs around you in nature to gauge when it is warm enough in spring to start sowing (buds swelling on trees and emerging bulbs, for example); and keep an eye on a maximum/minimum thermometer to spot a decline in temperatures that signals the time to start tucking up tender crops for winter.

Understanding your plot and animals takes time and experience, but keeping a daily diary can help you to spot emerging patterns. Note down the weather for the day, what you have done and anything that was ready for harvesting, transplanting, sowing, pruning and more. Compare your notes the following year and you will start to get a feel for the rhythm of the seasons and the cycle of nature.

Tailor the calendar to your needs

There are many crops which can be sown in regular succession throughout spring and summer, but if you do this you will be inundated with that one vegetable and may not have much room left in the vegetable garden to grow anything else. Sow all vegetables as and when it suits you (within their particular season), to get a reasonable amount and assortment of vegetables, rather than an ongoing glut of any one type.

Routine jobs in your plot

Remember that, in addition to the jobs described in this calendar, you must hoe the fruit and vegetable gardens regularly throughout the growing season to keep weeds under control and all crops must be watered regularly in dry weather.

Stake and tie plants as necessary to support them as they are growing, and protect emerging seedlings from birds by tying threads of cotton above them or by covering them with cloches. In addition, protect young crops from frost in the winter and early spring with cloches.

Inspect all crops regularly to make sure they are not suffering from any disease or pest infestation; if they are, deal with it immediately (*see* page 143) to prevent the condition getting worse or spreading, and burn any infected plants you pull up. Dig up and compost all healthy plants once the harvest is finished, so that the land can be used for another crop. Try not to allow any part of the vegetable garden to lie fallow, particularly during the main growing season.

Spring

As bulbs start emerging in the garden and buds begin to swell on the trees, it is time to venture back into the vegetable and fruit plots.

You may be able to harvest some early spring greens or rhubarb and overwintered root crops, but keep an eye on the weather and watch out for sudden spring frosts that can strip the blossom from fruit trees and destroy your budding crop.

As the season progresses and the soil warms up, seedlings, blossoms, insects and the promise of a bountiful harvest are all around you.

EARLY SPRING

In the greenhouse
- Water all greenhouse crops regularly throughout the spring
- Sow pepper, chilli and tomato seeds and raise them in a propagator

In the fruit garden
- Plant apricots, figs, vines and rhubarb
- Sow seeds of alpine strawberries under glass or indoors
- Prune apples, apricots, sour cherries, plums, gages and damsons
- Pollinate apricots
- Raise new plants of rhubarb
- Harvest rhubarb

In the vegetable garden
- Prepare seed beds and permanent growing sites for sowing as soon as weather

Get an early start with tomato seedlings sown and raised in a propagator in the greenhouse. Move them outside when the weather is better.

conditions allow
- Sow under glass or indoors seeds of globe varieties of beetroot, asparagus peas, leeks, self-blanching celery and ordinary celery
- Sow in seed beds seeds of calabrese
- Sow in permanent sites seeds of kohl rabi, maincrop carrots, parsnips, salsify and scorzonera, first-early peas, mange tout (snow peas) and petit pois, American cress, lettuce, radishes, salad and pickling onions, onions from seed and summer spinach
- Plant early potatoes and Jerusalem artichoke tubers
- Harden off summer cabbage and cauliflower
- Transplant to a permanent site red cabbage
- Harvest purple sprouting broccoli, savoy, red cabbage, kale, spinach beet, swedes (rutabagas), turnip greens, chicory, lettuce, celery, leeks, winter spinach
- Protect early crops and young

Follow the weather forecast and protect outdoor crops with horticultural fleece or cloches when spring frosts are expected so that they are not lost early in the year.

seedlings from cold weather with cloches as necessary

In the herb bed
- Sow in permanent sites seeds of burnet, chervil, fennel, dill, lovage, marjoram, parsley, rosemary, sage and thyme
- Divide roots of lovage to create new plants
- Plant bay trees and tarragon

MID-SPRING

In the greenhouse

- Transplant aubergine (eggplant) and cucumber seedlings to their permanent growing positions
- Sow melon seeds and raise them in a propagator
- Prune vines and established fruit trees. Train new growth on wires fixed to the greenhouse frame
- Pinch out growing tips of vines
- Start opening vents to increase ventilation as the daytime temperatures rise
- Damp down the greenhouse floor each time you water the plants to increase humidity

In the fruit garden

- Harden off alpine strawberries
- Train new growth of vines, peaches and nectarines
- Mulch apples, apricots, sour cherries, peaches and nectarines, pears, gooseberries, vines, raspberries and rhubarb. Put straw under strawberry plants
- Harvest rhubarb

In the vegetable garden

- Sow under glass or indoors dwarf French and haricot beans, tomatoes for outdoors, celery, celeriac, marrows, courgettes (zucchini) and pumpkins, okra, New Zealand spinach, sweetcorn
- Sow in seed beds seeds of purple sprouting broccoli, Brussels sprouts, summer cabbage and kale
- Sow in permanent sites seeds of kohl rabi, maincrop carrots, parsnips, salsify and scorzonera, spinach beet, turnips, broad beans, second-early peas, mange tout (snow peas) and petit pois, chicory, lettuce, radish, leeks, salad and pickling onions, onions from seed, onions from sets, garlic, summer spinach
- Plant second-early potatoes and globe artichoke suckers
- Harden off white sprouting broccoli, globe varieties of beetroot, asparagus peas, tomatoes for outdoors, celery, celeriac, leeks, onions from seed
- Transplant to permanent sites globe varieties of beetroot, carrots, turnips
- Harvest purple sprouting broccoli, spring cabbage, savoy, red cabbage, kale, spinach beet, swedes, turnip greens, lettuce, salad onions, leeks, winter spinach
- Begin earthing up emerging potatoes

In the herb bed

- Sow angelica, balm, borage, burnet, chervil, coriander, dill hyssop, pot marjoram, sage and summer savory

LATE SPRING

In the greenhouse

- Transplant pepper, chilli, melon and tomato seedlings to their permanent sites in greenhouse beds, pots or growing bags
- Mulch all greenhouse crops
- Shade greenhouse roof as necessary with shading paint, blinds or horticultural fleece
- Pollinate fruit trees under glass as necessary
- Support growing aubergine and cucumber plants

In the fruit garden

- Transplant to permanent site alpine strawberries
- Thin fruits of apricots and gooseberries
- Harvest rhubarb

In the vegetable garden

- Sow under glass or indoors seeds of cucumber and celery
- Sow in seed beds autumn and winter cabbage, savoy, cauliflower and white sprouting broccoli
- Sow in permanent sites seeds of kohl rabi, maincrop carrots, salsify and scorzonera, seakale beet, swedes, turnips, kale, broad beans, dwarf French and haricot beans, runner beans, late peas, mange tout (snow peas) and petit pois, cucumber (but protect with cloches), salad and pickling onions, onions from seed, okra (but protect with cloches), New Zealand spinach, sweetcorn (but protect with cloches)
- Plant maincrop potatoes, asparagus crowns
- Harden off dwarf French and haricot beans, runner beans, marrows, courgettes (zucchini) and pumpkins, okra, New Zealand spinach, celery, sweetcorn
- Transplant dwarf French and haricot beans, asparagus peas, celery, celeriac, onions from seed, okra, sweetcorn (but protect with cloches)
- Thin carrots, parsnips, turnips, dwarf, French and haricot beans, lettuce and all types of spinach
- Harvest purple sprouting broccoli, spring cabbage, swedes, turnip greens, broad beans, first-early peas, asparagus, lettuce, radish, salad onions, leeks, winter spinach
- Continue earthing up potatoes

In the herb bed

- Sow chervil, dill, pot marjoram and sage
- Harden off seedlings of basil and marjoram grown under glass and plant out into pots or the herb bed a few weeks later

Summer

The fruit and vegetable garden should, by now, be bursting with produce and growing fast. Summer is a season of hard work, but rich rewards – what could be better than collecting a basketful of fresh and delicious produce for your evening meal?

You will be busy throughout the fruit and vegetable patch in summer, watering, thinning and harvesting plants and checking thoroughly and regularly for signs of pests or disease. Feed plants regularly, too, to get the best out of them.

Check your crops daily, even if they don't require daily watering, so that you can spot and pick produce when it is at its very best. A young courgette can very quickly turn into a monster marrow, losing its delicious flavour overnight and becoming tough-skinned and watery; and soft fruits and tomatoes can over-ripen and begin to rot on the bush if they are not harvested promptly.

Preserving produce

At this time of year you may find yourself with a glut of one or more crops that have all matured at once. This spare produce can often be used to repay favours or store up future goodwill with friends and neighbours or you may be able to trade your surplus with another grower's different glut. But anything you cannot eat, swap or give away should be preserved to see you through the leaner winter months.

Many things – soft fruits in particular – can be frozen in their natural, harvested state or, with beans, for example, blanched quickly in boiling water first.

Freeze your produce on open trays to prevent individual berries or vegetables clumping together in a mass that must all be defrosted and used at once (*see* pages 210–11 and 222–3 for more on freezing).

The vegetable garden in summer is bursting with produce and there is daily work to be done, harvesting, thinning and watering.

Other crops can be preserved by cooking and then freezing or bottling. Turn a trug full of tomatoes into a pasta sauce, tomato ketchup, chutney or the basis of a ratatouille with leeks, courgettes and peppers. Or make jams, jellies, pickles and chutneys (see pages 214–17 and 226–9) that will last for months in a cool cupboard.

Carrots, potatoes, onions, apples and other crops can be stored for several months in a cool place if they are cleaned and packed carefully (see pages 207–8). And some root crops are actually best left in the ground if you do not need the space immediately for another crop.

Don't forget that some slightly spoiled produce that doesn't get picked in time or that falls from the bush before you pick it can still be used in chutneys or may be fed to your pigs. And anything that you miss until it is really too late for consumption should be added to the compost heap.

EARLY SUMMER

In the greenhouse
- Throughout the summer, water and feed all greenhouse crops regularly – twice a day, in morning and early evening, if necessary
- Pollinate grapes and melons
- Thin out tree fruits
- Support growing chilli, pepper, melon and tomato plants
- Harvest cucumbers
- Apply greenhouse shading to the glass if not already done in spring to protect plants from scorching

In the fruit garden
- Prune figs, peaches and nectarines, gooseberries, red and white currants
- Thin fruits of apples, plums and

gages, peaches and nectarines, gooseberries
- Harvest strawberries, blackcurrants, gooseberries and rhubarb

In the vegetable garden
- Water all crops regularly during dry spells
- Support growing plants
- Sow in seed beds seeds of red cabbage
- Sow in permanent sites seeds of Chinese cabbage, kohl rabi, globe varieties of beetroot, long-rooted varieties of beetroot, dwarf, French and haricot beans, first-early peas, asparagus peas, lettuce, radish, salad and pickling onions
- Harden off cucumbers
- Transplant to permanent sites purple sprouting broccoli, Brussels sprouts, autumn and winter cabbage, savoy, cauliflower and white sprouting broccoli, kale, runner beans, tomatoes

Pick perpetual spinach and leafy greens, like this ruby chard, regularly to encourage new growth of tender young stems.

for outdoors, cucumbers and pumpkins
- Thin Chinese cabbage, kohl rabi, salsify and scorzonera, summer spinach, New Zealand spinach, seakale beet and spinach beet
- Pinch out growing tips of trailing marrows and pumpkins
- Harvest globe artichokes, summer cabbage, kohl rabi, beetroot, carrots, broad beans, dwarf and French beans, first-early peas, mange tout (snow peas) and petit pois, asparagus peas, early potatoes, asparagus, American cress, lettuce, radish, salad onions, summer spinach

In the herb bed
- Sow in seed beds seeds of chervil and dill
- Harvest herbs as required for cooking

MIDSUMMER

In the greenhouse
- Thin out fruits of grapes and melons
- Harvest aubergines, cucumbers, tomatoes, peppers and chillies and tree fruits
- Water and feed crops regularly, looking out for signs of drought
- Inspect crops daily for signs of disease and treat promptly

In the fruit garden
- Plant strawberries
- Prune apples, peaches and nectarines and pears
- Thin fruits of pears (if necessary) and grapes
- Train blackberries, loganberries and raspberries
- Raise new plants of strawberries from runners
- Harvest apricots, sour cherries, peaches and

nectarines, strawberries, alpine strawberries, blackcurrants, blueberries, gooseberries, summer-fruiting raspberries, red and white currants and rhubarb

In the vegetable garden
- Sow in seed beds seeds of red cabbage
- Sow in permanent sites kohl rabi, globe beetroots, spinach beet, turnips, dwarf, French and haricot beans, salad and pickling onions, summer spinach
- Transplant to permanent sites purple sprouting broccoli, Brussels sprouts, autumn and winter cabbage, savoy, cauliflower and white sprouting broccoli and kale
- Thin kale, kohl rabi, beetroot (all varieties), parsnips, salsify and scorzonera, chicory, summer spinach, New Zealand spinach and swedes
- Pinch out growing tips of broad beans, tomatoes and New Zealand spinach
- Pollinate cucumbers, pumpkins and squashes
- Harvest globe artichokes, summer cabbage, kohl rabi, beetroot, carrots, turnips, broad beans, dwarf, French and haricot beans, runner beans, first-early peas, second-early peas, maincrop peas, mange tout (snow peas) and petit pois, asparagus peas, early- and second-early potatoes, American cress, lettuce, radish, garlic, marrows and courgettes (zucchini), salad and pickling onions, summer spinach and New Zealand spinach
- Shade lettuces in hot weather to

prevent them from bolting and running to seed

In the herb bed
- Sow in permanent sites seeds of chervil, dill and parsley
- Pinch out growing tips of bushy herbs, such as basil and marjoram to encourage growth
- Watch for herbs running to seed and pinch out the tips of plants that are bolting

LATE SUMMER
In the greenhouse
- Harvest aubergines, cucumbers, tomatoes, peppers and chillies, and tree fruits

In the fruit garden
- Continue harvesting as fruits ripen
- Cut back raspberry canes to just above ground level after fruiting
- Prune and train vines growing outdoors

A cherry tree is a froth of wonderful blossom in spring and will give a good crop of fruit in summer. Pick the cherries as soon as they are ripe.

- Raise new plants of strawberries by layering runners of established plants

In the vegetable garden
- Sow in seed beds seeds of red cabbage and lettuce
- Sow in permanent sites seeds of kohl rabi, spinach beet, swedes, turnips, turnip greens, corn salad, endive, lettuce, radish, winter radish, salad and pickling onions, onions from seed (overwintering varieties), summer and winter spinach
- Transplant to permanent sites cauliflower and white-sprouting broccoli, summer cabbage
- Thin Chinese cabbage and tie up outer leaves to encourage inner growth
- Thin kohl rabi, chicory, endive, summer spinach, spinach beet
- Blanch celery
- Harvest summer cabbage, kohl rabi, beetroot, carrots, seakale beet and spinach beet, swedes, turnips, broad beans, dwarf and French beans, runner beans, first-early peas, maincrop peas, late peas, mange tout (snow peas) and petit pois, asparagus peas, second-early potatoes, outdoor tomatoes, American cress, lettuce, radish, garlic, marrows and courgettes (zucchini), salad onions, shallots, okra, summer spinach, New Zealand spinach, sweetcorn

In the herb bed
- Sow in seed bed seeds of chervil

Autumn

Season of the traditional harvest festival, autumn – at its most crisp and clear – is one of the most pleasurable times of year to be in the garden. Enjoy the late gathering in of produce at the close of the growing year.

Autumn is the time to put much of your plot to bed for winter. Except for winter varieties of cabbage and cauliflower, Brussels sprouts and other winter greens, most green, leafy crops must be harvested before the first of the frosts ruins them. As your food mood starts to turn to warming casseroles and stews, pull up turnips, carrots and swedes.

Windfalls of apples and pears can be collected and used for cooking – or leave some on the ground for the birds as the season draws to a close. To avoid your crop spoiling, pick the fruit from the trees and wrap and store each one carefully.

Choose a fine day to clear and clean your greenhouse and to scrub off any shading paint applied for the summer. On another fair day, dig over any bare ground and sow a green manure or spread on a layer of well-rotted manure or compost to enrich the soil over the winter.

EARLY AUTUMN

In the greenhouse
- Water and spray all greenhouse crops regularly
- Harvest aubergine, cucumbers, tomatoes, tree fruits and grapes

In the fruit garden
- Prepare the ground for planting tree fruits and canes
- Mulch damsons, plums and gages and blackcurrants
- Thin fruits of figs
- Raise new plants of blackcurrants, gooseberries and other currants
- Harvest apples, damsons, figs, pears, strawberries, alpine strawberries, blackberries and loganberries, blueberries, grapes and autumn raspberries

In the vegetable garden
- Sow under glass or indoors seeds of cauliflower and lettuce for overwintering and forcing
- Sow in permanent sites corn salad, cress and winter spinach
- Thin corn salad, lettuce and winter radish
- Harvest calabrese, early Brussels sprouts, cabbages, cauliflower and white sprouting broccoli, kohl rabi, beetroot, carrots, parsnips, seakale beet and spinach beet, swedes, turnips, dwarf, French and haricot beans, runner beans, first-early peas, late peas, mange tout (snow peas) and petit pois, lettuce, radish, celery, courgettes (zucchini) and pumpkins, okra, summer spinach, New Zealand spinach, salad onions and sweetcorn

In the herb bed
- Sow angelica and lovage
- Take root cuttings of sage and grow under glass
- Harvest seedheads of fennel for drying

LATE AUTUMN

In the greenhouse
- Harvest aubergines, tomatoes, tree fruits and grapes
- Pull up and compost all annual plants when harvesting is finished
- Prune fruit trees and vines
- Clean and disinfect (*see* page 38), including cold frames, cloches, pots and trays
- Insulate if necessary to protect over-wintering tender crops

In the fruit garden
- Plant apples, apricots, plums, gages and damsons, peaches and nectarines, blackberries, loganberries, blackcurrants, gooseberries, red and white currants
- Prune blackcurrants and raspberries
- Protect strawberries with cloches to give a final late crop
- Harvest apples, damsons, figs, pears, strawberries, alpine strawberries, autumn-fruiting raspberries
- Lift roots of rhubarb for early forcing (*see* early winter)

In the vegetable garden
- Sow under glass or indoors over-wintering or forcing lettuces
- Sow in permanent sites broad beans (longpod) and garlic
- Thin corn salad and lettuce
- Blanch endive and force chicory
- Protect red cabbage with cloches and cauliflower curds by bending over the outside leaves
- Cut back asparagus foliage
- Harvest calabrese, Brussels sprouts, cabbage, cauliflower and white sprouting broccoli, kohl rabi, beetroot, carrots, parsnips, salsify, seakale and spinach beet, swedes, turnips, cress, lettuce, winter radish, garlic, celery, celeriac, leeks, spinach and salad onions

In the herb bed
- Sow chervil under glass for a winter crop

Winter

In winter, when there is less work to do in your plot, it is a good time to look back and reflect on the successes and failures of the year and to plan the next year's crops.

Make the most of fine days to finish pulling up, pruning and composting or burning your plants. Dig over bare earth in early winter to allow frosts to kill any pests that come to the surface and to break down compacted clumps of sod. By spring, you will just need to rake it. Clean your tools and oil any moving parts before putting them away.

Harvest root crops by the end of autumn and store them carefully in a cool place; freezing winter conditions will spoil them in the ground.

On days when the weather keeps you from all but the most pressing jobs outside, thumb through seed catalogues and the pages of this book to decide what to grow next year and start to make a plan so that you are ready in spring. As winter draws to a close you can even get a head start by sowing some early seeds under glass or indoors and by bringing them on so that they are ready to plant out as soon as the weather is mild enough.

EARLY WINTER

In the greenhouse
- Water vines and tree fruits throughout the winter

In the fruit garden
- Plant apples, apricots, sour cherries, pears and raspberries
  - Protect strawberries with cloches
  - Prune apples, apricots, peaches and nectarines, pears, currants, blueberries, gooseberries and grapes
  - Raise new plants of raspberries
  - Mulch red and white currants
  - Force rhubarb by planting roots lifted in late autumn in containers of moist compost

In the vegetable garden
- Force chicory
- Blanch endive
- Protect first-early peas and winter spinach with cloches
- Harvest Jerusalem artichokes, Brussels sprouts (and tops), autumn and winter cabbage, savoy, red cabbage, parsnips, swedes, turnips, salsify and scorzonera, spinach beet, chicory, American cress, lettuce, winter radish, celery, celeriac, leeks, onions, winter spinach and seakale beet

MIDWINTER

In the vegetable garden
- Sow under glass or indoors seeds of cauliflower
- Harvest Jerusalem artichokes, Brussels sprouts, autumn and winter cabbage, savoy, red cabbage, kale, parsnips, swedes, spinach beet, chicory, corn salad, American cress, endive, celery, celeriac, leeks and winter spinach

LATE WINTER

In the greenhouse
- Change the border soil
- Sow seeds of aubergine and cucumber
- Prune vines and tree fruits

In the vegetable garden
- Sow under glass or indoors seeds of Brussels sprouts, summer cabbage, cauliflower and white sprouting broccoli, early varieties of carrot, turnips, lettuce, radish and onions from seed
- Prepare seed potatoes for planting by chitting in a cool place
- Harvest Jerusalem artichokes, Brussels sprouts, autumn/winter cabbage, savoy, red cabbage, kale, parsnips, swedes, spinach beet, chicory, corn salad, lettuce, celery, leeks and winter spinach

GROWING
VEGETABLES

Growing Vegetables

Cultivating your own vegetables is one of the best money-saving activities in the garden and is often the first step for anyone thinking of trying to become more self-sufficient.

With some careful planning, even a small plot of land can yield enough vegetables to supply a family of four or five throughout the year. Some vegetables lend themselves to quick and easy methods of storage (*see* pages 207–11), so that they can still be eaten fresh or in their natural state for most of the year. Others may be dried or salted, and nearly all will freeze successfully. Your own frozen produce will taste better than shop-bought equivalents; not just because it represents your own hard work, but because it can be preserved within moments of being harvested if you are organised, maintaining all its freshness.

Use commonsense and instinct

Most vegetables are not difficult to grow; if you do find something particularly hard, abandon it in favour of others that suit your methods and your land better. The instructions given on the pages in this chapter must always be followed with commonsense, and will often have to be adapted to your particular soil and your habits. Few vegetables are so particular in their growing requirements that they cannot accommodate these kinds of small changes.

The weather is always a critical factor in any growing activity. It will often mean that sowing, planting out, transplanting and later, harvesting,

If you are a beginner, start small, with simple crops, like these fast-growing, fail-safe lettuces and expand the range of crops you grow as you gain in confidence and knowledge.

have to be delayed because conditions are not right or may be brought forward if crops have matured faster than usual.

Do not rigorously follow the sowing, tending and harvesting times given in this (or any other) book or on seed packets, but follow your instincts and be guided by experience as you grow in confidence. Far better to delay sowing, for example, for a week or two than to put the seed in wet, cold soil where it will not germinate.

In the same way, planting distances between rows and plants, or distances to which to thin out seedlings, are always approximate. It is a good idea to measure accurately when planning exactly what and how much to grow in your plot, but when doing the actual planting, most vegetable growers will judge spacings by eye, using experience to adapt them to suit the garden.

Pests and diseases

The pests and diseases outlined at the end of the groups of vegetables are seldom as much of a problem as they appear. You would be unlucky to experience most of those listed, so don't be put off growing a crop because of its possible problems. Few crops fail entirely because of disease or insect infestation, particularly if you tackle problems as soon as they arise. For more advice on diagnosing and treating plant problems, see the pests and diseases chapter on pages 140–51.

The main vegetable groups

Most individual vegetables can be categorised within a group, with other similar crops. In this book the groups are covered as follows:

- BRASSICAS
  Broccoli and calabrese, Brussels sprouts, cabbages, cauliflowers, kale and kohl rabi
- ROOT CROPS
  Beetroots, carrots, parsnips, salsify and scorzonera, seakale and spinach beet, swedes (rutabagas) and turnips
- LEGUMES
  Beans and peas
- POTATOES
- SALAD CROPS
  Chicory, cress, endives, cucumbers, lettuces and radishes
- OTHER OUTDOOR CROPS
  Globe and Jerusalem artichokes, asparagus, celery, celeriac, leeks, marrows and courgettes (zucchini), pumpkins and gourds, okra, onions, spinach and sweetcorn
- GREENHOUSE CROPS
  Aubergines (eggplants), peppers and chillies, indoor tomatoes and cucumbers

Raising Vegetable Seedlings

Nearly all the vegetables outlined in the following pages can be raised from seed. You can do this outdoors in seed beds or in the crop's intended growing position in the vegetable plot itself. Or sow them indoors in pots, pans or trays.

The method you choose will depend on a number of factors, including the prevailing weather conditions, the amount of space you have in the greenhouse, whether you have room for a dedicated seed bed, the type of seed and when you want to harvest each particular crop.

Asparagus, and both globe and Jerusalem artichokes are more usually raised from crowns, suckers and tubers respectively, and potatoes are grown from seed potatoes. These should all be planted directly where they are to grow, as they cannot be transplanted successfully during their growing period.

SOWING UNDER COVER IN POTS OR TRAYS

Giving seeds a start in potting compost is a way of bringing crops on early, and is a good option for those vegetables that take a long time to mature, leaving their space in the vegetable plot vacant for a while for quicker-growing crops.

This method is also useful for crops that are better raised individually, and tender plants that need higher temperatures to germinate.

Seeds grown this way must be planted in special soil-based or

SOWING OUTDOORS

Most vegetable seeds can be raised outdoors, although it is harder to produce early crops. Most seed packets will recommend a planting month or range of months in the instructions, but be guided by conditions where you live. Seeds need moisture and warmth to germinate, so the ground should be just damp (crumbly on the surface), not wet and cold.

The busiest sowing season is spring, but if you sow a little at a time through summer and into autumn, your crops will mature in stages, rather than as a glut of produce all ready at the same time.

1 Knock down the soil with a cultivator, rake it over and remove any large stones. Add top dressing and rake again to give a smooth surface.

2 Mark the correct planting distances along the plot and position a garden line along the first row to give you a straight guide to work to.

3 Create a seed drill the required depth using a draw hoe. Pull it down the soil in a succession of strokes, rather than dragging it the entire length of the row in one pass.

4 If the ground shows any signs of being dry, water the bottom of the drill well throughout. Put in any fertiliser dressings you wish to use, according to the crop you are sowing.

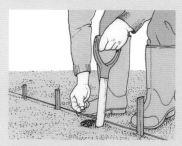

5 Using a dibber, sow the seed thinly. Even small seeds are best planted about two to each 2.5cm (1in). Use wooden stakes as distance guides.

6 Pull the soil back over the seeds and firm it gently with the back of the rake. Put labels at both ends of the row to remind you what you have planted.

RAISING SEEDS IN A PROPAGATOR

Electric propagators maintain the temperature of the soil at the optimum level for germination and growth. But any covered container can be used as a propagator, from seed trays with a clear lid to a simple pot sealed inside a plastic bag.

Once seedlings are established, remove the propagator lid and switch off the heat to an electric propagator. Left to grow in the warm and humid conditions of a propagator, seedlings will become tall and straggly, with weak stem growth and are likely to fail once you try to transplant them. With the lid removed, seedlings will grow at a slower rate, but will bush out and produce stronger young plants.

1 Squeeze some compost into a ball; it is wet enough to use if it cracks. For soil-less types some moisture should come out.

2 Place the compost in a seed tray or propagator tray and firm it down with your hand or the back of the trowel to about 2.5cm (1in) from the top of the tray.

3 Sprinkle seeds over the compost, keeping them 1cm (½in) apart; position larger seeds individually. Cover with a thin layer of compost, sieved if it is soil-based.

4 Cover the seed tray with a lid, a pane of glass or clear polythene bag and place it in a sunny spot.

5 Remove the cover when the seedlings begin to show through the compost and thin them out when they are large enough to handle.

soil-less seed or potting composts available at all garden centres. These have been specially prepared to provide the seeds with exactly the right growing medium; garden soil will not do – it contains too many weed seeds and is usually not a suitable texture for using in small containers. You can make your own seed and potting composts using loam (if you can get it), sterilised peat and sand; but it usually makes more sense to buy it.

Plastic containers are generally better than those made of wood or clay as they retain water better and this will cut down on how much you need to water the seedlings. Whenever possible, use fairly shallow ones as they will use less compost – the seedlings will not need much root space before they are ready to be potted on or planted out.

THINNING AND PRICKING OUT

When seedlings begin to appear, they will probably need to be thinned or pricked out to avoid overcrowding, which would result in weak, straggly growth and a higher risk of disease.

With outdoor plantings, if you were careful with your sowing there should be little thinning required and the minimum of disturbance to the growing seedlings. You should always sow enough to allow for some seeds to fail, so some thinning out will be inevitable, and you should do this in two or three stages.

The first thinning should be as soon as the seedlings are large enough to handle, and they should be thinned to a distance of about 5cm (2in) apart. The second thinning will be a few weeks later to

Pricking out seedlings will give them more room to grow into sturdy young plants. Hold them gently by a leaf and ease them out of the compost with a thin stick.

about 15cm (6in) apart and the third to the final, recommended spacing.

Seedlings from the first thinning are best discarded onto the compost heap; those from a second thinning can sometimes be transplanted if space permits; and those from the final thinning may produce actual baby vegetables – tiny carrots and turnips, for example – that you can use in salads or cook lightly.

Thin seedlings when the soil is damp; this reduces the disturbance to those left behind. Pull up the seedlings by their leaves, not the stem, if you intend to replant them – a crushed leaf will not harm the plant as much as if the stem is damaged.

Pricking out

Seedlings planted in containers must be pricked out when they begin to crowd each other. Gently hold a leaf and loosen the roots with a thin stick or a pencil. Plant them into further pots or containers giving them more room. Make a small hole with a stick or small dibber and bury the plants up to their first seed leaves.

TRANSPLANTING INTO THE GROUND

When seedlings are large enough to move from their containers or seed bed to their permanent cropping location, it is time to transplant them. This should be done carefully in order to lessen the shock and avoid damaging the stem or the leaves too badly. Don't move plants straight from a warm greenhouse into the soil on a chilly day. Make sure each plant has a strong growing tip in the centre before you transplant it – discard any that are unlikely to grow well.

1 Water the plants and new site well the day before. Choose a day that is mild and damp, but not windy. Dig up developing plants when they are about 10cm (4in) high, keeping some soil around their roots as you lift them out.

2 If the young plants are in containers, either dig them out of the seed tray or, if they are in individual pots, tip the pot upside down, supporting the plant carefully in your hand. If you use home-made pots from lengths of cardboard tube (above) or pots made out of newspaper, these can be put straight into the soil.

3 Make planting holes with a dibber or a hand trowel, ensuring they are slightly larger than the root ball with the soil attached and are set the correct distance apart.

4 Carefully set the roots in the hole and fill in the sides with soil. The plant should be set slightly deeper in the ground than it was before.

5 Firm in each plant and then gently tug a leaf to ensure that the plant is secure in the ground. Water well, sprinkling from the rose on your watering can to give a gentle flow.

Growing Brassicas

Although only seven different vegetables fall under this heading – broccoli, Brussels sprouts, cabbage, cauliflower, calabrese, kale and kohl rabi – the variety of shape, size and taste they offer is enormous.

There are so many types of cabbage that it is possible to harvest them the whole year round and most are very easy to grow. Lightly cooked or grated raw, cabbages do not deserve their reputation as an insipid, waterlogged vegetable. Broccoli comes in just two basic types: purple sprouting or white headed. The latter looks more like a cauliflower and is grown in the same way. In fact, it is often known as the winter cauliflower.

Purple sprouting broccoli, with its abundant purple-headed spears, is also easy to grow, although you need to keep pigeons away or they will destroy your crop. It is ready for picking in the late winter or early spring – a time when fresh produce from the garden can be in short supply. Its close relation, calabrese, yields large heads of tightly packed green flower buds in the late summer and early autumn. It is similar to broccoli, but with a shorter growing season and is less hardy.

Cauliflowers are the most difficult of the brassicas to grow, but with care and experience can be harvested all year round. Different varieties are available, but the only one that looks noticeably different from the classic white-headed type is the purple cauliflower.

Brussels sprouts are among the most dependable of winter vegetables. Early spring sowings will yield autumn crops, but if you really want to eat sprouts out of season it may be better to freeze some of the winter crop (which they take to well) and use your precious land for a crop that is quicker to mature.

Kale is often overlooked, and thought of as cattle food by many. But its distinctive taste, which is even better after a frost, has much to offer and it can be harvested throughout the lean winter months. Different varieties have crinkly or smooth, but deeply serrated, leaves. Curly kale is an extremely hardy winter crop, which will withstand very cold conditions and will provide you with fresh vegetables during winter and early spring.

Kohl rabi is another unusual vegetable. The round purple or green growths, with their long, tough, leaf-bearing stems, rest on the surface of the ground, where they can remain until they are needed. They are best harvested when they are the size of a tennis ball, though, as they can turn fibrous if left too long. Better to freeze them for storage or trim away leaves and roots and keep them somewhere cool and dry. They taste like turnip and can be cooked in the same way or used raw in salads.

GROWING TIMES AND HARVESTING MONTHS

Many types of brassicas – cabbages in particular – can be produced in your garden all the year round. The cropping season of others can be extended either by making sowings in succession over a period of weeks or months or by choosing to grow varieties that take varying times to mature (some have been specially produced to mature quickly).

Below is a chart which gives the shortest time each type of brassica will take to reach full maturity and the months in which they can be harvested (subject, of course, to timed sowing).

VEGETABLE	SHORTEST GROWING TIME	HARVESTING MONTHS
Purple sprouting broccoli	11 months	March–May
Calabrese	3–4 months	August–October
Brussels sprouts	8 months	September–early March (best in November and December)
Cabbage		
Summer	4 months	June–September
Autumn and winter	At least 6 months	October–February
Savoy	At least 5 months	September–May
Spring	8 months	April–May
Red	8 months	September–May
Chinese	3 months	September–October
Cauliflower and white broccoli	At least 4 months (most varieties take longer)	Can be harvested all year round; easiest to produce for autumn and winter
Kale	8 months	December–April
Kohl rabi	2 months	May–October

Choosing varieties

As well as the many different types of brassica, each crop has a wide choice of varieties, suited to different soil conditions, weather and timing. The best guide before buying is to read the seed packets, which will tell you the requirements of each particular variety.

Experiment to see which suit both your garden and your palate best. Try early and late varieties, and consider the new hybrids that appear on the market with each new year.

CULTIVATION

Comprehensive instructions for sowing, growing and harvesting brassicas are given in the chart overleaf. All brassicas like slightly alkaline, rather than acid, soil, so unless you know the soil to be alkaline, dress it with lime before planting to improve conditions.

Most brassicas thrive in good fertile soil, but often do best if they follow another crop for which the soil was manured. As most types take a number of months to mature and become ready for harvesting, it is a good idea to sow them in seed beds, leaving room in the main vegetable plot for some quicker-growing crops that can be harvested before the brassicas are ready to transplant into their cropping position.

After harvesting, plants should be dug up and the roots burnt. The leaves and stems can be composted, but cut up or crush anything woody first, as the thick stems can take years to break down. If there is any hint of disease in the crop, burn the plants; if they are composted, the infecting bacteria will thrive and multiply, and then spread when the compost is used.

CULTIVATION OF BRASSICAS

1 Because brassicas are not a quick-maturing crop, sow the seeds in a seed bed first.

2 Thin seedlings as they appear. Transplant them carefully when they are large enough to handle.

3 Plant out large crops in their final cropping site on a mild, damp day, using a garden line as a guide.

4 Support tall plants, such as Brussels sprouts (below) and broccoli, with large stakes, tied in with twine.

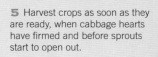

5 Harvest crops as soon as they are ready, when cabbage hearts have firmed and before sprouts start to open out.

6 Cabbages growing in the winter may need to be protected from harsh weather with cloches. All brassicas need netting to protect them from birds.

PESTS AND DISEASES

Brassicas are susceptible to a number of pests and diseases, but in most cases, the diseases can be controlled or eliminated by treating the soil with various shop-bought sprays or preparations.

Brassica plants, broccoli in particular, are irresistible to hungry birds. Protect young seedlings by stretching black cotton along the rows. It may even be necessary to net broccoli plants later.

Slugs can often be a problem too, eating their way quickly through an entire line of seedlings. They can be controlled by scattering slug pellets on the ground. However, these pellets contain poison that can be harmful to animals, so put them under a flowerpot and prop up one side of it, so only the slugs can enter. Better still, try to encourage wildlife

CULTIVATION OF BRASSICAS

VEGETABLE	SOIL/POSITION	SOWING	DRILL DEPTH
Purple sprouting broccoli and calabrese	**Soil:** Firm, heavy, loamy soil that is well-dug and manured **Position:** Open and sunny, but with some shelter	Sow in seed beds mid-April to May. Calabrese sowings can begin in late March	1cm (½in)
Brussels sprouts	**Soil:** Rich loam – a firm soil which has been well-manured **Position:** Prefer an open site, but do not mind partial shade	Sow under glass in February for early crops. In seed beds from mid-March to April	1cm (½in)
Cabbage	**Soil:** All types like well-drained, fertile, non-acid soil, preferably following a crop for which the ground was manured. They will grow successfully in most well-cultivated soils **Position:** Open and sunny	**Summer cabbage:** Sow under glass or in boxes from January to February. In seed beds from late March/April to May **Autumn and winter cabbage:** Sow in seed beds from April to May **Spring cabbage:** Sow in seed beds in summer **Savoy:** See winter cabbage **Red cabbage:** Sow in seed beds from April to early September **Chinese cabbage:** Sow in ultimate cropping site mid-June/early July	1cm (½in)
Cauliflower and white sprouting broccoli	**Soil:** Deep, well-drained, well-cultivated, rich soil **Position:** Open and sunny, but sheltered	**Early varieties** **Caulilower:** Under glass in September, or in seed boxess in heated position in January **Broccoli:** Under glass in late February to March **Maincrop varieties:** Sow in seed beds in regular succession from late spring to early summer	2cm (¾in)
Kale	**Soil:** Rich loam but will grow in most well-cultivated soil **Position:** Any, but particularly likes an exposed site	Sow outdoors in cropping site or in seed beds from April to May	1cm (½in)
Kohl rabi	**Soil:** Fertile, well-drained **Position:** Any, but not too shaded	Sow outdoors in cropping site at monthly intervals from March to August	1 cm (½in)

into your plot that will control your pests for you, such as hedgehogs.

Good garden hygiene will do much to keep disease at bay. This means ensuring that dead plants are removed from the ground and composted at once. Never leave them in the soil once they have yielded their full harvest. Equally, burn all infected or diseased plants and ensure all the tools and equipment you use are clean.

Some of the common pests and diseases that attack brassicas are listed here; for more information on identification and treatment, see the relevant pages. Mealy cabbage aphid (page 147), cabbage root fly (page 148), cabbage white butterfly (page 144), flea beetle (page 144), gall weevil (page 147), cabbage whitefly (page 150), club root (page 148), downy mildew (page 146), wire stem (page 148), whiptail (page 145).

PLANTING OUT/TRANSPLANTING	PLANTING DISTANCES (between plants/rows)	CULTIVATION	HARVESTING
Thin regularly; plant in cropping site when plants are 10–15cm (4–6in) tall (about six weeks after sowing)	**Broccoli:** 60 x 65cm (2ft x 2ft 6in) **Calabrese:** 45 x 60cm (18in x 2ft) Calabrese plants can be planted closer together to give a large harvest of small spears	Hoe regularly between rows to eliminate weeds. Protect from birds by netting. Water well if at all dry. Stake plants, tie loosely to support if weather is windy, and draw soil up around the stems for extra support	In both cases, cut while flower buds are still tightly closed. Cut from the centre, taking central heads with 10–12.5cm (4–5in) of stem. Cut just above a side shoot to encourage more growth. Harvest side shoots as they appear
Thin regularly; plant in cropping site when plants are 10–15cm (4–6in) tall (about six weeks after sowing)	65 x 65cm (2ft 6in x 2ft 6in). Stagger the rows	Pull soil around stems a month or so after planting to firm plants. Stake plants and tie loosely. Water freely. Break off the lower leaves as they turn yellow	Pick while still small and tightly knotted, preferably after the first frost. Start at the bottom of the stem. Pick off top leaves and cook as greens (this brings on sprouts at the top of the plant)
Summer cabbage: Those sown under glass should be planted out in seed beds in March to harden off **Other cabbage:** Should be transplanted to cropping site when 10–15cm (4–6in) tall (about six weeks after sowing) **Red cabbage:** Sown in September. Can be left in seed bed through winter, protected by cloches **Chinese cabbage:** Thin seedlings progressively, so they are correct distance apart when plants are 10cm (4in) tall	**Summer cabbage:** 45 x 45cm (18 x 18in) **Autumn and winter:** *Cabbage and savoy:* 60 x 60cm (2 x 2ft) **Spring cabbage:** 22 x 45cm (9 x 18in) **Red cabbage:** 60 x 60cm (2 x 2ft) **Chinese cabbage:** 30 x 45cm (1ft x 1ft 6in)	**For all cabbages:** Hoe regularly between rows to discourage weeds and keep plants well-watered. Remove any decaying leaves as they appear **Chinese cabbage:** Gently pull any drooping outside leaves up around inner ones and tie loosely to encourage thicker growth inside	**For all cabbages:** Cut when heads are firm and leave stumps in ground (except spring ones) to give a few extra subsequent cuts of greens **Spring cabbage:** Cut cabbages in March and use as spring greens
Early varieties cauliflower: Prick out those from heated boxes and put in cold frame to harden off Plant all varieties in cropping site when 10–15cm (4–6in) tall, using a dibber	**Early varieties:** 45 x 45cm (18 x 18in) **Maincrop varieties:** 60 x 75cm (2ft x 2ft 6in) in staggered rows	Hoe between rows to discourage weeds. Water frequently if at all dry. When curds form, bend outside leaves over them. This protects from sun, frost or staining from soil – all of which discolour the curds	Cut when curds are formed, but are tightly packed. Cauliflowers are best picked in the morning, when the dew is still on them. If more ripen at one time than you need, pull them up and hang by the roots in a cool, dry place. They will keep for up to three weeks
Thin as seedlings appear. Transplant from seed bed when plants are about six weeks old. If sown in cropping site, thin to recommended distances	60 x 60cm (2 x 2ft)	Hoe between rows and plants to eliminate weeds. Tread round plants to firm ground. Stake and tie if necessary	Cut from early January, taking from the plants' centre to encourage more growth
Thin progressively until required planting distance is achieved	25 x 40cm (9 x 15in)	Hoe between rows and keep plants well-watered	Pull out bulbs (which you can see on the ground) when about 7.5cm (3in) diameter. If larger than this, they will be woody

Growing Root Vegetables

The term 'root crops' covers a wealth of vegetables. Included here are beetroot, carrots, parsnips, salsify and scorzonera, spinach beet, seakale beet, swedes (rutabagas), turnips and sweet potatoes.

Swedes and turnips are, strictly speaking, members of the brassica group, but their growing habits and requirements mean that they are often grouped with root vegetables.

Sweet potatoes are also not true root crops; and, despite their name, they are only very distantly related to the common potato, with quite different cultivation requirements,

so they are rarely grown together. They are actually an herbaceous perennial vine, although they are grown from tubers or 'slips', pieces of the tuber that will produce roots and new plants.

Beetroot, is most frequently thought of as a salad vegetable, cooked and then eaten cold, or pickled, but it is also delicious eaten hot or in soup and can be grated and eaten raw (the young ones are the most palatable). There are many different-shaped varieties, but also some that are golden in colour.

Carrots come in myriad shapes from round, or finger-shaped, to conical, or elongated – far more interesting than the supermarket variety. Like most roots, they store well (*see* page 207), so can generally be eaten fresh all the year round. Their cooking possibilities are

endless, even as a sweetener in some puddings and they make a deliciously moist cake.

Parsnips, too, have more uses than just as a side vegetable. They are one of the most common ingredients of home-made wine. Varieties bred to yield small roots are very useful for people who have only a small amount of land to devote to vegetable production.

Try something different

Salsify and scorzonera are two unusual root vegetables which are well worth growing for the tasty interest they can give to family meals. Both produce long, thin roots; salsify looks a little like an elongated parsnip, while scorzonera is similar in shape but has a black skin. They take up quite a lot of land for a good six months or more, but if you have space for them in your overall vegetable garden plan, they make an interesting change on the table.

Seakale beet and spinach beet are perhaps a little more unusual too. Although they are both root crops, they are grown for their leaves rather than their roots. Seakale beet is a form of spinach beet, with wider leaf stalks and midribs. Its leaves have a dual purpose; the green leafy part may be torn from the stem to be cooked and eaten as greens, and the white midrib can then be cooked and served on its own.

Spinach beet is often known as perpetual spinach and is the easiest of all spinaches to grow, having a higher yield and a greater tolerance to dry conditions. It also has a less acidic taste than true spinach. As its

GROWING TIMES AND HARVESTING MONTHS

Continuous crops of roots can be produced in the garden by regular sowings and experimenting with the various early- and late-maturing varieties. Many root crops are sown in two main stages: one planned to give the early, small, sweet crops, with a heavier sowing to follow, giving the main crop through the winter.

VEGETABLE	SHORTEST GROWING TIME	HARVESTING MONTHS
Beetroot	4 months	June–October
Carrot	3–4 months	June–October
Parsnip	7–8 months	End September–February
Salsify and scorzonera	6–7 months	October–November
Seakale beet	3–4 months	August–November
Spinach beet	4 months	August–April
Swede (rutabaga)	Early sowings take about 3 months. Later May/ June sowings take about 5 months	July/August–April
Sweet potato	4–5 months	September–October
Turnip	At least 2 months	July–November (Greens: November–April)

Beetroot is a rich source of vitamin B, when eaten raw – grate it into salads to make the most of its goodness. The roots store well in a cool place or can be pickled, whole or sliced.

name suggests, perpetual spinach can be harvested for most of the year. These vegetables cannot be stored like other root crops, but they take very well to being frozen.

Earthy crops for warming stews

The swede has a surprisingly delicate taste for such a hardy vegetable. If you have more space in the ground than in your storage sheds, the crop can be left in the ground all winter with no ill effects.

Turnips come in all manner of shapes, sizes and colours. They may be round like a ball or flattened on the top and bottom. In colour, they may be white or golden, or green, red or purple-topped. They grow so fast that they make an excellent 'catch crop' between rows of longer maturing vegetables and they can also be grown for their leaves, harvested through the winter and early spring, which can be cooked like spring greens.

Sweet potatoes will not reliably grow outdoors in colder regions of the UK, although new varieties are being bred all the time that

could make this possible. But they will grow in pots or borders in the greenhouse or outdoors in milder climates. Do not attempt to grow plants from tubers bought in the supermarket, as they are likely to be tender varieties from overseas; instead, look for tubers or slips sold by mail order that are bred for the UK climate. They may have pinkish or orange flesh and produce attractive flowers, similar to the Morning Glory vine.

CULTIVATION TIPS

The cultivation details for the root crops included in this section are given on pages 70–71. Most favour a similar type of soil and not one that has been freshly manured, which encourages the roots to fork and split. Stony ground can also cause forking of the roots as they grow around obstacles in the soil.

It is usual to sow seeds of root crops straight into the cropping site. Make sure the soil is well prepared for sowing and is dry and crumbly; it is

Hoe carefully between rows. Keeping weeds at bay is important, but it is easy to damage the tops of the developing roots, which are usually very close to the surface.

better to delay planting than to sow seeds into wet, sticky, cold soil.

Getting a double yield

Most root crops take less time to mature than the brassicas; even so,

---

CULTIVATING ROOT CROPS

1 Prepare the ground by raking in a general-purpose fertiliser. Sow the seed in shallow drills, as instructed on the seed packet. Take care to allow the correct spacing between rows.

2 Water young plants well to prevent the developing roots from forking in search of water.

3 Regularly weed between rows of growing plants, taking care not to damage the growing roots.

4 Thin plants progressively. The third thinning may produce tiny vegetables.

a catch crop of quicker-maturing vegetables such as lettuce can be sown between the rows of the longer-maturing varieties in the early stages of growth. Another way of making the land yield twice is to sow radish seed together with parsnip along the same rows. The radish seeds germinate much faster; thus indicating where the parsnip seedlings will later emerge, as well as giving an extra crop of radishes that you can harvest before the parsnips start to crowd them out.

Routine care

All root crops should be watered freely if there is any danger of their drying out. Those deprived of water will be woody and fibrous as a result; they may also fork if allowed to dry out and are then subjected to a heavy rainfall.

Hoeing between the rows is necessary to keep down the weed population, but take extra care not to chop through the developing vegetables with the hoe.

Harvesting and storage

Most roots can be harvested over a fairly long period, the early pullings providing small, but delicious, sweet-tasting baby vegetables. Pull these by hand and then lift later crops with a fork, being very careful not to damage and bruise the roots.

Some, such as parsnip and swede can be left in the ground until they are wanted (provided you do not want the land for anything else) and their flavour is actually often improved by enduring a frost. Others, such as turnips, do not take so kindly to this treatment and should be lifted and stored (see page 207). Roots are among the best types of vegetables for storing, although they also freeze well.

Sow catch crops between slow-maturing root vegetables. Here, lettuces are growing alongside the carrots to their left, but will be harvested before the carrot leaves bush out.

PESTS AND DISEASES

Root crops are prone to pests and diseases, which can often be controlled with one of the many treatments available to buy. Consult your local garden centre for advice on tackling a particular problem.

Paying attention to good garden hygiene and destroying infected plants immediately (see page 143) will help to keep your crop healthy and strong enough to shrug off disease and pest attacks.

One of the most virulent pests is the carrot fly (which, despite its name, may also attack parsnips). Early crops of carrots are likely to escape attack as they may be harvested before the maggots hatch and burrow into the ground in search of the tasty roots. Carrot fly are attracted by the smell given off by leaves when handled, so avoid touching the plants as much as possible. For the same reason, destroy any thinnings, or remove them from the ground immediately.

Cover crops with horticultural fleece to prevent the flies from laying their eggs on the crop.

Flea beetle presents the greatest danger to swedes and turnips. Avoid growing all these crops on land which you know is still harbouring club root, because the vegetables will be swollen, distorted and inedible. Both beetroot and carrots can suffer from violet root rot.

Some of the common pests and diseases that attack root crops are listed here; for more information on identification and treatment, see the relevant pages. Carrot fly (page 151), beet fly (page 151), wireworm (page 151), black slugs (page 151), celery leaf fly (page 145), cutworm (page 147), parsnip canker (page 151), rust (page 146), white blister (page 145), club root (page 148) and violet root rot (page 148).

CULTIVATION OF ROOT CROPS

VEGETABLE	SOIL/POSITION	SOWING	DRILL DEPTH
Beetroot	**Soil:** Light, but deep loam that has been well-dug and cultivated **Position:** Will grow in most places, but avoid heavily shaded sites	**Globe varieties:** Sow under glass in March. Harden off before transplanting. Sow in cropping site from April to July **Long-rooted varieties:** Sow in regular succession in cropping site from May to June. Beetroot grows from clusters of three or four seeds. Space these about 5cm (2in) apart	1cm (½in) 2–2.5cm (¾–1in)
Carrot	**Soil:** Well-cultivated and deeply dug sandy loam, but will grow in any light soil, providing it is free of any large clods of earth or big stones **Position:** Any which is not heavily shaded. Early crops like an open, sunny spot	**Early varieties:** Sow under glass in February **Maincrop:** Sow in regular succession in cropping site from late March to July. Sow two seeds at a time, 2.5cm (1in) between pairs	0.5cm (¼in)
Parsnip	**Soil:** Deeply dug, light loam, free from large stones **Position:** Any which is not heavily shaded	Sow in cropping site late February/March to April. The surface of the soil must be dry and fine	2.5cm (1in)
Salsify and scorzonera	**Soil:** Deeply dug, light loam **Position:** Open and sunny	Sow in cropping site from March/April to May	2cm (¾in)
Seakale beet and spinach beet	**Soil:** Any well-cultivated soil; these vegetables particularly dislike being waterlogged **Position:** Any which is not heavily shaded	**Spinach beet:** Sow in cropping site in April and again in July and August **Seakale beet:** Sow in cropping site in May	2.5cm (1in)
Swede (rutabaga)	**Soil:** Light, fertile loam that is well-drained but not too dry. Does not like acid soil **Position:** Open and sunny. React badly to overshadowing	For an early crop, sow in cropping site in early spring; otherwise sow in cropping site in May/June. Sow two seeds to 2.5cm (1in)	2cm (¾in)
Turnip	**Soil:** Well-cultivated, light loam **Position:** *see* Swede (rutabaga)	Sow under glass in February. Then in cropping site in regular succession from March/April to July/August. Late sowings provide winter maincrop **Turnips for greens:** Sow in cropping site at end of August	1cm (½in)
Sweet potato	**Soil:** Fertile and free-draining, with manure or compost dug in the previous autumn **Position:** Sheltered spot in full sun	Pot cuttings in mid-spring/early summer. Keep slips under glass or in a propagator until roots appear, then pot into individual pots of compost	1cm (½in)

THINNING/TRANSPLANTING	PLANTING DISTANCES (between plants/rows)	CULTIVATION	HARVESTING
Thin seedlings under glass to 15cm (6in). Plant out in cropping site end April. Thin seedlings when about 2.5cm (1in) high then again to final spacing when roots are 2.5cm (1in) in diameter.	**Globe:** 12.5 x 30cm (5 x 12in) **Long-rooted:** 20 x 45cm (8 x 18in)	Protect seedlings from birds and slugs. As they grow, hoe between rows and water plants well.	Begin by pulling out every other plant. Those that remain can be left until wanted, but globe varieties should not grow more than 7.5cm (3in) across or they will turn woody. Lift in late autumn before the frosts. Twist off the leaves just above the root to seal in the juices.
Early varieties: Thin to 2.5cm (1in) apart, then 7.5cm (3in). **Maincrop:** Thin to 7.5cm (3in) when first proper leaves appear, then to final spacing when carrots are as thick as a finger. Never leave thinnings lying on the ground – they attract carrot fly	**Early:** 7.5 x 22cm (3 x 9in) **Maincrop:** 15 x 30cm (6 x 12in)	Water after sowing to aid germination. After thinning draw soil up around base (top of carrot should not show through soil). Hoe between rows to check weeds	**Early crops:** Pull every other plant. Pull young carrots by hand **Maincrop:** Lift carefully with a fork, no later than October. If storing (see page 207), trim off the top (compost this immediately), remove the soil from the carrots, but do not wash them before they are stored, or they will rot
Thin to 5cm (2in), then to final recommended spacing. Do not try to transplant thinnings as it is rarely successful	15 x 40cm (6 x 15in)	Hoe between the rows to keep weeds in check. Water plants if they are at all dry	Dig up parsnips as wanted – the flavour improves after the first frost. They can stay in their cropping site until spring, otherwise, dig them up and store them
Thin twice to recommended distance	**Salsify:** 20 x 30cm (9 x 12in) **Scorzonera:** 30 x 30cm (12 x 12in)	Hoe between rows and water plants in dry spells to prevent them running to seed. Pull the soil up around the base of the plants	Lift carefully from mid-October onwards. Although both are hardy and can be left in the ground, it is better to harvest them and freeze them. If space permits, you can leave some salsify in the ground until spring; the new growth can be picked and cooked like spring greens
Thin progressively to recommended distance, beginning as soon as the plants are large enough to handle. Later thinnings can be eaten	15 x 20cm (6 x 9in)	Hoe to eliminate weeds. Water plants freely if there is any danger of them drying out.	Pick the early sowing in summer and the later sowing through autumn and winter. Do not pick autumn plants too heavily if you want a good supply through the winter months. To harvest, take the outer leaves gently away from the root, leaving the young, central leaves to encourage more growth
Thin regularly to recommended distance	30 x 45cm (12 x 18in)	Hoe in the early stages to control weeds; this will not be necessary when the leaves cover the ground and smother the weeds	If you want small, sweet-tasting swedes, you can begin harvesting two to three months after the first sowing. Most will be allowed to grow bigger and can be harvested as needed. Leave in the ground through winter, or lift and store
Seedlings under glass: Thin when about 10cm (4in) high **Other sowings:** Thin to 10cm (4in) when first true leaves appear. Thin to 20cm (8in) when turnips are just large enough to make cooking worthwhile **Turnips for greens:** No need to thin, just leave plants to grow	20 x 30cm (8 x 12in) **Greens:** rows 20cm (9in) apart (see Transplanting)	Hoe to eliminate weeds	Pull early sowings when turnips are 5–7.5cm (2–3in) in diameter. Check by pulling the foliage aside to see the top of the turnip. Lift maincrop in mid-October to November. Twist off tops and store. **Greens:** Cut leaves when they are about 20cm (8in) long. They can be picked end October/early November, but are more usually left until spring
Grow young plants in a frost-free place until mid-summer. Harden off for 2–3 weeks before planting outside. Shelter with cloches or fleece for a further 2–3 weeks	30 x 75cm (12 x 30in)	Keep the plants well-watered, but not too much, as this can cause the tubers to split. Allow the foliage to spread over the soil to smother the weeds	Pick leaves and cook like spinach once at a usable height. Harvest tubers from end August; they will rot in cold, wet soil. Cut off the vines before carefully lifting the tubers, which bruise easily. Do not wash until you want to cook them. The flavour improves if stored in a humid place for two weeks after lifting

Growing Pulses

Although this section includes only two main groups of vegetables – peas and beans – they are two of the most useful and varied crops in the vegetable garden. Both groups of plants are quick to mature and their roots manufacture valuable nitrogen, which they release into the soil, enriching it for the following year.

Pulses yield their main harvest through the summer and autumn, but both peas and beans can be produced especially for drying and all types also freeze well, so they can be enjoyed all year round.

Peas and beans need stakes to support them as they grow. When mature, the plants will have completely smothered this framework with lush foliage and a crop of beans.

Choosing beans
Among the bean group are broad, French, dwarf, haricot and runner beans. The large, kidney-shaped

Purple-podded beans look stunning, although the beans inside are a conventional white and the pods usually lose their extraordinary colour when they are cooked.

broad beans sometimes have a reputation for being tough, but eaten straight from the garden when they are young, they are delicious and mouth-wateringly tender. Another little-known fact about broad beans is that the top foliage can be picked and cooked like spinach.

There are endless varieties of broad beans, suitable for sowing at different times of the year. They also include dwarf varieties suitable for small vegetable plots. Most types are hardy and will yield heavy crops.

French and dwarf beans are virtually the same species, although dwarf ones are a little hardier and produce very heavy yields. Both these beans are available in many varieties, from those with a waxy finish and yellow pods to deep purple varieties and those that are flat or round-podded. Haricot beans are a type of French bean grown specifically for drying and the white-seeded varieties are best for this. Borlotti, pea beans, cannellini beans

GROWING TIMES AND HARVESTING MONTHS

Peas and beans are largely a summer and autumn crop, but there is no reason why all types should not yield heavy harvests throughout these seasons. Many different varieties are available – both early- and late- maturing. Sow a good selection for maximum cropping, but make sure you sow the right variety at the correct time.

VEGETABLE	SHORTEST GROWING TIME	HARVESTING MONTHS
Broad beans	5 months	Late May/June–August
Dwarf and French beans	2–3 months	June–October
Runner beans	3 months	July–September
Soya beans	3½ months	August–September
Peas *First early:*	2½ months	End May–June and September–October
Second early: *Maincrop:* *Late:*	3½ months 3 months 3 months	July July–August August–September
Mange tout and petit pois	2½ months	June–September
Asparagus peas	3 months	June–August

and some varieties of runner bean – such as 'Czar', which is used and eaten like a butter bean – are also often grown specifically for drying. Give the crops the longest possible growing season for the best yield.

Runner beans usually mature after dwarf beans, although they can be grown to be harvested simultaneously. They are easy to grow and pretty enough to be incorporated into a flower garden on a wigwam system (*see* page 78). Dwarf varieties will also need the support of stakes.

Soya beans are an excellent source of protein, particularly valuable to vegetarians, but do best in a warm site. Young pods can be eaten whole, but to pod more mature beans you should blanch them in boiling water first for five minutes, cool then break open the pods and remove the beans inside before cooking them properly.

Pea varieties

Peas also produce endless varieties and different types will grow to different heights. They are divided into four main groups – first early, second early, maincrop and late – all with different qualities. Some are hardier than others and can withstand earlier sowing, but a succession of planting can produce harvests of succulent young peas right through the summer and into the autumn. Wrinkle-seeded varieties, known as marrowfat, are considered to be better flavoured, but they are less hardy than the round-seeded types.

In addition to the common garden peas mentioned above, mange tout (snow peas) and petit pois are also very popular. Mange tout are harvested while the peas are barely formed and are eaten, pods and all. Petit pois are very small, sweet-tasting peas, which can be cooked in the pod and shelled afterwards, or shelled first like other peas. Less well-known is the asparagus pea, which is a member of the pea family, but looks quite different. It is sometimes known as the winged pea because of its crinkly, double pods.

Asparagus peas are also cooked whole and get their name because they taste a little like asparagus.

CULTIVATION

All legumes, or pulses, grow best in soil that has been heavily manured for a previous crop. Failing this, for peas and runner beans in particular, dig some well-rotted manure at least one spit deep into the ground a month or two before sowing. The roots will quickly grow down in search of this, giving the plants a firm anchorage.

Peas and beans are sown deeper into the soil than most other crops, the drills for sowing being a good 5cm (2in) deep. When sowing, the soil should be forked over to a depth of at least 10cm (4in), making sure that it is crumbly, with no big clods or stones. Scrape out wide drills of 15–20cm (6–8in), using the width of the draw hoe blade, and rake the soil loosely back over the seeds.

Mice often dig up and eat the seeds, but you can discourage them by sprinkling some holly leaves in the drill, dousing the seed in paraffin, setting traps along the rows or keeping a good, hungry, garden cat.

Sow seeds at the correct distance apart, as no thinning is usually required, but to ensure a full crop, either sow two seeds at each station and pull out the weakest one as the seedlings emerge, or sow some extra seeds at the ends of the rows and use the resulting seedlings to fill in any gaps as the others germinate.

Most legumes need some sort of support. Dwarf varieties can be left

THE SELF-SUFFICIENCY MANUAL

Mange tout (or snow peas) are picked when the peas inside the pods are only just developing and they are eaten whole.

Thinning out is only necessary with peas and beans if you planted extra seeds to insure against the failure of a few.

to grow straggly and bushy with no supports, but not only will the pods become very mud-splashed, they are not always easy to find in the tangle of foliage. Various ways of supporting them are shown on page 78.

Except for varieties grown specifically for drying, all peas and beans should be harvested when young for the best flavour. The more you pick a plant, the more pods it will produce, so pick heavily and regularly, freezing any surplus vegetables you may have.

Legume roots make valuable nitrogen, so they can be left in the soil after the plant has yielded its full harvest. Cut off stems at ground level and compost the leaves.

PESTS AND DISEASES

Mice are one of the biggest threats to peas and beans. Slugs (page 151) will also attack seeds and seedlings. If the plants are not well-watered, including their foliage, the flowers fail to set, so pods do not form, and plants will wilt and die quickly if allowed to dry out. In wet weather, particularly if it is cold too, peas are vulnerable to downy mildew (*see* page 146).

CULTIVATING PULSES

1 Sow seeds in evenly dug rows in their cropping sites. Make sure the ground is watered.

2 Protect the emerging seedlings against birds by covering them with chicken wire or cloches.

3 If you planted two or three seeds at each station, you will have to thin the seedlings.

4 Most peas and beans will need to be supported as they grow to stop them straggling. Train them up poles.

5 Pinch out the tips of the broad bean plants to discourage the pest, black fly. Destroy any infected leaves.

6 Most peas and beans are best when picked young and tender. This will also encourage the plants to grow.

The most common pests and diseases to affect pulses are listed here; turn to the relevant pages in the pests and diseases chapter for more information on diagnosing and treating the various problems. Pea and bean weevil (page 150), pea moth (page 150), red spider mite (page 146), pea thrips (page 150), black fly (page 144), bean seed fly (page 150), foot rot (page 148) and chocolate spot (page 150).

CULTIVATION OF PULSES

VEGETABLE	SOIL/POSITION	SOWING	DRILL DEPTH
Broad beans	**Soil:** Good, rich loam, but will grow in any well-cultivated, well-drained soil **Position:** Prefer a well-sheltered site	Sow in cropping site at the recommended planting distances in October/early November for longpod varieties, February/April for summer crops and May for autumn crops. In cold, exposed gardens sow indoors in boxes 5cm (2in) apart or singly in biodegradable pots in late January/early February	5cm (2in)
Dwarf, French, haricot beans and other beans for drying	**Soil:** Light, well-drained, non-acid loam **Position:** Open and sunny, but sheltered	Sow indoors in boxes or under glass March to April: in cropping site in May, or slightly earlier if protecting with cloches, then regularly until early July. Put seeds in pairs 2.5cm (1in) apart or sow singly 7.5cm (3in) apart	4–5cm (1½–2in)
Runner beans	**Soil:** Rich, well-cultivated, well-drained, deep soil **Position:** Open and sunny, but sheltered	In cropping site in late April if well-protected with cloches. To be safe, plant in early May (mid to late May in cold districts) or indoors in April. Seed will not survive frosts	5cm (2in)
Soya beans	**Soil:** Well-cultivated, well-drained loam **Position:** Open and sunny; preferably warm	Sow in cropping site in late spring, or wait until early summer in cooler regions. Sow seeds 8cm (3in) apart. Under glass, sow four seeds to a pot in late spring	2.5–5cm (1–2in)
Peas	**Soil:** Most medium loam that is well-cultivated, well-drained and non-acid **Position:** Open and sunny	Flood drills with water if dry and sow when water has soaked through. Sow seeds 5–7.5cm (2–3in) apart or in a V-shaped drill, 7.5cm (3in) deep **First early:** Sow in cropping site in late October/early November (protect with cloches through winter) or March/April and again in June **Second early:** In cropping site in March/April **Maincrop and late:** Sow in cropping site in May	5cm (2in)
Mange tout (snow peas) and petit pois	**Soil:** see Peas **Position:** see Peas	In cropping site from March – June. Follow general instructions for sowing	5cm (2in)
Asparagus peas	**Soil:** see other peas, but soil must be really well-drained. **Position:** see Peas	Under glass in cropping site in late March/early April or in May/June. Sow two seeds together every 25cm (10in)	5cm (2in)

THINNING/TRANSPLANTING	PLANTING DISTANCES (between plants/rows)	CULTIVATION	HARVESTING
Outdoor sowings don't need thinning; fill any gaps with extra plants. Harden off indoor sowings from the end of March and plant in cropping site as soon as soil conditions allow, usually in April. Stand biodegradable pots in water first and plant so that the rim is beneath the soil surface	**Tall varieties:** Double rows 20cm (8in) apart with 20cm (8in) between plants. Stagger seeds in the two rows. Leave 60cm (2ft) between double rows. **Dwarf varieties:** 20cm (9in) between plants; 45cm (18in) between rows	Protect seedlings from birds, stake growing plants and hoe between rows to control weeds. Pinch out growing tips when plants are in full flower, when the first pods form or when the first black fly appears (see page 144). This helps to control black fly and keep the plant bushy	Begin as soon as beans are big enough to cook or sooner, before the beans are properly formed, if you like to eat the pods as well. Pick the bottom clusters first and continue regularly picking as beans become ready. Old beans will be tough, but can be used for next year's seed
Harden off seedlings in boxes or under glass in early May and plant out at the end of the month. If sown outdoors, pull out the weaker seedlings as soon as germination has occurred, or thin to recommended distance	**Smaller varieties:** 15 x 40cm (6 x 15in) **Larger varieties:** 20 x 45cm (9 x 18in)	Hoe to eliminate weeds and draw the soil up around the stem of the plants to firm them. Water plants freely and mulch with compost or farmyard manure if ground is prone to drying out. Support larger plants	Begin harvesting when beans are 10cm (4in) long and pick regularly to encourage growth **Haricot beans and other beans grown for drying:** Leave to ripen fully on plant. In late summer, pull up entire plant and hang upside down in a dry, airy place to finish drying. Pod beans and store them when quite dried
Indoor sowings: Harden off in May. Plant out in June **Outdoor sowings:** Those sown in cropping site need no thinning; fill any gaps with extra plants	Depends on method of support (see page 78). **For crossed poles:** Two staggered rows, plants 25cm (10in) apart; rows 75cm (2ft 6in) apart. If more than two rows, allow 1.5m (5ft) between them. **Vertical stakes:** Single rows 30 x 75cm (1ft x 2ft 6in) **Wigwam:** Six plants spaced round 1m (3ft) circle	Decide on your plan for support before you sow (page 78); supports should be 2.5–3m (8–10ft) high. Encourage plants to grow up them by entwining tendrils around stakes as soon as they appear. Hoe between rows and water freely, mulching ground if it tends to dry. Spray foliage to help to set flowers and pinch out top growing tips to encourage side growth	Pick regularly while pods are young and tender – freeze or salt the surplus rather than leaving them to get tough on the plant. As soon as beans swell in the pod, they will make tough eating
No need for thinning. Plant out seedlings grown under glass in early summer	Single rows, 8cm (3in) between plants and 25–30cm (9–12in) between rows	Protect seedlings from birds with black cotton, tunnels of wire mesh or cloches. Support plants with stakes	**For eating fresh:** Pick in late summer and autumn when the pods are green. Harvest each plant all at once. When pods change to a creamy colour, only eat the beans inside **For drying:** When foliage dies, lift plants and hang upside down. Shell pods when completely dry
Seedlings are not thinned, but allowed to grow thickly as sown. Fill in any gaps as seedlings appear with the extra seeds sown	5–7.5cm (2–3in) between plants. Distance between rows about the same as the height of plants – consult the seed packet	Protect seedlings from birds with cotton, wire mesh tunnels or cloches (remove as they grow). Hoe between rows until growth covers the ground. Water freely and mulch if soil tends to dry. Push thin twiggy supports into soil when you sow so tendrils can entwine around them easily	Pick as soon as peas are swollen in the pod and use or freeze at once. Leave some peas on the plant to ripen fully for drying. Treat in the same way as for haricot beans
No need to thin. Fill in gaps with extra plants	5–7.5cm x 1m (2–3in x 3ft)	See Peas	**Mange tout:** Pick when pods are 5cm (2in) long, before peas have formed properly. Use at once **Petit pois:** Harvest as other peas
Those under glass: Harden off ready for planting out in May **In cropping site:** Pull out weaker seedlings as they emerge	25 x 45cm (10 x 18in)	General cultivation is similar to other peas. Support emerging seedlings or leave to grow bushy over the ground	Gather when pods are about 2.5–5cm (1–2in) long

SUPPORTING PULSES AS THEY GROW

Practically all varieties of peas and beans need some kind of support as they grow, with the exception of dwarf varieties.

1 The most common way of staking peas is to push pea sticks into the ground near the growing plants. The wispy tendrils will wrap around the sticks.

2 To support broad beans, tie string between poles which are staked at the ends of each row. The plants are then loosely tied to the strings.

3 & 4 Runner beans can be grown up wigwam supports consisting of four or more poles positioned on the ground in a ring or square and pulled together and tied at the top. They can also be grown along rows of poles angled together like triangles and crossed at the top. By the time of harvesting, the runner beans will have reached the top of their supports.

5 & 6 Search carefully through the leaves of the plants for any concealed beans. If left, they will grow too large and become tough.

Growing Potatoes

Although potatoes take up quite a lot of space in the vegetable plot, they earn their keep. Not only are they a staple ingredient in the kitchen, they are also said to 'clean' the land, particularly in a new vegetable plot, leaving the soil ready-prepared for growing other crops the following year.

The 'cleaning' is actually brought about by the thorough digging that you must do before planting a potato crop, and the earthing up during the plants' growth, which helps to prevent weeds. This leaves you with well-cultivated, weed-free ground.

The various varieties of potato produce types that are round, oval or kidney-shaped. The skins may be yellow, pale brown, red or white and the flesh may be floury (and good for mashing) or waxy. Even if you have a strong preference, it is wise to consult a local supplier to find out which is most suitable for your land.

Potatoes are divided into earlies, second earlies and maincrop varieties, depending on when you plant and harvest them.

Soil and position

All potatoes do best in a fertile, well-drained, well-cultivated soil and, unlike most other vegetables, favour acid conditions (they grow best in a pH of 5.5 – see page 24). Ideally the ground should be double dug (see page 29) and a good supply of well-rotted manure added, especially on light, sandy soils. Dig some bonemeal into the top layer, too.

Choose an open site. Heavy shading can lead to light top growth and a disappointingly small crop.

Fresh new potatoes are one of the delights of early summer. Just dig enough for a meal at a time: lightly scrubbed and steamed with their tender skins still on, they are delicious.

Planting potatoes

Potatoes are grown from seed potatoes. Although these come from the previous year's crop, always buy them rather than saving some of your own crop, which are likely to harbour disease. For the same reason, do not use potatoes sold for eating. Instead, buy seed potatoes that are certified disease-free. Late winter is the time to buy them.

Seed potatoes should be about the size of an egg. For earlies, put

Good potato varieties

FIRST EARLIES
• **Rocket** Easy to grow; heavy cropper

• **Epicure** Excellent flavour; floury 'new' potato that resists frost well

SECOND EARLIES
• **Maris Peer** White varierty; versatile for cooking.

MAINCROP
• **Desirée** Pink-skinned tubers of varying shapes. Cood for cooking

• **King Edward** Pink and white skinned tubers of high quality

CULTIVATION OF POTATOES

1 Plant individual potatoes in holes and gently cover with soil. Shoots should be facing upwards.

2 Alternatively make drills with a draw hoe and plant rows of potatoes with shoots uppermost.

3 When leaves first appear, cover bases of the potatoes with more soil and water the growing plants well.

4 When the stems are large enough, begin to earth up the potatoes at 2–3 week intervals.

5 Harvest first earlies by hand, leaving the smaller crops in the soil to grow more. Lift tubers carefully so that you do not damage them with the fork.

6 Harvest maincrop when tops have died down. Leave crops on the ground to dry out before storing the potatoes in a cool, but frost-free, dark place.

the potatoes in shallow boxes, with the eye pointing upwards. Leave in a light, warm place for a few weeks until the shoots appear – a process known as 'chitting'. Two or three will probably grow close together. Leave two shoots and rub off any others; alternatively, if possible, cut the potatoes in half to give two pieces with two shoots, but only do this just before planting. Potatoes that are put in too warm or dark a place may develop long, spindly shoots. These will not be so healthy or easy to plant without damaging the shoots.

Make drills in the soil with a draw hoe (using the entire width of the hoe) or plant the potatoes individually with a trowel (*see* below for planting depths and times). Put the emerging shoot uppermost and pull the soil loosely over the potato; do not pack it tightly because you might damage the shoots.

CULTIVATION TIPS

Potatoes are unlike any other plant in the way in which they are planted and tended, but their needs are easily met and potatoes are usually an easy and trouble-free crop.

Immediately after planting, hoe between the lines and draw the soil up over the tubers very slightly. This mound of earth will protect them from any late frost. When the first

POTATO PLANTING TIMES, DEPTHS AND DISTANCES

	PLANTING DEPTH	DISTANCE BETWEEN TUBERS	DISTANCE BETWEEN ROWS	WHEN TO PLANT
Earlies	7.5cm (3in)	25cm (10in)	60cm (2ft)	Early spring
Second earlies	10cm (4in)	30cm (12in)	70cm (2ft 4in)	Mid-spring
Maincrop	12.5cm (5in)	40cm (15in)	75cm (2ft 6in)	Late spring

Chit seed potatoes to encourage shoots to grow. Plant them, shoots uppermost, and cover gently to avoid damaging the growth.

leaves appear, either cover the plants with straw or dried bracken or draw some more soil lightly over them, allowing just the tips of the shoots to peep through the surface.

When the stems are 20–25cm (8–9in) high, start earthing up. This process is done by gently drawing up the soil on either side of the rows to surround the stems. Earthing up encourages the plant to develop more roots and, therefore, more potatoes. It also keeps the developing potatoes well covered in soil so the light does not reach them and turn them green. About 15cm (6in) of leafy growth should show above the ridge at all times. Keep the top of the ridge broad rather than narrow, and tapering. A pointed ridge makes it more likely that the potatoes will be exposed. Repeat the earthing up process every few weeks so that deep trenches develop between the rows. This process also helps to control weeds and improves drainage in the soil.

A general-purpose fertiliser can be added to the soil at the first earthing up and this can help to boost your crop. In dry spring weather, make sure the potato plants are kept well-watered.

Harvesting

Start harvesting the first early potatoes in early summer. The very first harvests can be done by hand, feeling and delving into the soil and taking the largest potatoes (even these will be very small) and leaving the others to carry on growing. Make sure those left behind are well covered over with soil.

Later earlies can be dug up, using a broad-tined fork. Push this into the ground well clear of the plant, so as not to spear the potatoes. Turn the plant into the trench, then collect all the potatoes by hand.

When the earlies have run out, towards the middle of summer, start harvesting the second earlies. They should yield good-sized potatoes until late summer.

The maincrop should be lifted in early autumn on a fine, dry day. Leave them on the surface of the ground for several hours to dry off, particularly if they are wanted for storing. Then rub off any large clods of earth and store the potatoes.

Clearing the plot after harvest

Put the old plants on the compost heap when you dig up your potatoes, unless they were diseased, in which case they should be burnt. Avoid using compost made with potato plants on ground in which potatoes or tomatoes will be grown the following year, because it might still harbour harmful bacteria common to these vegetables.

Make sure you have removed all the potatoes from the ground. It can then be used straightaway for another vegetable crop.

PESTS AND DISEASES

Potatoes are subject to a number of pests and diseases, but many can be avoided by using certified, disease-free seed potatoes. Observing a strict crop rotation will also help to reduce the likelihood of disease hitting your potato crop.

The most common problems to affect potatoes are potato blight (page 151), potato cyst eelworm (page 151), potato scab (page 151), wart disease (page 151), black leaf (page 151) and wireworm (page 151).

Alternative growing methods

One alternative to the traditional method of growing potatoes is to place them on the ground and cover with black polythene. Anchor the edges with stones or earth.

Make slits in the polythene directly above each growing plant. Watch for slugs, which thrive in these conditions. Roll back the sheeting for harvesting.

Potatoes also do well in pots. You can use ordinary large, deep pots, planting the seed potatoes in around 20cm (8in) compost at the bottom and adding more compost on top to bury the plants again as they grow. Special potato pots are also available, which allow you to add another strip of plastic at the top of the pot each time you need to earth up the growing plants.

Look out, too, for strong plastic bags, corrugated plastic towers, woven surrounds to disguise utilitarian containers and many more options for raising a crop of potatoes in a pot.

Growing Salad Vegetables

Salad crops are a delight of the summer and early autumn months, but it is also possible to grow many of them in winter and spring too, and they can often be cooked in stir-fries as well as eaten cold in a conventional salad. Many vegetables could be classed as salad crops, but those included here are chicory, corn salad, American cress, cucumber, endive, lettuces and radishes and some of the more modern salad leaves, such as rocket, Mizuna mixture and pak choi.

Chicory is a useful winter salad vegetable that may be eaten raw or cooked. It is grown in two stages, first in the plot, and then in large flowerpots. This second stage is known as forcing and it is at this time that the light-green, spear-shaped heads or chicons are produced.

Corn salad and endives also provide fresh leaves for winter salads, when other salad crops are not in such abundance, although both can be produced through the summer too. Corn salad has small, dark-green leaves and is a small plant; endive is much larger and may either have deeply crinkled and curly leaves or ones that are waxy and indented. Endive is blanched during growth to reduce its otherwise rather bitter taste.

Mustard and cress

Mustard and cress are usually grown indoors. Do this either by sprinkling the seed on saucers containing dampened blotting paper or sheets of kitchen paper, or in shallow, compost-filled containers. Keep these in a dark place until the seed has germinated, then move them to a light windowsill. Cut and use when the stems are about 4cm (1½in) high, which will be take about two to three weeks.

GROWING TIMES AND HARVESTING MONTHS

It is possible to produce some salad crops in your garden throughout the year, although summer and autumn are the principal seasons. Lettuces can be grown all year round, but winter and spring crops are harder to produce successfully.
Choose lettuce varieties to suit your taste and those you find easiest to produce. The different crops all include varieties suitable for sowing variously throughout the year. The chart below shows the quickest time in which it takes these crops to reach maturity – remember this will vary according to the month of sowing and the weather conditions – and the months in which they can be harvested.

VEGETABLE	SHORTEST GROWING TIME	HARVESTING MONTHS
Chicory	*To lifting:* 5 months *Forcing to harvesting:* 1 month	November–March
Corn Salad	4 months	December and January
American cress	2 months	March–December
Cucumber	4 months	Late July/August–September
Endive	*To blanching:* 3 months *Blanching to harvesting:* 2–4 weeks	October–November
Lettuce	2½ months	December
Salad leaves	4–6 weeks	April–November and January–March all year round
Radish *Ordinary* *Winter*	1 month 4 months	April–November October–December

American cress is a much easier to grow alternative to watercress, which should be grown in a running stream. American cress has smaller, rather more symmetrically arranged leaves, but its flavour is very similar.

Lettuces and leaves
The two main types of lettuce – cabbage and cos – have countless subdivisions. As well as normal-sized lettuces in all different shades of green, there are dwarf varieties, those with very crisp leaves that curl over each other and others with soft leaves that form loose hearts. Choose according to the type you like and the time of year in which you want to grow them. There is always a wide selection of lettuce seeds in garden centres in early spring.

Many salad leaves are grown as cut-and-come-again crops. They grow as individual leaves, which are picked as required. More grow in their place, so that you can continue to harvest over a long period. You could grow a dedicated crop of rocket, for example, or choose a packet of mixed seeds that will give a variety of leaves, often including rocket, Lamb's lettuce, ornamental mustards and more colourful varieties, such as Bull's blood beet and red salad bowl. Mizuna mix is a widely available and popular choice, or you can experiment with creating your own mixtures.

Pak choi is harvested like a hearted lettuce, but is included with cut-and-come-again leaves here, as it requires the same care.

Other salad ingredients

Radishes are actually brassicas, but are included here as they are grown and eaten as a salad crop. Ordinary radishes grown throughout the summer may be round, bomb-shaped or conical, and brilliant red, red and white or even pure white. Winter radishes are parsnip-shaped, black-skinned and can grow up to 15cm (6in) long.

Cucumbers are often thought of as a greenhouse crop, and many varieties do best under glass, but outdoor varieties are also available, although they tend to be shorter and have tougher skins.

Tomatoes are such a varied salad crop that they are covered separately in greater detail on pages 87–90.

CULTIVATION TIPS

The comprehensive cultural details for the salad crops in this section are listed overleaf. Nearly all these crops do best in a fertile soil which is rich in organic material.

This need for fertile soil is particularly true of cucumbers, which can be

successfully grown on a mound of well-rotted compost or farmyard manure covered with 7.5–10cm (3–4in) of good topsoil. The roots of cucumber plants need to be kept very moist, but the crop will fail if they are waterlogged. Cucumber plants can be left to trail over the ground (but remember they take up quite a lot of space), or trained to grow up a vertical trellis.

Lettuces as catch crops

As most salads are quick to mature, they can be sown as catch crops – that is, between rows of slower-maturing vegetables. Alternatively, lettuces can easily be grown in odd spots in a flower garden or even in pots on the patio. Sow all types of salad crop very thinly and in rapid succession. As salad crops cannot be stored, it makes more sense to have a small, steady flow, rather than to be swamped with a glut of say, radishes and lettuce, all at once.

Salad crops need to be kept well watered whilst growing. Most must be grown rapidly both for the best

Add colour and interest to your salads when you grow your own crops. You need not be restricted to the bland green varieties available in the supermarket when you can raise your own radishes (above left) and colourful leaves like radicchio, Bull's blood beet and red salad bowl lettuce (above).

taste and to stop them running to seed. Once harvested, pull up the roots quickly and compost them. The land can be used immediately for another crop.

Winter salads

Both endive and corn salad are usually thought of as autumn and winter vegetables, but they can be sown in early spring to crop in summer. Remember that you should have an abundance of lettuce through the summer, and only grow this extra cropping if you prefer them over other salad leaves.

Winter crops may need to be protected from harsh weather with cloches and even though weeds are not as abundant at this time of year, it is still good practice to hoe regularly to keep them at bay.

CULTIVATION OF SALAD CROPS

VEGETABLE	SOIL/POSITION	SOWING	DRILL DEPTH
Chicory	**Soil:** Deep and well-cultivated. Appreciates some well-rotted manure or compost dug in deeply before sowing **Position:** Any, but does not like to be heavily over-shadowed	Sow thinly in cropping position from April to June	0.5cm (¼in)
Corn salad	**Soil:** Any well-cultivated soil **Position:** Open and sunny	Sow thinly in August/September	1cm (½in)
Cress, American	**Soil:** Damp, full of well-rotted manure **Position:** Moist and shady	Water the drills well and sow seed thinly in March; then again in September	0.5cm (¼in)
Cucumber	**Soil:** Good soil which has been well enriched with manure or compost shortly before planting **Position:** Sunny and sheltered	Sow indoors in individual peat pots in late April. Keep in warm place. Sow under glass in cropping site in mid-May, or unprotected in cropping site from the end of May. Sow three seeds in a 10-15cm (4-6in) group, every 60cm (2ft)	1–2.5cm (½–1in)
Endive	**Soil:** Light, well-drained and fertile soil **Position:** Any, but prefers a well-sheltered spot	Sow in cropping site late June to early August, or in a seed bed if more convenient	1 cm (½in)
Lettuce	**Soil:** Fertile, well-drained light soil. Crisp varieties like soil with lots of organic matter incorporated to help make them water-retentive **Position:** Open and sunny. Will not generally grow well if trees are shading the site	**Required harvesting time:** *May to November:* outdoors in cropping site, thinly, every two weeks from March to early August. *May to July:* indoors in boxes January/February. *April to May:* choose hardy over-wintering varieties and sow under cloches end September/October. *November to December:* choose forcing varieties; sow in seed bed in August in rows 15cm (6in) apart *March to April:* choose a forcing variety and sow in a cold frame or under cloches in October	All drills 1cm (½in)
Salad leaves and Pak Choi	**Soil:** Any fertile, well-drained soil; pots of multi-purpose compost **Position:** Open and sunny	Sow in cropping site at three to four week intervals from early spring to mid-autumn. Sow seed thinly	0.5cm (¼in)
Radish	**Soil:** Any fertile, well-cultivated soil, preferably containing well-rotted organic matter. This is particularly necessary if soil is light and sandy **Position:** For spring sowing: open and sunny, but sheltered. Over-shadowing may result in radishes that are woody and hot. For summer sowing: cool, shady site	**Ordinary radish:** Sow in cropping site in succession from March; sow very thinly every two weeks until August/September. If you want radishes even earlier (for late March), sow under cloches in January/February. Put cloches in place a fortnight before sowing to warm ground **Winter radishes:** Sow in cropping site in July/August. If ground is dry, water base of drill before sowing	1cm (½in) 0.5cm (¼in) 2cm (¾in)

THINNING/TRANSPLANTING	PLANTING DISTANCES	CULTIVATION	HARVESTING
Thin progressively to recommended spacing	20 x 40cm (8 x 15in)	Hoe between rows and water if plants show signs of drying. In October/ November, when the leaves have turned yellow and died down, dig up the long roots. Cut off leaves at about 2.5cm (1in) and rub off all the lower end of the root to make it about 20cm (8in) long. Force at once (see Harvesting) or store covered in dry soil in a dark place until wanted	**To force:** plant roots in compost-filled flower pots, so there is 2.5–5cm (1–2in) between them and the tops are visible above the soil. Water and cover pot with another pot the same size, inverted. Put in a warm place and leave for about four weeks. The heads are ready when they are 12.5–15cm (5–6in) high. Cut as required and then compost the roots
Thin to recommended spacing	10 x 15cm (4 x 6in)	Water freely and hoe between rows to eliminate weeds. Protect from frost by packing straw round plants. Alternatively, place cloches on top	Begin to harvest when at least six leaves have formed. Pick older leaves first or pull up the whole plant. Usually ready by the end of December
Thin progressively to recommended spacing	20 x 30cm (8 x 12in)	Water freely. Mulch the ground if there is any likelihood of it drying out	Pick outer leaves first. As these become tough, use the centre leaves
Harden off those grown indoors in May. Plant out in early June, spacing as recommended. If sown outside, pull out the weaker seedlings as they emerge, leaving one strong plant at each station	60 x 90cm (2 x 3ft)	Water freely. It helps to encourage side shoots if you pinch out the growing tips when four or five leaves have formed. Pollinate female flowers by pushing pollen-bearing male flowers into their centres or using a small brush. As young cucumbers form, pinch out shoots that have no cucumbers beyond the seventh leaf	Cut the cucumbers while they are still young. More will form
Thin progressively to recommended spacing if sown in cropping site. If sown in seed bed, transplant to cropping site when seedlings are 5–7.5cm (2–3in) high	30 x 40cm (12 x 15in)	Hoe to eliminate weeds and water freely. Give a liquid feed to encourage growth if necessary. Blanch centre leaves after about three months (see page 86). Alternatively, cover the row of endives with black polythene or white-painted cloches	If harvesting in autumn, plants will take 10 days to blanch. In winter, leave them for twice this time. Lift all plants before any danger of frost. They will keep for a few weeks in boxes of soil in a dark shed or cellar, but are best used immediately
Prick out seedlings from early sowings. Thin all crops as large enough to handle; transplant to cropping site when 10cm (4in) if raised in seed bed or boxes. Thin progressively to recommended distance, transplanting second thinnings and eating third thinnings as appropriate	From 15–30cm (6–12in) between plants: check seed packet. Distance between rows is usually 30cm (12in)	Protect all seedlings from birds with threads of black cotton or polythene tunnels. Summer crops need constant watering: they will bolt if allowed to dry out. Winter lettuces need less watering, but must be sown in well-cultivated soil. To encourage a cos-type lettuce to form its centre heart, draw up the outer leaves and tie round the plant loosely	Cabbage-type lettuces are ready when the heart is well formed. Feel it gently, but do not pinch it. Crisper varieties are ready when the centre leaves have curled over each other and this part feels hard and compact. Cos types are ready when the centre leaves are well developed. Cut all lettuces as required, but do not allow them to run to seed
If sown thinly, no thinning should be necessary. If you need to thin out the crop, pull seedlings when they are large enough to eat	20–30cm (8–10in) between rows	Water freely and hoe between rows. Cover early crops and late sowings with cloches in cold regions to protect from harsh conditions. Some will run to seed if left to grow for too long or if allowed to dry out	Pick leaves as required
Ordinary radish: Little thinning will be necessary, providing seed was thinly sown **Winter radish:** Thin to recommended spacing as seedlings emerge	**Ordinary radish:** 2.5 x 25cm (1 x 9in) **Winter radish:** 20 x30cm (8 x 12in)	**Ordinary radish:** Water well – crops depend on rapid growth. In dry conditions, radishes will be woody and very hot-tasting. Summer-sown crops are prone to very rapid bolting. Provide shade with plastic tunnels in very hot weather **Winter radish:** Hoe between rows to eliminate weeds	**Ordinary radish:** Pull largest ones first (you can check by pushing aside leaves and stems), beginning when they are 1cm (½in) in diameter. Pull up in succession quickly **Winter radish:** Start harvesting in November. Can be left in the ground through winter, but are better stored like other root crops (see page 207)

GROWING VEGETABLES · SALADS

Pick salad crops a little and often. They will not keep well and are far better eaten when they are absolutely fresh. Many salad leaves will grow again to replace what you have cut.

PESTS AND DISEASES

Their fast growth and prompt harvesting means that salads are generally less affected by pests and disease than many other crops.

Slugs (page 147) will chew their way through leaves. Look out, too, for cutworms (page 147) and downy mildew (page 146). Radishes, which are brassicas, will be subject to the brassica diseases (*see* page 65); flea beetle is the worst. Do not grow radishes in ground infected with club root. The most common problems to look for are grey mould (page 146), mosaic virus (page 146), greenfly (page 144), root aphids (page 148) and swift moth (page 151).

FORCING CHICORY

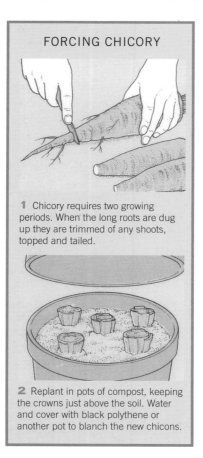

1 Chicory requires two growing periods. When the long roots are dug up they are trimmed of any shoots, topped and tailed.

2 Replant in pots of compost, keeping the crowns just above the soil. Water and cover with black polythene or another pot to blanch the new chicons.

BLANCHING ENDIVE

1 Loosely tie raffia around the stems of fully-grown plants. This keeps the lower tresses off the ground and reduces the risk of them rotting.

2 Cover the drainage holes of flower pots to exclude light and place over plants to blanch the inner stems. Allow ventilation around the base of the pot.

ENCOURAGING CUCUMBERS

1 Pinch out any growing shoots when enough cucumbers have formed on the plant, to prevent any further crops growth.

2 If necessary, hand pollinate the female cucumber flowers, either with a brush or by pushing the male flowers into the centres of the female flowers.

Growing Tomatoes

The many hybrid varieties of tomatoes available today have made it possible to grow tomatoes outdoors successfully in many areas. Failing this, a good-sized crop can often be produced on a small paved area, on a windowsill or in a garden room or conservatory.

The varieties of tomatoes are endless, from round ones of all sizes – those that are scarcely bigger than a sugar lump to those that are almost too big to hold in the hand – to plum- or pear-shaped ones that may be yellow, striped green and red, or yellow and red.

The most usual way of growing tomatoes outdoors is on a single-stemmed plant known as a cordon, but there are also bush and dwarf varieties, the latter growing to a height of no more that 15cm (6in) but sprawling extensively over the ground. Dwarf varieties can also be successfully grown in hanging baskets, where they will drape over the edges and there are vareities specifically bred for this situation.

Soil and position

For tomatoes, the ground should be well-cultivated and well-drained soil, into which well-rotted organic matter (leafmould is ideal) has been incorporated the previous autumn. If the ground is freshly manured just before planting tomatoes, the plants will be very leafy but bear few fruits. Tomatoes will grow well in potting composts and growing bags, although they will need regular liquid feeding in the later stages of growth.

Sunshine is the main requisite for a good crop of juicy tomatoes, so choose the sunniest spot you can. South-facing walls or fences make the best sites, because they also act as windbreaks.

Tomatoes grown outdoors usually have better flavour than indoor fruits. Choose from the many outdoor varieties available.

SOWING AND PLANTING

Tomatoes can be grown successfully from seed and there are many dozens of varieties to choose from. Make sure you buy an outdoor variety if you do not intend to grow them in a greenhouse.

Sow tomatoes in boxes or pots filled with seed compost in early spring. Sow seeds 2.5cm (1in) apart or two seeds to each 7.5cm (3in) pot. Damp the compost well and cover with newspaper until the seed has germinated. Put the containers in a warm, darkened place and, as soon as the seedlings emerge, remove the newspaper and move the containers to a warm, south-facing windowsill in full sunlight. When the first leaves appear, transplant strong seedlings from boxes to individual pots filled with potting compost, or just remove the weaker seedling of the two if they were sown in individual pots.

From mid-April, begin to harden off the plants by putting them in

Good tomato varieties

OUTDOOR CORDON

• **Moneymaker** Very popular heavy cropper with medium-sized fruits

• **Sungold** Sweet, cherry-sized fruits that are golden in colour

OUTDOOR BUSH

• **Red Alert** Delicious small and early fruits

• **Sigmabush** Excellent fruits and high yield

DWARF

• **Tumbling Tom** Small, sweet fruits; red or yellow. Ideal for baskets

CULTIVATION OF TOMATOES

1 Sow the seed in boxes filled with seed compost in late March/early April. Dampen the compost, cover the boxes with newspaper and leave them in a warm, dark place.

2 When the seedlings begin to grow, prick out the strongest and plant in individual flower pots filled with potting compost. Water the seedlings lightly, but regularly.

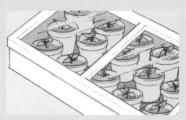

3 Harden the seedlings off either by placing them in cold frames in mid-April, or in cloches in May. If necessary, pot on any seedlings which are out-growing their pots.

4 Plant out the seedlings when they are about 20cm (8in) high. Tip them out of their pots, holding them carefully by their rootballs, and plant them in the soil.

5 Space plants 45cm (18in) apart. As they grow taller they will need to be supported with canes, loosely attached with soft garden string.

6 Water the plants regularly to prevent them wilting. Take care with plants in growing bags, as too much water can rot their roots.

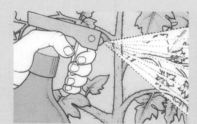

7 Give a regular liquid feed from about the end of July, once they begin to bear fruit. Irregular feeding and watering may make the fruits grow unevenly and split.

8 Remove any yellow leaves and tie back others that are shading tomatoes from the sun. Place straw on the ground to protect lower trusses from the mud.

Healthy tomato seedlings will have a strong stem and deep green, robust leaves; discard any that are weak and straggly. It takes about seven weeks from sowing the seed to the plants being ready to plant out into the garden.

cold frames. If you don't have one, put them under cloches in mid-May, or keep indoors until early June. If necessary pot the seedlings on to bigger pots as they grow. Keep the compost damp, but not waterlogged.

Planting out established plants

Many people prefer to buy plants from a nursery rather than raise their own from seed. Buy them when they are about 20cm (8in) high, making sure you buy sturdy-looking plants, bred to grow outdoors. They should be dark green and short-jointed; avoid those that look weak or have large gaps between fern-like leaves.

Plant tomatoes carefully; tip them out of the pot and hold them by the rootballs, not the stems. Plant with the rootball and compost intact, so the top of the rootball is 1cm (½in) below the surface of the soil. Plants should be about 45cm (1ft 6in) apart. If growing more than one row, place rows 75cm (2ft 6in) apart.

CULTIVATION TIPS

Tomatoes need food and water throughout their growing period. Irregular watering can lead to split fruits and a poor harvest.

Water the seedlings immediately after planting. A good way to keep tomato plants evenly moist is to sink a 10cm (4in) flowerpot into the soil near the root and fill this to the top with water once a week. This allows water to get straight to the roots and to seep into the soil slowly and gradually. Irregular or over-watering can do as much damage as insufficient watering.

Push strong canes about 1.5m (5ft) long into the ground close to the plant and as the plant grows, tie the stem loosely to the cane (giving

Growing tomatoes in pots and containers

Planting in pots means that you can position your tomatoes in the sunniest, most sheltered spot.

Containers

Any good-sized container will house a tomato plant, although you will need to be vigilant as pots dry out faster than garden soil. Make sure that pots are sturdy and have a broad base, as the tall plants and heavy trusses of fruit make tapering pots unstable.

Hanging baskets

Cherry tomatoes are the best choice for hanging baskets, as the fruit will not get so heavy that it risks breaking the plant's stems. Add slow-release fertiliser and water-retaining gels to reduce the need for feeding and watering in awkward spots.'Tumbler' tomatoes are the best for baskets.

Growing bags

Some are formulated specifically for tomatoes and you may not need to feed the plants as often. They will still need staking; look for wire frames that slide beneath the bag and curve over the top; you feed your cane through the supports to make it more secure.

Planting in a ring

Ring culture pots help to promote strong growth and maximum flavour.

Bed the ring pots into the top of a growing bag and plant your tomato in the raised 'pot', using a few handfuls of potting compost to surround it. Apply feed directly into the compost at the top and this will be taken up quickly by the feeding roots near the surface. Water into the lower ring and this will soak through into the growing bag, to be taken up by the water roots, which grow down from the plant. This gives the maximum strength of feed to the plants, without it being diluted by regular watering and lost into the soil.

the stem room to expand without damage from the ties).

Pinching out

As growth progresses, pinch out the side shoots that grow in the leaf axils – that is, the little shoots appearing between the leaves and the stem (*see* page 90). This helps to ensure that strong flower trusses (on which the fruits will form) develop, instead

of a number of long, useless side shoots. The flower trusses grow from the main stem, not the leaf axils and these unnecessary shoots will take up valuable water and nutrients.

When the plant has developed about four trusses (usually towards the end of July), prevent further upward growth by pinching out the central growing tip. The plant's energies will then be directed into

Every two weeks, pinch out any shoots growing in the leaf axils to prevent them from taking valuable nutrients from the developing fruit.

developing the trusses. Pinching out is not necessary on dwarf or bush tomato varieties.

Tomatoes will benefit from regular liquid feeding from now on; you will need to begin earlier if growing in pots or growing bags, as the fertiliser in the compost will soon be exhausted by the growing plants. Spray or syringe the plants with water and liquid feed, as well as watering through the ground.

Good housekeeping, healthy plants
Remove any leaves that turn yellow as soon as you spot them and, as the fruits begin to form, tie back any lower leaves that are shading them from the sun. Plants with a lot

of leaf growth can become prone to disease, as air cannot circulate within the plant and moisture builds up, encouraging mould. Tomatoes on lower trusses can be kept clean by putting a layer of straw beneath them to protect them if their stems bend down to the ground.

Harvesting
Begin picking the tomatoes as soon as they are ripe, supporting the fruits in the palm of your hand and pressing the stem just above the fruit. It will snap, leaving the calyx on the end of the tomato.

In autumn, any fruit still remaining should be picked, even if it is green – it will not survive early frosts and will be lost entirely if left too long. Pull up the plant and hang either the whole thing, or just the tomato-bearing trusses in a warm, preferably sunny, spot indoors, or in a greenhouse, to allow the tomatoes to ripen. Alternatively, if space permits, leave the plants in the ground, but untie them from their supports, lie them down gently on a bed of straw and cover with cloches until the tomatoes ripen.

Green tomatoes can also be picked off the plant and put carefully into trays, placed in a cool, darkened

place. They will ripen gradually over the next few months, and will be encouraged to do so if you include one red tomato with every batch. Alternatively, use the green tomatoes to make chutney or relish (*see* pages 214–17).

PESTS AND DISEASES

The tomato is closely related to the potato and therefore is likely to suffer from many of the same problems. It may be affected by the potato cyst eelworm (*see* page 151) and is likely to get blight if you handle tomato plants after tending potatoes. Always wash your hands between the two operations.

Apart from those diseases mentioned below, young plants put out too soon may show signs of distress. If growth is slow and plants look sickly shortly after planting, protect them with cloches. Tomatoes grown outdoors, however, are usually far less susceptible to problems than their hot-house equivalents.

The most common problems to look for when tending your tomatoes are blossom end rot (page 150), buck eye rot (page 150), leaf mould (page 150) and splitting (page 150).

HARVESTING TOMATOES

1 Pick tomatoes by supporting the fruit in the palm of your hand and gently snapping off the stem above the calyx.

2 If picking whole trusses of green tomatoes at the end of the season, leave them on a bed of straw under cloches, outside, to ripen.

3 Alternatively, the trusses can be cut and hung up in a warm, sunny spot indoors, or ideally in a greenhouse, until they are ripe.

Other Outdoor Vegetables

Included on the following pages are some of the many other vegetables you may choose to cultivate, including globe and Jerusalem artichokes, asparagus, celery and celeriac, leeks, onions and garlic, marrows, courgettes (zucchini), pumpkins, okra, spinach and sweetcorn.

There are two main types of celery – ones that must be blanched during growth and others that are self-blanching. Self-blanching celery is easier to grow and demands less work, but it will not survive the heavy frosts that the other types can withstand and is generally said to be less tasty. Celeriac, known sometimes as the turnip-rooted celery because of the edible swollen bulb that grows at the bottom of the plant, is easier to grow than celery and can be eaten raw or cooked.

Artichoke varieties

Globe artichokes are perennial plants, and their silvery green leaves make them an attractive addition to the plot. Each plant yields about six flower heads (the edible part) a year and will crop for about six years, although it is best to renew plants after three or four years, as the heads start to become smaller and tougher. You probably don't need more than a few plants, but growing your own will give you more opportunities to eat this delicious vegetable, which is often considered to be something of a delicacy.

Jerusalem artichokes are grown for their tubers, which have a distinctly earthy taste. The plants

Globe artichokes are a delicious treat for the table, but worth growing for their striking beauty, too. These stately, silvery plants bear fantastic purple flowerheads in summer.

GROWING TIMES AND HARVESTING MONTHS

The chart below gives the shortest time it takes for these other outdoor crops to reach maturity, and the months in which they are generally harvested. As with other vegetables, cropping seasons can be extended by regular sowings at intervals of a couple of weeks or a month, or by sowing different varieties that take varying times to reach maturity.

VEGETABLE	SHORTEST GROWING TIME	HARVESTING MONTHS
Celery:		
Self-blanching	5½ months	End August – end October
Blanching	6½ months	End September – March
Celeriac	6½ months	October–November
Courgette (Small zucchini)	2½ months	July–September
Marrow (Large zucchini)	3 months	July–October
Pumpkin	3 months	July–October
Leek	8 months	Early October–April
Onion – salad	3 months	June–mid November
Onion	6–10 months	September–November
Shallot	4 months	Late July–August
Okra	3 months	August–early October
Spinach:		
Summer	2 months	May–October
Winter	2½ months	November–April
New Zealand	1½ months	Mid-June–September
Sweetcorn	3 months	August–September

resemble sunflowers (to which they are related), and they grow tall enough to form an effective screen to hide a shed or compost heap. They will grow in almost any soil.

Courgettes, marrows and squash

Courgettes are actually young marrows, but they have become so popular in their own right, that plant breeders have developed many varieties specifically to produce heavy crops of these smaller fruits, and it is better to grow these than to harvest small marrows.

You will find green and yellow varieties, most in the conventional long, thin shape, but some globe shaped vegetables, too. The cultivation for all kinds of both marrows and courgettes is the same. Marrows, in particular, are available in bush and trailing varieties, which can be trained to grow up vertical supports if space is at a premium.

Also related to the marrow is the pumpkin and other edible squashes. These are generally easy to grow, but greedy of space. Gourds also belong to the same family and may be grown in the same way, although most types are purely ornamental and not edible. To harvest for eating, squashes should be cut in late summer and put in a warm, sunny place to dry.

The onion family

Leeks, onions and garlic are all members of the same family, but leeks are the easiest to grow and the hardiest, as they will withstand heavy frosts. Growing them also helps to break down heavy ground and improves its texture for other crops the following year.

Onions can be produced the whole year round, but they need protection from hard frosts if they are to survive the winter. More usually they are harvested in the autumn and then stored (*see* page 208), so they are available through the winter. They are grown from onion sets, small bulbs planted into the ground – a more successful and higher-yielding method than trying to grow from seed. Each set swells into one large bulb for harvesting. When the leaves turn yellow, bend them over the bulbs and leave the onions to finish ripening. Once they are harvested, they must be dried, preferably by hanging them in the sun in bunches or plaits.

Okra, spinach and sweetcorn

Okra is a less commonly grown and eaten vegetable in the UK, but can be used to flavour soups, stews and curries as well as being served as a vegetable accompaniment. It is also known as ladies' fingers or gumbo. Because it originated in Africa, it grows best in hot, sunny and humid conditions, so it will need protection with cloches if you wish to grow it outdoors in most of the UK.

Spinach is one of the fastest growing of all leaf vegetables, making it a good intercrop vegetable when

Okra is an unusual crop to find growing in Britain, but with protection from the cold you can try something a little different.

Harvest spinach leaves when they are young for their best flavour. Larger leaves develop woody, stringy stems and tough greenery.

you have an area of empty ground. The two main types are summer and winter spinach, but New Zealand spinach is usually grouped with them, although it is not a true member of the spinach family. It has smaller leaves which are less shiny, and it is not as hardy – it will be killed by frost. However, New Zealand spinach will flourish in drier conditions, so is a useful alternative in sandy, free-draining soil. Perpetual spinach, or spinach beet, is included with root crops, (*see* pages 66–71).

Sweetcorn is traditionally a hot-weather vegetable, but there are now varieties that can be grown in more temperate climates. Given a sheltered position, plants will give a reasonable yield, making them well worthwhile growing for at least one year to see whether they suit your soil and palate.

CULTIVATION OF OTHER OUTDOOR CROPS

VEGETABLE	SOIL/POSITION	SOWING	DRILL DEPTH
Globe artichoke	**Soil:** Rich, well-drained soil which was manured the previous spring. Apply lime about two months before planting if soil is acid **Position:** Open, sunny, but sheltered	If raising from seed, sow outdoors in a seed bed in March/April. If raising from suckers, plant them into a spare area in April	1cm (½in)
Jerusalem artichoke	**Soil:** Will grow in almost any soil; the richer it is, the heavier the crop. Enrich poor soil with manure the winter before planting **Position:** Sunny, but will tolerate partial shade. Can be grown as a screen	Plant tubers into the cropping site in February to March	10–15cm (4–6in)
Celery	**Soil:** Deeply dug, rich, well-drained soil with lots of well-rotted organic matter. Self-blanching types will grow in poorer soils **Position:** Open and sunny	**Both types:** Sow seeds under glass in mid-March and again in mid-April to stagger the crop. Keep in a warm place to germinate	
Celeriac	**Soil:** Richly cultivated and well-drained. Will grow in poorer soils than celery, but bigger vegetables are produced in rich soil **Position:** Sunny	Sow under glass in mid-March and keep warm until germination	
Garlic	**Soil:** *see* Onions **Position:** *see* Onions	Divide garlic bulbs into individual cloves and plant, growing tip upwards, just below the soil at intervals from March to May and in October	*See* Onions
Leek	**Soil:** Well-cultivated and well-drained soil, which was manured the previous winter. Leeks are not as demanding as onions in their soil requirements **Position:** Any, but they dislike heavy shading	Indoors in February/March or outdoors in a seed bed in March/April, sowing three seeds every 2.5cm (1in).	1cm (½in)

THINNING/TRANSPLANTING	PLANTING DISTANCES	CULTIVATION	HARVESTING
Thin seedlings as they appear, discarding the weaker ones. The following spring, transplant into cropping site at recommended spacing. Transplant plants grown from suckers at this time, too	75–105cm (2ft 6in x 3ft 6in)	Mulch plants one month after planting out. Water well in dry spells. Remove flower buds as they appear in the first year. In subsequent years, allow plant to develop four to six flower buds, picking off any extra ones. In early winter, cut main stems to ground level, leaving small leaves at the centre to protect the plant. Cover the plants with straw or draw soil up around them	In the second and following years, pick the heads in summer when they are plump, but green, and the petals are tightly grouped. There should be no brown tips to the scales. Use secateurs to cut them and begin with the central, largest, head. After harvesting, cut the stems back by half
Prick out into boxes or pots when large enough to handle. Harden off seedlings from early sowing late April and plant out in May. Harden off later sowing in May and plant out in June	38 x 75cm (1ft 3in x 2ft 6in)	Hoe to control weeds and pinch out growing tips to prevent flowers forming. Stake plants if necessary and cut the stems down in early winter	Lift tubers as required from October. You can leave the crop in the ground or dig them up and store. Save some tubers from the crop to plant out the following year
For blanching: In April dig trenches 40cm (15in) wide and 30cm (1ft) deep. Make them 30cm (1ft) wide for a double row of celery and plant in pairs. Dig manure into the bottom to leave trench 15cm (6in) deep. Plant seedlings in the trench at recommended spacings and time **Self-blanching:** Plant in a block rather than rows, so inner plants are blanched naturally.	**For blanching:** 15cm (6in) between plants **Self-blanching:** 25 x 25cm (9 x 9in)	Water all plants liberally after planting and during dry spells. **For blanching:** When plants are 30cm (1ft) high, tie paper or black polythene around their stems, water and draw earth up around stems to exclude light. Make sure the leaves remain exposed. Continue earthing up regularly for six to eight weeks. **Self-blanching:** Remove side growths as they appear; when plants are 30cm (1ft) high, pack straw around the outer stems	**For blanching:** Harvest from early autumn; flavour is improved after the first frost. Dig up plants from one end of the trench, shake off soil and cut off roots. Make sure those left for later harvest are well earthed up **Self-blanching:** Harvest from end August until the first frost. Pack straw around plants exposed after lifting others. Harvest as for blanching types
Treat as celery seedlings, pricking out and hardening off for planting out in late May/June. Plant directly into the cropping site with roots well buried so plants are firm in the soil	30 x 20cm (12 x 8in)	Hoe to control weeds and keep well watered. Feed fortnightly with liquid manure to keep growth even. From August, remove any side growths and yellowing leaves to ensure the roots develop to their full potential	Begin lifting when roots are large enough (usually from the end of October), as required. Harvest the entire crop by the end of November and store any that are not required for immediate use
No thinning necessary.	15 x 30cm (6 x 12in)	Hoe to control weeds and water well in dry spells. When flowers appear, feed fortnightly with liquid fertiliser	Harvest when leaves turn yellow. Those planted in March will be ready from October. Those planted in October will be ready the following July/August
Prick out indoor seedlings when large enough to handle and harden off in mid-March. Transplant into a seed bed when seedlings are 15–20cm (6–8in) high, then thin to about 5cm (2in) apart when large enough to handle. Transplant to cropping site in June/July. **To transplant:** Trim off top third of the leaves with scissors. Make holes in the ground with a dibber at the recommended spacing and drop leeks into them so the tips of the leaves just show. Do not firm the soil around them; instead just water them well. This will firm them into the ground sufficiently once the water drains away	25 x 30cm (9 x 12in)	Hoe to control weeds and draw soil up around stem as plants grow. This helps to blanch the stems, but try not to let the soil go in between the leaves	Dig up leeks as you need them from September to April, easing them gently out of the soil with a fork. Lift them in spring when you want the ground for some other crop, and put the leeks in a shallow trench in a patch of spare ground. Just cover the roots and stems with soil, with the leaves protruding. In this way, the leeks will not begin to grow again, which makes them go to seed. Use as required

CULTIVATION OF OTHER OUTDOOR CROPS

VEGETABLE	SOIL/POSITION	SOWING	DRILL DEPTH
Marrow and courgette (zucchini)	**Soil:** Rich and moisture-retentive. It should have lots of well-rotted manure added to it **Position:** Sunny or partial shade. Can be grown on a compost heap; trailing varieties can also be grown up and along a fence	Indoors, sow two to a pot in early April. Outdoors, sow directly into the cropping site in mid-May, but protect with cloches in cold areas. Sow seeds at 15cm (6in) intervals, the pointed end pushed down into the soil	2.5cm (1in)
Onion No onion seed or seedlings should be sown or transplanted until the soil has really dried out after winter. If it sticks to your boots, it is still too wet. Firm the ground and rake it to a fine tilth	**Soil:** Well-cultivated, deeply dug soil which has been manured the previous autumn. Pickling onions are better grown in lighter, not so rich, soil or they will grow too big **Position:** Sunny and open	**Salad and pickling:** Sow into cropping site at monthly intervals from March to September **Onions from seed:** 1. Sow under glass in January to February 2. Sow outdoors in seed bed or cropping site from late February to early April 3. Sow over-wintering varieties in seed bed in mid-August for harvesting the following summer **Onions from sets:** Trim off wispy growth and push sets into the soil at the recommended distance in March/April. Alternatively, sow in shallow drills	1cm (½in) 0.5–1cm (¼–½in)
Pumpkin	**Soil:** Very rich with lots of well-rotted organic matter incorporated **Position:** Warm and sunny. Will grow in light shade, but the vegetables will be smaller	Indoors, sow two to a pot in early April Outdoors, sow directly into the cropping site in late April/mid-May. Protect with cloches	2.5cm (1in).
Okra	**Soil:** Light, which has been well-cultivated to ensure good water retention **Position:** Warm and sheltered. A south-facing spot is ideal	Sow indoors under glass in April. Sow direct into cropping site in mid-May, but protect with cloches or polythene tunnels	1cm (½in)
Spinach	**Soil:** Rich, moisture-retentive soil (this is particularly important for summer spinach) **Position:** Summer spinach: full sun or partial shade; Winter spinach: sheltered site	**Summer spinach:** Sow directly into the cropping site at fortnightly intervals, early March to July **Winter spinach:** Sow directly into cropping site in August and again one month later	2.5cm (1in)
New Zealand spinach	**Soil:** Light and well-drained **Position:** Sunny	Sow indoors in late March/early April Sow directly into cropping site in early May. Sow two seeds together every 15cm (6in) along row	2.5cm (1in)
Sweetcorn	**Soil:** Well-cultivated, rich soil. Improve light soils by incorporating lots of well-rotted organic matter **Position:** Warm, sunny and sheltered, but not shaded	Sow indoors in individual peat pots in late April/ early May. Sow directly into cropping site in mid-May. Plant two or three seeds at each station (*see* Spacing)	1–2 cm (½–¾in)

THINNING/TRANSPLANTING	PLANTING DISTANCES	CULTIVATION	HARVESTING
Pull out weaker seedlings as they emerge. Harden off pot-grown seedlings in May and plant into cropping site at the end of May/ early June	**Marrows, bush:** 90 x 90cm (3 x 3ft) **Marrows, trailing:** 90 x 120cm 3 x 4ft) **Courgettes:** 60 x 60cm (2ft x 2ft)	Hoe until leaves smother weed growth. Water well, soaking the surrounding ground. Protect young plants from slugs. Pinch out growing tips of trailing marrows when they have four or five leaves to encourage side shoots to grow. Pollinate by hand (see page 98)	Cut courgettes when 10cm (4in) long; keep cutting to encourage more to grow. Cut marrows at 20cm (8in) long, and tender. Test by pressing a rib close to the stalk – it should yield slightly. Harvest marrows when young, at the end of July and cut them all by mid-October, before any danger of frost
Salad and pickling: No need to thin **Onions from seed:** 1. Prick out when large enough to handle. Harden off in mid-March and plant in cropping site mid-April 2. Thin to 5cm (2in) when large enough to handle. Thin a month later to 10cm (4in), using thinnings for salads or small onions. Thin to final spacing a month later or transplant to cropping site 3. Do not thin, but transplant to cropping site the following March. Plant onions so that half the stem is underground **Onions from sets:** Need no thinning	**Salad and pickling:** 25–30cm (9–12in) between rows **All others:** 15 x 30cm (6 x 12in). If growing a large-bulbed variety, increase distance between bulbs to 25cm (9in)	**Salad and pickling:** Hoe to control weeds and protect September sowings with cloches to give winter crops **All others:** Hoe to control weeds. Keep well-watered, and if any plants produce flower heads, pull them up and use the onions straightaway. When plants are fully grown and leaves begin to turn yellow, bend the leaves over just above the bulbs	**Salad and pickling:** Pull onions from about March when they are about 15cm (6in) high. Leave some to get a little larger for pickling. Pull these when appropriate size and leave in the sun to ripen **All others:** A week or two after bending over leaves, dig up onions gently to break their roots, but leave them in the ground for another two weeks. Then dig up completely and leave in the sun to ripen. Store as described on page 208. Onions for winter storage should be lifted by late September
Pull out weaker seedlings of those in pots as they emerge. Harden off for planting out in late May/early June. Thin outdoor seedlings to final recommended spacings	90 x 120cm (3 x 4ft)	Water well and give fortnightly feeds when fruits start to swell. Pinch out growing tips when three leaves have formed. Pollinate as for marrows. Put young fruits on wood or a slate to discourage slugs and keep them clean. Leave on the plant to ripen	Cut pumpkins when they have fully ripened. This is usually in early autumn, although small-fruited varieties will be ready in late summer. If there is any danger of frost, cover the plants with a sack at night
Prick out indoor seedlings into pots as they emerge. Harden off in early May and plant out into cropping site in late May. Thin those sown in the cropping site progressively until you reach the recommended spacing	50 x 60 cm (1ft 8in x 2ft)	Hoe to control weeds and keep plants well watered. Give plants feeds of liquid fertiliser at 14-day intervals when the flowers have appeared	Cut fruits when 15–20cm (6–8in) long. Regular picking encourages growth. Plants will be killed by the first frost, so harvest all the fruits by then. Freeze any surplus
Both types: Thin seedlings to 7.5cm (3in) when large enough to handle. Thin to final spacing one month later. (Thinnings may be eaten.)	**Summer:** 30 x 30cm (1ft x 1ft) **Winter:** 15 x 30cm (6 x 12in)	Hoe to control weeds. **Summer spinach:** Water well. Will run to seed in hot, dry conditions **Winter spinach:** Protect with cloches or straw from November	Pick leaves by pinching the base of the leaf stalk as soon as they are large enough. Take only half the leaves from a plant at one time, picking the largest first. Summer spinach can be picked harder than winter
Prick out indoor seedlings when large enough to handle. Harden off in early May and plant out in late May/June. Remove the weaker seedlings of the outdoor sowing to achieve recommended spacing	45 x 60cm (1ft 6in x 2ft)	Water plants constantly through any dry spells. Pinch out the' central growing tips. This encourages the growth of side shoots which bear more leaves	Pinch off young shoots when they have two or three good-sized leaves. As with summer and winter spinach, do not strip the plant
Harden off indoor seedlings when 15cm (6in) tall. Plant into cropping site in late May and protect with cloches for a month or so. Pull out weaker seedlings of outdoor sowing as they emerge. Grow sweetcorn in a block rather than in rows. This gives a better chance of good pollination	45 x 60cm (1ft 6in x 2ft)	Remove cloches when plants are established. Hoe to control weeds and draw soil up around stem to firm plants in. Water well, and feed weekly with liquid fertiliser. Stake plants if need be. Remove side shoots at the base of the stem. When three cobs have formed, remove any others that appear	When the hairy tassels protruding from the top of the cobs turn dark brown, test the grains of the cob for ripeness. A milky liquid should ooze out when you press a grain with a fingernail. Grains should be a pale yellow colour. Snap off the cobs and use immediately or freeze

CULTIVATION TIPS

The charts on pages 94–97 give the basic cultivation advice for the vegetables covered here, but there are some additional tips that can help to ensure a good harvest.

Globe artichokes may be grown from seed, but it is quicker and easier to grow them from suckers, cut off existing plants, or bought. Jerusalem artichokes are grown from tubers. It is important to plant new tubers each year, as this reduces the chance of disease, and stops them taking over the land.

Celery that needs blanching is grown in deep trenches. Self-blanching celery is usually grown in a block to blanch the stems (of the inner plants, at least) naturally. You can also grow them in a cold frame with the top removed. The walls of the frame give shade to the plants, blanching their stems.

Sweetcorn is also grown in a block, to increase the chance of good pollination between the top flowers and those that form the cobs.

CULTIVATING CELERY

1 Before earthing up, wrap newspaper, cardboard or black polythene around the stems of each plant to keep them free from dirt and to blanch, if necessary.

2 Plant out celery seedlings in trenches at the required distance and water well.

3 Begin the earthing up process, keeping the leaves exposed. Continue to water well.

4 Take care when harvesting celery not to damage the plants.

CULTIVATING MARROWS

| **PLANTING** | **PINCHING OUT** | **PROTECTING** | **POLLINATING** |

Use a dibber to make holes in the soil, with a garden line as a guide. Sow seeds individually.

Pinch out the growing tips of marrows to encourage the side shoots to grow and the plant to spread.

Place plants on pieces of wood, slate or polythene to protect the fruits from mud.

Marrows must be pollinated to bear fruit. There are two ways of transferring the pollen from the male to the female plants: either use a soft paintbrush dabbed inside each flower or insert the male flower itself into the centre of the female (above).

Onions may be grown from seeds or sets, tiny, immature onions which will each produce one large onion. Sets are easier to grow, but keep them in a cool, dry place if you cannot plant them immediately, to discourage premature sprouting. Shallots are also grown from sets, but in this case each bulb multiplies to produce about six new ones. After harvesting, keep some of the shallots to plant for the following year's crop.

PESTS AND DISEASES

There are many potential pests and diseases in the garden; some of the most likely problems are listed here.

Celery leaf fly, which attacks parsnips (*see* page 145) is a major pest of celery and celeriac. Affected plants will recover more quickly if they are given a feed of liquid fertiliser.

Dry growing conditions and poor soil can make globe artichokes small, woody and unpalatable. Apply a general fertiliser to the soil and mulch with well-rotted organic matter to improve conditions.

Marrows and courgettes that are kept short of water, or spinach grown on poorly drained land, may suffer mildew on their leaves. If this is not severe, it will not affect the size of the crop, and infected leaves can be picked off spinach plants. Mildew is less likely if spinach plants are thinned early, as recommended. Marrows can also suffer from mosaic virus (*see* page 146).

Other potential problems to look out for on your crops include leek moth (page 146), frit fly (page 145), onion fly (page 148), eelworm (page 145), slugs (page 151), petal blight fungus (page 145), neck rot (page 151), white rot (page 151) and celery leaf spot (page 146).

Growing Asparagus

Growing your own asparagus is a cheap way to put this often expensive ingredient on your plate. It does take a while to get established – three years if you start from seed – but the same plants will then go on producing yields for up to 20 years.

French varieties tend to be whiter-stemmed than the English ones, but your choice may depend on whether you want to grow from seed or crowns. If you buy two-year-old crowns, you will be able to start cutting stems the second season after planting. Growing from seed will take a little longer.

Soil and situation
The most important requirement for asparagus is that the soil is well-drained. Ideal conditions are a deep, rich, light sandy loam. As the site is so permanent, it should be well prepared by digging in lots of organic matter the autumn before planting and all perennial weeds must be removed. If the soil is acid, lime it to give a pH of 6.5–7.

When choosing where to put your asparagus bed, select an open sunny site, well sheltered from the wind. South-facing is usually best.

Sowing and planting
To raise asparagus from seed, sow it in a seed bed in early spring. Sow in drills about 5cm (2in) deep and 30cm (1ft) apart. The seed is slow to germinate, so soak it in water for a day first to soften it.

Water the emerging seedlings well through the summer and thin them to 15cm (6in) when they are large

Asparagus doesn't have to be an expensive luxury. If you have space for a dedicated asparagus bed you can harvest your own.

enough to handle. The following spring, you can plant them out following the directions given below.

Asparagus is more usually grown from one- or two-year-old crowns. Two-year-old crowns may produce asparagus quicker, but one-year-old crowns are cheaper and less likely to suffer during transplanting. If you cannot plant them immediately, cover the roots in damp compost or a damp sack: they must not dry out.

To plant the crowns, dig a trench 20cm (8in) deep and 30cm (1ft) wide. If you have any coarse sand, scatter some at the base to improve the drainage. Put a little soil back into the trench to form a mound about 7.5cm (3in) high. Spread the crowns over this, so the roots are splayed out on either side of the ridge. Then cover them with about 7.5cm (3in) of soil. Leave 45cm (18in) between plants and 1.2m (4ft) between rows.

CULTIVATION TIPS

Good preparation and care when the plants are getting established will pay dividends in subsequent years with a prolific crop.

Fill in the trench gradually as the plants grow, always keeping the crowns just covered. As the foliage grows in spring and summer, you may find it better to support it than to let it grow really wild and straggly. Do not be tempted to cut back the foliage, as this will reduce the crop.

Keep the bed well-watered; it must never dry out. For the first year, weeds can be controlled by hoeing; thereafter, they are best pulled out by hand, because hoeing could damage the plants' delicate roots. Treat any perennial weeds with a weedkiller.

After the first frost, in early autumn, cut down the foliage to 7.5cm (3in). It should have turned yellow by now. Do this before any berries start dropping to the ground and pick up and destroy any that have already fallen; if they germinate, they will crowd the plants already established.

If you like blanched asparagus stalks, pull the soil up around the crops in autumn and spring, making a mound of about 5cm (2in). Each spring, apply a general fertiliser to the soil, and each autumn a mulch of rotted compost or manure.

Harvesting

If you planted one-year crowns, do not cut any spears the first spring

CULTIVATING ASPARAGUS

1 Plant crowns on top of mounds dug in trenches and carefully cover with soil.

2 For the first year, do not cut the foliage, but continue to water the plants well. Control weeds by hoeing.

3 After the first frost, cut down the foliage before any berries begin dropping to the ground.

4 In the following spring, apply fertiliser and a mulch of compost or farmyard manure in the autumn.

5 If growing two-year-old crowns, cut a few spears the following spring, but do not harvest too many.

6 Established plants may need to be supported with stakes, but take care not to damage the crowns.

(one year after planting). Two-year-old crowns will give a small harvest the following year, but pick this sparingly – no more than one spear from each crown. When the plants are four years old, you can harvest the spears for four weeks, and in following years, for six weeks. The plants are ready for harvesting when the spears start to form.

Cut the spears using a special curved knife, about 7.5cm (3in) below the surface of the soil. The spears should have about 12.5cm (5in) showing above the ground if they are to be tender and succulent. Any taller than this, and they will be woody and stringy to eat. Always stop cutting in late spring to allow

the plants to build up their resources again before the next growing season. Contain the summer foliage if it gets unruly and cut it down each autumn as described above.

PESTS AND DISEASES

The most common problems to look for in asparagus beds are black slugs (page 151), asparagus beetle (page 144) and violet root rot (page 148).

Watch out for changes in the foliage that can signal an attack: distorted, patchy brown leaves indicate asparagus beetle, while yellowing foliage can be a sign of violet root rot.

Greenhouse Vegetables

A greenhouse is not an essential item of equipment for those who want to grow their own garden produce. But even in warmer regions one can boost your yield and the quality of some crops, speed up the time between sowing and maturing and broaden your range of possible crops for growing.

Before you buy a greenhouse, weigh up the cost plus the maintenance of heating it (if you choose to do so) against the value of the crops you will produce. You may feel it is worth it even if the arithmetic does not agree, but it could be many years before a harvest of peppers will pay you back. For more information on choosing and looking after a greenhouse *see* pages 34–38.

AUBERGINES

This Mediterranean plant can be grown in a large pot on a sunny, sheltered patio, where it can be protected from harsh weather, or even temporarily moved inside, but you will get a better crop if you grow aubergines under glass, in a greenhouse or even a conservatory.

Sow seeds in early spring and put them in a propagator to germinate; if you don't have a propagator, sow in spring and put them on the side of the greenhouse which gets the most sun. When the seedlings are large enough to handle, prick them out into small pots filled with soil-less potting compost. When they are 15cm (6in) high, put them into their permanent site – large pots, growing

You may be surprised how easy it is to grow exotic crops like aubergines in Britain. Take the opportunity to try some unusual varieties.

bags or straight into the border soil, if you have any. Space plants 45cm (18in) apart.

When the plants are 25cm (9in) high, pinch out the growing tips to encourage side growth. As the fruits form, pinch out the tips of the branches so that there are no more than two or three fruits on each branch. Remove any side shoots. As the fruits begin to swell and become heavy, you may need to support the plant with stakes to stop it drooping.

Water the plants well – they dry out easily. The fruits will be better if you feed the plants each week with a liquid fertiliser. Syringe the leaves

with water in warm weather as this discourages red spider mite – the most virulent pest in the greenhouse.

Pick the fruits when they are swollen and a shiny, deep purple colour (some varieties are mottled or have creamy-white stripes, too). Cut them free of the plant with scissors or a sharp knife, handling them carefully to avoid bruising.

CUCUMBERS

Instructions for growing outdoor cucumbers are given with the salad vegetables on pages 82–86, but the fruit of greenhouse plants will be larger and have less tough skins.

If cucumbers develop from male flowers, they will be bitter, so either remove male flowers as they appear or choose self-pollinating varieties which produce only female flowers. Tiny cucumbers form behind the female flowers, while the male flowers just have a simple stem, making them easy to distinguish.

Raise seed in late winter in a propagator and pot on in the same way as for aubergine seedlings. Plant them in their permanent site when the seedlings have begun to develop their rough leaves, spacing them about 60cm (2ft) apart.

Growing bags and rings

Growing bags are very useful in a greenhouse. Raise the plants in the usual way and transplant them into the growing bag, with its rich mixture of compost, fertiliser and water-retaining substances.

Besides growing greenhouse tomatoes in border soil or bags, they can also be grown in a ring culture

system (*see* page 89). You can use rings that fit into a growing bag, or bottomless pots or rings that are filled with compost and placed on a bed of gravel or crushed stones. The roots grow down into the gravel searching for water, while fertiliser is applied to the compost in the ring to be taken up by the 'feeding roots'.

Staking and support

As the plants grow, you will need to support them. This can be done in one of two ways. When the plant is about 25cm (9in) high, tie a string very loosely a round its base and take this up to the top of the wall of the greenhouse, attaching it to another string running up the roof.

As the plant grows, pinch out the side shoots and train the main stem up the string by twisting it gently. To do this, the string should not be too tight, and the plant will need very careful handling to ensure you do not break the stem. When it reaches the top of the wall of the greenhouse, you can continue taking it up the string that runs parallel with the sloping roof.

The other method is to put a stake into the ground alongside the plant and let it grow level with the top of this, tying the main stem loosely to the stake to support it. Fix horizontal wires or strings at intervals up the stakes, then pinch out the growing tip of the cucumber when it reaches the top of the stake. As the laterals grow, train them along the strings, twisting them carefully around them.

Routine care

Keep plants well watered, and spray them if it is very hot. You will get better cucumbers if you feed the plant with liquid fertiliser when the fruits are beginning to swell, but this is only necessary once a fortnight.

Cucumbers will be ready for harvesting from about mid-summer, and it is best to pick them as soon as they are ready. This is when they have nice straight sides, not when they have reached their maximum size. Picking cucumbers at this stage will also encourage the development of more fruits.

Hints on growing greenhouse crops

- Sow the seeds thinly in seed boxes, pricking out later into individual pots.

- Most greenhouse crops will need to be trained up some form of support to prevent the plants getting straggly.

- The growing tips of many greenhouse crops, tomatoes in particular, should be pinched out.

- Continue to spray the plants with water to increase humidity and discourage pests. Give liquid feeds.

- As soon as any of the crops in the greenhouse are ready, harvest them to make room for the remaining crops.

- Do not leave crops until they have reached their maximum size before picking. Always cut them with a knife.

TOMATOES

Many tomatoes can be successfully grown outdoors (*see* pages 87–90), but you will probably get a heavier yield of better-tasting fruit in the greenhouse.

Tomato seedlings are raised from seed in the same way as the other crops so far discussed and the seed should be sown in early spring. They can be set in their permanent site when they are about 10cm (4in) high, with about 45cm (18in) between the plants and 60cm (2ft) between the rows. Stagger the plants in the rows so they are not directly in line with one another.

The easiest and most efficient way of supporting tomatoes growing in a greenhouse is to tie strings loosely round their bases and take these up to a horizontal string hung across the greenhouse, level with

the top of the walls. As the plants grow, gently twist the main stems around the strings, taking great care not to snap the stems. Nip out the side shoots that emerge from the leaf axils (*see* page 90) and pinch out the growing tips when the plants near the top of the horizontal strings.

Feeding and watering

Mulch the tomato plants when you plant them and then water them once a week. Even, regular watering is important with tomato plants; if you allow them to dry out and then give them a healthy drink to compensate, you are likely to get split fruit. Feed with liquid fertiliser every 10 days or so when the tomatoes have begun to develop.

As the plant grows, the leaves at the base will begin to turn yellow and die back. At this point it is best to pick them off. This makes it easier to pick the fruit and water the plants.

Take care not to strip off too much foliage, or you will leave the plant with no means of manufacturing foodstuffs for the growing tomatoes.

Harvesting and ripening

You can pick tomatoes as they ripen, or you can take them green from the plant and ripen them on windowsills or in other warm, sunny places. Tomatoes that are still green at the end of the season can often be ripened successfully in the fruit bowl, with some bananas. Harvest the tomatoes by supporting them in your hand and nipping off the stem just above the calyx.

PEPPERS AND CHILLIES

Hot-house conditions are ideal for these hot-weather crops. Peppers will be sweeter and chillies more fiery when the plants are grown in the heat of a greenhouse.

Round, sweet, capsicum peppers and the thinner, longer and very much hotter chilli peppers can be grown successfully in a greenhouse and are treated in the same way as these other greenhouse crops.

Sowing and care

Sow the seeds in spring and raise the seedlings in a propagator. Thereafter treat the young seedlings exactly the same as those of aubergines and cucumbers, planting them in their permanent site when they are about 10cm (4in) high. If growing in border soil, put them about 45cm (18in) apart and push a heavy stake into the soil alongside each plant. The

Fiery chillies will thrive in a greenhouse; if you don't have one, try growing them on a sunny windowsill or in a conservatory.

fruits can be very heavy and plants will need support to prevent them drooping as the fruits develop.

These plants need very little attention; just water them regularly and feed them with liquid fertiliser every week or so when the fruits begin to appear. Support them by tying them loosely to the cane as this becomes necessary.

You can either pick peppers when they are green (in mid-summer) or you can leave them on the plant to ripen still further. They will either turn red or yellow, depending on the variety. Cut the fruit off the plant using scissors or a sharp knife in the same way as aubergines.

GREENHOUSE MANAGEMENT

The conditions in a greenhouse that are so good for the crops are also ideal breeding grounds for pests and disease. So pay extra attention to the crops you have under glass and nip any problems in the bud before they get beyond your control.

Crops may be grown in the greenhouse in the border soil, in large pots or in fertilised growing bags. Tomatoes may be grown in a special system known as ring culture (*see* page 89), in which the plants are actually grown in bottomless pots filled with compost and set on a bed of gravel or sterile aggregate or bedded into a growing bag.

The easiest method is to grow in the border soil, but if you mainly use the greenhouse for growing tomatoes, you must either change the soil each year or sterilise it before planting again. If you grow tomatoes in the same soil in the greenhouse for two years running, they are very prone to various diseases.

You can follow tomatoes with a different crop, such as peppers or cucumbers, which will not be diseased in the same way, but be prepared for tomato seedlings to sprout alongside. The soil should be changed after these crops have been harvested, and tomatoes can be grown in the site the following year.

Changing the soil

In early summer, dig out and swap the soil in the greenhouse borders for some in the garden. Mix in plenty of well-rotted farmyard manure at the same time, and you should have even better tomatoes the following year. You can put the old soil back into the greenhouse after a year, when it has been thoroughly exposed to the elements and has had a chance to be washed through by the rain. To sterilise soil, sprinkle it with a solution of formalin and cover with sheets of plastic, so the fumes do not escape.

Avoiding pests and disease

Always keep the inside of the greenhouse scrupulously clean and tidy (*see* page 38); if weeds do appear, pull them out straight away and check over all the crops each day. Regular watering will not just prevent plants from drying out, but can also discourage pests, which thrive in hot and dry conditions.

Growing Herbs

Although growing herbs may not always represent the same saving in cost as vegetables, they are so important in adding interest and flavour to your cooking that it is well worth producing a selection of the ones you like to use the most.

Herbs are easy to grow. Although they mostly flourish best in rich, well-drained soils and sunny, sheltered positions, they will generally grow in almost any type of soil or garden site. In addition, of course, individual herbs take up only a small amount of space and they can be grown in any convenient spot, even in pots on a windowsill, step or patio.

Herbs are ideally sited close to the kitchen, so they are quickly to hand when you need them. If this is not possible, they can be grown at one end of the vegetable garden, or scattered individually around the flower beds. Many are decorative enough to grow in a border or bed and, besides adding colour, they will also help pollination among the flowers by attracting bees.

Many herbs can be preserved for out-of-season use, either by drying, making into jellies, freezing or making herb-infused oils and vinegars. See the chapter on Preserving your Produce (pages 204–36) for more advice.

Planning a herb bed

A formally planned and well laid out herb garden was once a common feature of many gardens. Lack of space has made them less common, but if there is room, they can become a charming and productive addition to your vegetable plot or

TAKING HERB CUTTINGS

Many new herb plants can be raised by taking cuttings from existing plants or by digging up part of the plant or bush and dividing the roots.

1 Take heel cuttings by removing side shoots from the main stem.

2 Dip the cut end in hormone rooting powder then push into pots of compost. Cover the pots with miniature cloches or a clear plastic food bag or stand them in a propagator until the cuttings are well established.

3 Dividing the roots gives you more established plants, but fewer new ones. Dig up the existing plant and carefully tease the rootball apart, taking care not to damage the roots. Disentangle the stems and replant the original plant and the new ones immediately.

kitchen garden. Traditionally, herb gardens followed geometric shapes – triangles, circles, squares and so on – in the style of an Elizabethan knot garden. Each small area would be bordered by a neatly clipped edging of box (*Buxus*) or other small-leaved evergreen. Creating an elaborate scheme like this is a long-term plan, waiting for the herbs to establish and the evergreens to grow, but you can use a wooden framework to divide a bed or create a patchwork of different herbs that does not need a formal edging.

If you are planning a herb garden, bear in mind that the taller herbs should be placed at the back so they do not put others in perpetual shade. Some herbs like partial shade and will grow happily when planted close to their tall companions.

Where space is at a premium, herbs can be grown successfully in tubs, pots or other containers, placed anywhere that there is room, from patios and terraces to kitchen windowsills or the side of a flight of outdoor steps. Some herbs will even grow in narrow gaps between paving stones in a path or terrace, but not in heavy traffic areas, where they will be repeatedly trodden on.

Choosing what to grow

The choice of herbs to grow is likely to depend on individual taste, although those most widely used in cooking are probably chives, parsley, thyme, rosemary, marjoram and sage. Try some of the more unusual ones as well though – they are usually no more difficult to grow and can be much more interesting in the kitchen.

Many herbs are perennial, although in some instances it is best to treat them as annuals and start them again each year to ensure that you have a good supply of fresh young leaves and stems, rather than woody growth. Few will withstand very heavy winter picking, so allow any you wish to keep for next year to rest over winter.

CULTIVATION

Growing advice for a variety of common herbs is given on pages 106–7. As most herbs do best in similar soils and situations, they do well planted together in a dedicated herb bed.

The spacings given overleaf refer to space between plants; in most domestic situations, you will not need to plant more than one row of any particular herb; in fact, one plant of each herb will provide sufficient leaves or seeds for most families.

Parsley is the most notable exception to this rule, as it is so widely used in the kitchen and is often used in large quantities when you need it, many households find they need several plants to fulfil their regular needs.

Sow herb seeds very sparingly, and thin the seedlings progressively, discarding the weakest ones until you are left with the number you need. If sowing indoors, sow two or three seeds to a pot, and discard the weaker seedlings as they emerge.

Pests and diseases

As a rule, herbs do not suffer too much from pests and diseases, and these will be kept to a minimum if normal garden hygiene is observed.

When herb plants are affected, it is probably best to dig up the affected plants and burn them, planting fresh seeds or plants to replace the lost ones.

Herb plants are pretty as well as productive – and a useful ally in the fight against pests. Thyme and lavender will give off a delicious scent and attract insects that help to control aphids.

GROWING VEGETABLES · HERBS

CULTIVATION OF HERBS

HERB	SOIL/POSITION	SOWING	SPACING
Balm (evergreen perennial)	**Soil:** Any **Position:** Sunny, but will tolerate some shade	Indoors in pots or direct into cropping site April/May, in 1cm (½in) drills	45cm (1ft 6in)
Basil (annual)	**Soil:** Any that is well-drained **Position:** Sunny and sheltered. Bush basil may be grown in pots indoors for winter	Indoors in pots or direct into the cropping site in May, in 0.5 cm (¼in) drills	30cm (1ft)
Bay (evergreen perennial)	**Soil:** Any **Position:** Sunny and sheltered. Grows very successfully in a large tub or pot	Buy a young plant or take 15cm (6in) cuttings in spring and grow in potting compost until established	One tree is sufficient
Borage (annual)	**Soil:** Any that is well-drained **Position:** Sunny	Directly into cropping site in April and again in August. Sow in 1cm (½in) drills	30cm (1ft)
Chervil (biennial)	**Soil:** Any that is moist and water-retentive **Position:** Sheltered, in partial sun	Directly into growing site at regular intervals from March to August in 0.5cm (¼in) drills	30cm (1ft)
Chives (perennial)	**Soil:** Any that is moist **Position:** Sunny or partial shade	If raising from seed sow directly into cropping site in 0.5cm (¼in) drills in March	30cm (1ft)
Coriander (annual)	**Soil:** Rich and well-drained **Position:** Sunny; near dill and chervil	Directly into cropping site in April and August, in 0.5cm (¼in) drills	30cm (1ft)
Dill (annual)	**Soil:** Well-drained **Position:** Open and sunny	Directly into growing site in March and April in 0.5cm (¼in) drills	25cm (10in)
Fennel (perennial)	**Soil:** Rich and well-drained. Will grow on well-cultivated chalky soils **Position:** Warm and sunny. Does not flourish well if grown near coriander	If raising from seed, sow at regular intervals from March to May in 1cm (½in) drills. New plants may also be obtained by division	30cm (1ft)
Horseradish (treat as an annual)	**Soil:** Deeply dug light loam which is well-drained **Position:** Sunny or partial shade	Plant roots or root cuttings 12.5cm (5in) long in March so they are 5cm (2in) below the ground	45cm (1ft 6in)
Marjoram or Oregano (treat as an annual)	**Soil:** Light and well-drained **Position:** Sunny but sheltered	Directly into cropping site in April and/or early September or raise from cuttings	25cm (10in)
Mint (perennial)	**Soil:** Most, but likes rich, moist soil best **Position:** Full sun gives best flavour	Plant young plants in March in a bucket or similar container to contain the pervasive roots. Mint is very hard to grow from seed	15cm (6in)
Parsley (treat as an annual)	**Soil:** Rich and well-drained, but moist **Position:** Sunny	Sow into growing site at intervals through spring and early summer, in 0.5cm (¼in) drills. Pour boiling water along the drills to aid germination. Raise indoors in pots	20cm (8in)
Rosemary (evergreen perennial)	**Soil:** Light, sandy or chalky. Well drained **Position:** Sunny but sheltered. Near sage	Sow into growing site or seed bed in April, or raise from heel cuttings taken early summer	
Sage (biennial)	**Soil:** Well-drained **Position:** Sunny, but sheltered	Sow in seed bed April–June in 0.5cm (¼in) drills. Raise from heel cuttings in summer	Two plants 30cm (1ft) apart
Tarragon (perennial)	**Soil:** Well-drained **Position:** Sunny and warm	Buy a young plant and plant in March or October, or raise from cuttings taken in spring or autumn or from root division	Only one plant is needed
Thyme (perennial) The different types are all cultivated in the same way	**Soil:** Light, sandy, but well-drained **Position:** Sunny	Sow in growing site from April to July in 0.5cm (¼in) drills or indoors in trays. Raise new plants from heel cuttings taken in May/June or by root division	25–30cm (9–12in)

THINNING/TRANSPLANTING	CULTIVATION	HARVESTING
Plant out pot-grown plants in early autumn. Thin sowings in cropping site when large enough to handle	Water well in dry spells. The year after planting, cut back plants in early summer. In autumn, cut to just above ground level	Pick very sparingly the first summer. Thereafter, pick as required throughout late spring and summer. Pick leaves for drying in early summer
Harden off plants for outdoors in May and plant out in early June.	Water well in dry spells. Pinch out growing centres to encourage bushy, leafy growth and pinch out flowers as they form	Pick leaves as required through the summer. The first frost will kill outdoor plants
Thin sowings in cropping site when large enough to handle	Bay can be trimmed into a variety of shapes in summer. Trees grown in containers are best put in a light, airy shed in the winter	Pick leaves as required. For drying, cut branches on summer mornings
Thin when seedlings are large enough to handle	Keep weed growth in check. Borage grows very quickly and reseeds itself readily	Pick as required. For drying, pick undamaged leaves in the morning after the dew has evaporated
Thin to recommended spacing as seedlings emerge	Water well in dry spells and pick off flowering stems as they appear	Pick as required. For drying, pick sprays from mature plants on a sunny morning
Thin to recommended spacing as seedlings emerge	Water well in dry spells and pick off flower heads to help prevent early dying back. Dig up and divide in spring or autumn	Pick as required, cutting leaves at the base. Picking encourages heavier growth
Thin when seedlings are large enough to handle	Hoe to control weeds and water in dry spells	Gather seeds by picking flower heads when they smell spicy and seeds have turned from green to beige. Dry heads in boxes, trays or racks, then shake out seeds
Thin seedlings when large enough to handle. Leaves from thinnings may be used	Hoe to control weeds and water in dry spells. Stake plants as they grow.	Pick leaves as required before flowers appear, cutting to the base to encourage growth. Leave some plants to flower and produce seeds
Thin to recommended spacing when large enough to handle	Needs no special attention	*See* Dill
Plant no more than three or four, because they spread	They need no special attention except for watering in dry spells. Dig up all plants each year and replant new ones	Dig up roots from August to November. Lift all plants and store roots as described on page 207
Thin to recommended spacing when large enough to handle	Need no special attention	Pick leaves as required before flowers form through summer and autumn. Leave the young central leaves
	Water well after planting. Dig up some roots in autumn and grow in pots over winter. Cut plants to ground in October	Pick as required through spring and summer. Young leaves have the most flavour. For drying, cut stalks as the first flower heads appear
Thin seedlings twice to achieve recommended spacings	Water well in dry spells and protect plants with cloches in winter if trying to keep them until following spring	Cut out flowering stems to encourage leaf growth. Pick leaves sparingly until plants are established, then pick them hard, leaving only the green centre. For drying, cut from mid-summer onwards
Gradually discard seedlings until one healthy plant is left	No special attention	Pick fresh as required (do not pick too heavily during winter). For drying, pick as plants come into flower
Thin seedlings as they emerge and transplant in autumn	Pinch out flower heads and growing tips to encourage bushy growth. Cut back hard after flowering	*See* Rosemary. The flavour is at its best in mid-summer
	Water well in dry weather. Plant dies down in winter: protect in cold areas with straw	Pick fresh leaves as required through summer and autumn. For drying, pick leafy sprays from fully grown plants in the morning
Thin to recommended spacing. Prick out indoor sowings to individual pots an plant out in autumn when well-established	Water growing plants well and cut back after flowering. Pinch out growing shoots to encourage more leaf production and bushy growth	As for Rosemary. Do not cut too heavily in the autumn or the plant may not survive the winter

GROWING FRUIT

Growing fruit

By and large, fruit falls into two categories – tree (or top) fruit, and soft fruit. You don't need to plant an orchard: almost all gardens will have room to grow some fruit and with more than a couple of trees you can easily find yourself with more fruit than you can possibly eat. Plant breeders have developed a wide range of varieties that have made it possible to grow even top fruit in very small spaces.

Fruit is generally seen as less of an essential than vegetables in a self-sufficient gardening scheme, but a couple of fruit trees and a handful of bushes will produce a surprisingly large quantity of fruit that will make a significant contribution to your family's table. Most are easy to freeze and to preserve in other ways that will see you through the winter.

A row of raspberry canes can be used as a productive windbreak to shelter more tender plants behind, an apple tree makes a charming addition to the ornamental garden rather than just the cultivation plot, and many tree fruits or vines can be trained against a wall as espaliers or in a fan shape. They are not hard to incorporate into an established vegetable plot or to fit into a new garden plan.

Fruits in two main groups

The tree fruits covered in this book include apples, pears, peaches, nectarines, plums, damsons, gages, apricots, cherries, figs and citrus fruits. The soft fruits include raspberries, loganberries, blackberries, blueberries, red, white

and blackcurrants, gooseberries and strawberries.

Grapes, melons and rhubarb do not fit into either category – grapes grow on perennial vines, melons are annual plants and rhubarb grows from tubers, but they are all popular fruits and you will find all the growing advice you need in these pages.

You will need a greenhouse or orangery to grow melons successfully in the UK. Grapevines will also produce a sweeter and better crop under glass, but a south-facing wall will also do, particularly in the warmer, southern regions. There are some successful commercial vineyards in southen Britain, where, of course, the grapes are grown outdoors.

Modern and compact top fruit

Top fruit grown on traditional standard or half-standard trees can reach heights and spreads of six metres (20ft) and more which, apart from anything else, makes picking difficult and possibly dangerous. Even if a garden is big enough to take a couple of these trees, it is rarely an efficient allocation of

Soft fruits are the taste of summer. Most plots have room for a wide variety, including blackcurrants, strawberries, gooseberries, raspberries, blackberries and red currants.

space which would be far more productively used growing other fruit and vegetables or supporting livestock.

Most top fruit bred for planting in domestic gardens now is produced by grafting the different varieties onto special 'dwarfing' roots. This restricts the tree's growth in order to keep it manageable, but also gives quicker fruit production. Where once it took 10 years or so for trees to start to bear fruit, most modern trees will now do so in their third year.

Make sure when purchasing top fruit, that the trees you buy are growing on dwarfing rootstocks, which are numbered according to their size. Check the plant label for a guide to the ultimate size of the tree in maturity.

Keeping trees healthy

To make sure that your fruit trees remain healthy and productive, they must be pruned regularly. This will help to minimise the risk of disease, which is greater when branches are crowded or crossing within the tree, but will also concentrate the tree's energy into producing fruit, rather than unnecessary branches and leaves. Left to their own devices, trees will continue to produce an abundance of fruit, but the quality and taste will almost certainly deteriorate with each year.

Sweet and simple soft fruit

Soft fruit has no such size problems. The different types grow either on bushes (blueberries, red, white and blackcurrants and gooseberries), or canes (raspberries, loganberries and blackberries). Although these also need regular pruning and training if they are to be fully productive, this is a far less complicated procedure than for tree fruit.

Strawberries grow on neither bushes nor canes, but on low, spreading plants, which put out runners that produce new plants as they grow. These new plants can be separated from the parent plant and transplanted elsewhere or passed on to friends. Save some to renew your plants every couple of years.

Choosing what to grow

There are endless varieties of all types of tree and soft fruit. The best way to make a choice of what to grow in your particular plot is to consult a local nursery to see what grows best in your locality. You will find most nurseries stock a limited number of varieties, because over the years they have established which types are the most successful for them and for their customers. Unless you have a real preference for some other specific variety, it is wisest to restrict your choice to the ones already stocked.

Planting Out

Most fruit are bought as trees, bushes or canes, rather than being grown from seed. They should be planted during winter, when they are dormant, but not when the ground is frozen or waterlogged. The ideal time is in early and mid-winter, but planting can be done any time through to the following spring. It is best to buy two- or three-year old top fruit trees and soft fruit bushes, and one-year-old fruit canes.

If you will not be able to plant the fruit for a few days after buying it, leave the roots encased in their protective wrapping and keep the plant in a cool shed. The day before planting, inspect the roots and if they are dry, soak them in a bucket of water for a few hours.

Planting a bush

Dig a hole wide enough to take the roots of the bush and fork well-rotted organic matter into the bottom. Place the bush in the hole, spread out the roots and cut off any that are growing upwards.

Fill in around the roots with soil and firm it down. When planted, the base of the bush should be just covered with soil. Apply a mulch of compost, straw or leafmould all around the base.

PLANTING A FRUIT TREE

1 If the roots of the tree are dry, soak them in water before planting. Place a layer of compost in a wide hole, position the tree and spread out the roots.

2 Mix soil with compost and fill in around the roots. Shake the tree to settle the soil. Firm gently with your feet, top up if necessary; firm again.

3 Water around the roots well and give the soil a mulch of garden compost, straw or leafmould. Secure the top of the stem to a supporting stake with a tree tie or adjustable strap.

Planting canes

Raspberry and other fruit canes look like unpromising sticks when you buy them, but they will bush out.

Fork well-rotted organic matter into the bottom of a trench. Position the canes, spreading out the roots and keeping the canes upright. Pack around the roots with soil to firm the cane into the ground, then finish replacing the remaining soil dug out of the trench and firm it down again. Cut back the canes to around 25cm (9in) high.

Apply a mulch of compost, straw or leafmould along the row.

Cut back canes to just 25cm (9in) after planting to encourage vigorous new growth.

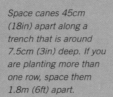

Space canes 45cm (18in) apart along a trench that is around 7.5cm (3in) deep. If you are planting more than one row, space them 1.8m (6ft) apart.

Protecting plants

Since the best time for planting trees, bushes and canes is in the winter, the plants may need to be protected against the harsh weather or birds in search of food while it is scarce elsewhere. Windbreaks may help or the plant may need to be isolated in a polythene cage against frost or wind. Soft fruit, in particular, will need to be protected from birds by being grown in cages of mesh or wire (below).

Supporting canes

Drive stakes into both ends of the trench where you have planted raspberry or other soft fruit canes. Stretch three evenly spaced strands of wire between them and train shoots to these wires as they grow.

Heeling in

Do not plant a tree until the weather conditions are right. If they are not, keep it temporarily in the shed; if it is a bare root tree, keep the roots in damp straw until you are ready to plant it. A better option for a bare-root tree is to heel it into the soil in a sheltered part of the garden. Do this by planting it in the soil at an angle (left), covering the rootball with soil to help it to retain moisture.

Growing Apples

Just about every garden will have room for an apple tree or two. Early-maturing varieties will be ready for picking in late summer and the late varieties in mid-autumn, but they will keep well for eating through the winter until mid-spring if you are careful as you pick, wrap and store them.

Apples are not self-pollinating, so it is essential to grow at least two trees (that blossom at the same time) unless you have a near neighbour who has a number of apple trees. An alternative, if you really feel you only have room for one tree, is to grow a family tree, which has two or more cross-pollinating varieties grafted onto a single rootstock.

There are myriad varieties of apple, divided into two basic types:

How many trees do you need

The four different forms of apple tree (see pages 116–17) give the following approximate yields when they are at full capacity.

• **Cordon** Up to 4.5kg (10lb), but with an average of 1.8kg (4lb)

• **Open centre bush tree with four main branches** Up to 27kg (60lb), with an average yield of 13.5kg (30lb)

• **Espalier** The yield depends on the size of the tree. Expect about half the amount of a bush tree grown on the same rootstock.

• **Spindlebush** 13.5kg (30lb)

cookers and dessert apples. Before buying trees, decide which type you want to grow. Choose varieties according to your taste, their cross-pollination compatibility and what is known to grow well in your area. Avoid Cox's Orange Pippins where the soil is poor or if you live in a cold area, for example. This variety was developed in the South of England and will not withstand harsh, northern weather. Late-flowering varieties are best for cold gardens.

Soil and position
Apples like deep, fertile loam, but will grow in most well-cultivated soils providing they are not waterlogged or too acid. Choose an open sunny position that is well-sheltered from prevailing cold winds and avoid planting in pockets or hollows where frost collects and lingers.

Planting and routine cultivation
Make sure the ground is completely free of weeds (particularly perennial ones) before planting and keep the area round a newly-planted tree weed-free, particularly through the first year. Remove weeds with gentle hoeing or by hand, taking care not to damage the young roots.

Water new trees very heavily in the first growing season, and thereafter water all trees in dry spells – trees are good at finding and taking up water, but will still be weakened in periods of drought and this can affect the blossom and, later, the quality and quantity of the fruit. Mulch the ground around the tree in spring until it is well established.

When you buy apple trees, ask the nursery for advice about how far apart to plant them. This differs so much with the variety, the form in which the tree is to be grown, the type of soil and the

For the best and sweetest fruit, thin out clusters of apples in the early stages of their growth to just one or two fruits.

SEASONAL GROWING GUIDE

Late autumn to early spring	Winter pruning Cut back hard to invigorate new growth
Early summer	Thin out fruit Pick off developing fruits to leave no more than two apples in each cluster
Midsummer	Summer pruning Cut out new growth to improve shape and avoid overcrowding
Late summer to late autumn	Harvest fruit Pick fruits as they ripen. To store for later use, individually wrap perfect fruits only in paper

rootstock on which it is grafted, that it is not practical to give specific measurements here.

TRAINING AND PRUNING

The eventual shape of any top fruit tree is established by the pruning and training done in the first four years of its life. If you buy two- or three-year-old trees, the training will have already begun at the nursery.

The aim in pruning is to maintain the shape you have established, to allow a good penetration of light to reach all parts of the tree and to maintain a constant good balance between growth and fruit. Enough new wood must be allowed to develop to turn into next year's fruiting growth and old wood should be cut out after its second or third season.

Be bold, and prune hard

Most people do not prune established trees hard enough – open centre bush trees and spindlebush trees in particular should be reduced by a third each winter. Winter pruning is invigorating – the harder you prune, the harder the tree will grow. Summer pruning is restricting as you are cutting out new growth as it forms.

SPUR- OR TIP-BEARING

Apple trees are either spur- or tip-bearing – depending on the variety, the apples are either borne on the spur wood that grows from the leaders and laterals, or on the end of the previous season's shoots.

When pruning spur-bearing varieties, the leaders should be cut back by

half each year and all the laterals cut back to three or four growth buds to induce the spurs to grow.

An alternative method to this is to operate a three-year cycle, which works on the principle that the second and third year wood produces the best fruit. For this you need a framework of up to six strong branches growing off a central trunk. The laterals, which will bear fruit in their second and third years, grow from these permanent branches. After their third year, cut out the entire lateral, so that a new one will grow in its place.

Tip-bearing tips

In tip-bearing varieties, it is obviously important not to cut off the shoots bearing the terminal buds, as it is these that will form the following year's fruit. The difficulty, is how to keep the tree bushy and compact without cutting out the fruiting wood.

This is best done by sawing out entire big, old branches when they have ceased to be productive. This will shape up the tree and allow new branches to grow in their place. Do not just snip at the tree, as a light trim will have little effect – make big cuts which will count.

CULTIVATION TIPS

Apples, like other fruit trees, will produce fruit year after year without your help, but with some care and attention you can increase the quality and quantity of your crop.

If large clusters of apples are produced after a bumper blossom season, these should be thinned. It may seem contrary to remove fruit from the tree, but if you leave it all to mature, the results will probably be small and sour and prone to

---

GOLDEN RULES FOR PRUNING

A few simple rules will help to ensure that your pruning improves the health and vigour of your trees, rather than introducing disease or damaging the plant.

• Always make a positive cut with sharp, clean secateurs or loppers. Do not tear the wood.

• Seal any cuts you make with wound-protecting paint to prevent disease entering.

• Always cut back to either a new growth bud or flush with the branch.

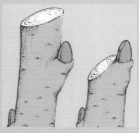

• Never cut between buds or cut so close that they might be damaged.

TERMS USED IN PRUNING

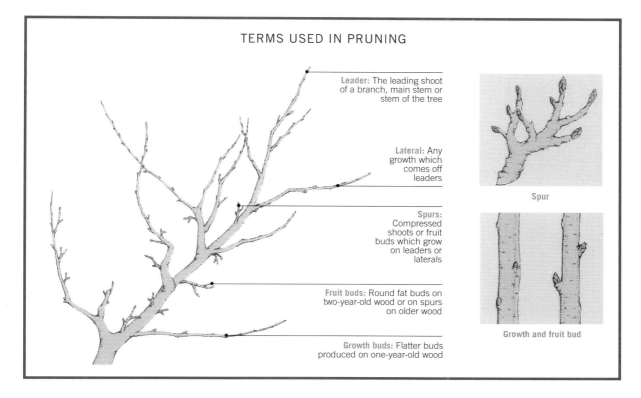

Leader: The leading shoot of a branch, main stem or stem of the tree

Lateral: Any growth which comes off leaders

Spurs: Compressed shoots or fruit buds which grow on leaders or laterals

Fruit buds: Round fat buds on two-year-old wood or on spurs on older wood

Growth buds: Flatter buds produced on one-year-old wood

Spur

Growth and fruit bud

disease due to overcrowding on the tree. Thinned out, you will get fewer apples in all, but they will be far better tasting.

Trees will naturally thin their own crop in early summer – a process known as the June drop – but check the tree after this and cut out (with scissors) any damaged or misshapen apples that remain to leave one, or at the most two, to each cluster. Ideally, you should aim to keep the apples about 15cm (6in) apart.

Harvesting and storing

Test fruit for ripeness by supporting the apple in your hand and gently lifting it. If it is ripe it will come away easily from the tree.

Always handle apples very gently, particularly if you want to store them for eating later in the year, as any blemishes will spoil the fruit and this can spread to the whole box in

storage. Pick apples with the palm of your hand, not your fingertips, which can bruise the fruit.

Some varieties of apple can be kept for many months, provided they are stored correctly. The most important rule is to only use perfect fruit and to store it in such a way that no apple touches another, by wrapping them individually in tissue or newspaper, for example. For preserving apples, see page 222.

PESTS AND DISEASES

There is a frighteningly long list of pests and diseases that can affect apple trees, but the main ones to fear are apple mildew (page 149), apple scab (page 149) and canker (page 148).

Old-fashioned protection practices, such as tying grease bands round

the trunk of the tree in summer and early autumn, can help trap and therefore deter pests such as the codling moth, which climbs up the trunk of the tree to lay its eggs.

Some gardeners still recommend regular spraying with various chemical preparations through the spring and summer, but in most domestic situations (particularly if strict garden hygiene is observed) this should not really be necessary.

If your trees are showing signs of disease, consult a local commercial grower, if you can, on what action to take. Otherwise, ask advice from within your local gardening club or from neighbours with trees. Remember that over-spraying can do the tree as much harm as good.

If birds attack your crop the only remedy is to cover the tree with netting. You could leave windfalls for the birds to eat instead.

TRAINING AND PRUNING APPLES AND PEARS

There are four common tree shapes: cordon, espalier, open-centre bush and spindlebush.

Training a Cordon

This allows trees to be planted close together, making them easy to manage.

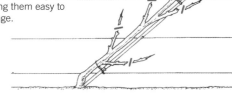

1 In winter, erect posts and wire system. Plant maiden tree at an angle of 45°, the union uppermost. Tie trunk of tree to a bamboo stake, and tie that to the wires. Cut any side shoots (feathers) back to three buds. Do not prune the leader unless it is a tip-bearing cultivar, which should be pruned back by half. It is best to buy a feathered maiden.

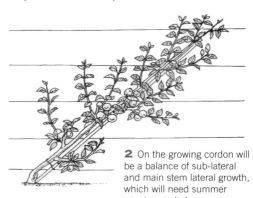

2 On the growing cordon will be a balance of sub-lateral and main stem lateral growth, which will need summer pruning, as below.

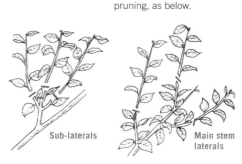

Sub-laterals   Main stem laterals

3 Start the summer pruning; cut back sub-laterals to 2.5cm (1in) or one leaf, to encourage the formation of fruiting spurs. Prune laterals growing from main stem back to three leaves beyond the basal cluster. If the spur system becomes too crowded the spurs should be thinned in the winter, by removing some and cutting back others.

Training an Espalier

An espalier is a decorative feature and is often planted to mark boundaries between different parts of the land, such as the fruit and vegetable gardens.

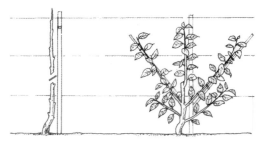

1 Erect stakes and wire. Plant maiden (unfeathered) in early winter, and cut back to a good bud with two buds facing outward beneath it, 30cm (12in) from the ground.

2 During summer, train the centre shoot up the stake and tie side shoots to canes set at 45° to the main stem. Secure the bamboo canes to the horizontal wires.

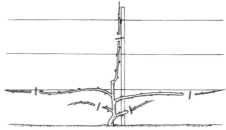

3 In winter, bend down side growths and tie to the horizontal wires. Prune them back to one third and the main stem to three good buds, two of which should face in opposite outward directions. These will form the next tier, 30cm (12in) from the lower one. Cut side shoots down to three buds.

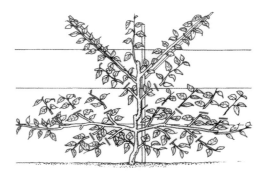

4 In summer, tie new tier to 45° canes. Start summer pruning on lower tiers by cutting back laterals on horizontals to three leaves to encourage fruiting spurs and cut sub-laterals to 2.5cm (1in) or one leaf, like cordons. Cut growths from the main stem to three leaves. On established espaliers cut back main stem and horizontals to ripe wood.

Training an Open-centre bush

This shape is used for growing apples, pears, peaches, plums and sour cherries. However, it may take up to five years to train the tree into its required shape.

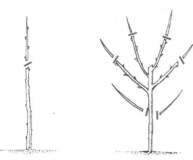

1 In winter, plant maiden tree; and cut it back to 60cm (2ft) at a point where there are four buds well positioned around it.

2 Next winter, cut back the four primary leaders by a third, to an outward-facing bud. Remove any other growths.

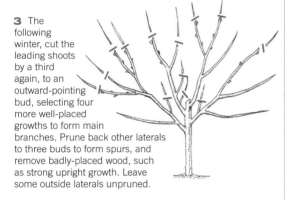

3 The following winter, cut the leading shoots by a third again, to an outward-pointing bud, selecting four more well-placed growths to form main branches. Prune back other laterals to three buds to form spurs, and remove badly-placed wood, such as strong upright growth. Leave some outside laterals unpruned.

4 Cut back the leader and laterals to give a strong framework to support the fruiting growth and strengthen it. Cut back the laterals to good flower buds. Once the tree is established, aim to keep the centre of the tree open. Replace the leading shoots by cutting them back to new laterals when they are about three years old.

Training a Spindlebush

If planning to train the tree in this way buy a feathered maiden. The growth comes easily from the central leader, and forms a flat A-shape.

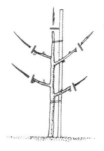

1 In winter, plant a feathered maiden. Prune back three or four laterals by one third to outward-facing buds. Laterals should be about 60cm (2ft) from the ground. Cut out other laterals, and cut back leader to two buds above the top lateral.

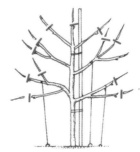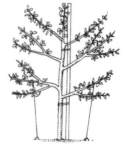

2 In summer, if growth of laterals has been good, tie them with soft string to 30° above the horizontal.

3 In winter, cut back main leader to an opposite growing bud. Remove any unright growth. Tip remaining laterals to a downward bud.

4 Remove ties when branch angle is set. Keep tying in new laterals, check that string is not too tight and restricting. Incorporate new horizontal laterals but keep those at the top of the tree short to allow the sun to reach lower branches. When tree is 2m (7–8ft) high, cut back main leader to a weaker lateral, and tie it to the stake. To maintain A-shape remove vigorous upright growth.

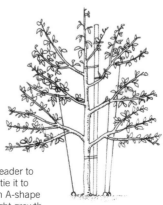

Growing Pears

The cultivation of pears is very similar to apples. Garden varieties are grafted onto dwarfing rootstocks of quinces, which produce larger trees than the smaller rootstocks of apples.

Pears are not generally self-pollinating, although family trees of two or more varieties are available. You are likely to get better results, however, by growing two or more trees of different varieties. Varieties can be divided into those that mature early, mid-season or late.

Pears grow best in a sunny, warm and sheltered site. A south-facing wall is an ideal place for training a pear as an espalier.

Soil, position and cultivation

Pears like a deeply cultivated loam which is moisture-retentive, particularly in the summer. They need a more sheltered spot than apples, and it should be warm and sunny. As they come into blossom early, do not plant them in a hollow or pocket where frost collects. Pear trees do not grow well with grass round their roots, and the soil around them should be kept well-cultivated and perpetually free of weeds.

Early winter is the ideal time to plant. If you are planting more than one tree, leave approximately 4m (13ft) between them. Mulch the area round the roots in spring and make sure the trees are kept well watered in dry weather. They like more nitrogen than apples, and this should be supplied in a spring feed.

Thinning out

Like apples, pears need some thinning; clusters should generally be reduced to one or two fruits as the fruitlets begin to turn downwards. Remove smaller fruits but don't leave any infested by the pear midge.

Training and pruning

Pears are trained and pruned in the same way as apples (*see* pages 117–18), but, once established, can take harder pruning.

Harvesting

Early maturing varieties should be harvested while the pears are still hard (in late summer). They will not part easily from the tree, so cut stalks with secateurs. If left on the tree, the pears will ripen unevenly. Lay them in trays and boxes and keep in a cool place until ripe.

Later varieties should be picked when they part easily from the tree and then ripened as above.

PESTS AND DISEASES

Pears are not vulnerable to many pests and diseases. Maintain good hygiene in your garden and prune the trees appropriately and you will avoid inviting problems.

The main pest is pear midge (page 149), although this is only a threat in certain areas. Pear leaf blister mites (page 145) can also be a problem. Look for shrivelled leaves or flowers that could indicate fire blight (page 146), a serious disease that must be notified to Defra.

SEASONAL GROWING GUIDE

Early to late winter	Winter pruning Cut back hard to invigorate new growth
Early summer	Thinning Pick off developing fruits to leave no more than two in each cluster
Midsummer	Summer pruning Cut out new growth to improve shape and avoid overcrowding
Late summer to late autumn	Harvesting Pick when the fruit is still hard and ripen off the tree

Other Tree Fruit

Tree fruit takes a longer time to become established than soft fruit and needs more room to grow. However, it has a longer fruiting season and can also become a decorative feature of the garden.

Damsons, gages, plums and cherries are hardy choices that will thrive in most areas and conditions, whereas peaches, nectarines and apricots need a warm and sheltered spot to produce their best fruit.

DAMSONS, GAGES AND PLUMS

These all belong to the same family, but vary in size and colour, from small, deep-purple damsons to juicy plums that can be pinkish yellow as well as purple.

Damsons are the smallest of the fruits in this group and taste sour, so they are generally cooked before eating. They make excellent jams and are delicious stewed or in pies. Gages may be eaten fresh, but are very often cooked; although they are usually known as greengages, you can also grow yellow varieties.

Plums offer the greatest variety, with both dessert and cooking types. Only a few are self-pollinating, so if you want to have only one tree, make sure you choose one of these.

Soil, position and cultivation
All these trees will grow on most soils, but they like it to be well-drained. If it is wet and heavy, add lots of well-rotted organic material when preparing the ground for planting. Avoid planting in a spot where frost collects – particularly

for plums and gages, which flower early. These trees will give their best crops if grown against a south-facing wall. Damsons can withstand more inclement weather conditions.

Planting essentials
Plant all three fruits as early as possible in the planting period and if the soil is dry, soak it well the day before planting.

Keep the surrounding area free of weeds by hoeing, but try not to disturb the roots of the trees, as this will encourage the tree to put out suckers, diverting water and nutrients from the fruiting branches. If suckers do form, tear them off: cutting will only encourage further growth. Regular autumn mulches of well-rotted organic matter should give improved yields.

You don't need a lot of trees and certainly not a whole orchard to produce a wide variety of delicious tree fruit.

Growing a fan-shaped tree

For many tree fruits that originated in hotter climates, a brick wall can provide the warmth and shelter they need to fruit reliably and well. Most fruit trees can be trained to grow against a wall, where they will benefit from heat that radiates from the wall on cold nights following long and sunny days. Apricots, peaches and nectarines are particularly well-suited to this style of training. Growing fruit trees in this way is also a very economical use of space if you have a suitable area of wall. Many other fruit and vegetables will not grow so well close to a high wall, so it is soil that would otherwise be left bare, and the trees themselves take up far less room like this than as trees grown in the open.

Training a fan In winter, erect a wire support system. Plant maiden tree and prune to three buds 30–45cm (12–18in) above ground.

In summer Tie laterals to poles at 45° angles, which are attached to wires. Remove other side shoots and cut and seal main stem.

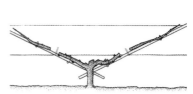

In winter Cut back the two laterals to give two good buds on the top, one at the end, and one underneath at the end.

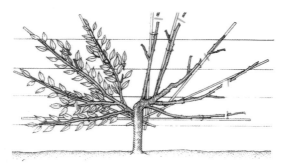

Next summer Train laterals to grow evenly-spaced. Tie each shoot to an angled cane. Prune back sub-laterals to 7.5–10cm (3–4in).
In winter Cut back all leaders by one third to suitable buds.

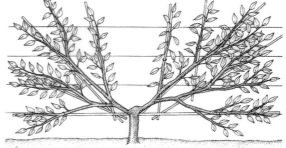

Established tree The tree is considered to have covered the wall space when it has a good framework of branches, each rib having a fruit-bearing lateral at 10cm (4in) intervals, every fourth one being a fruit-bearing lateral.

Pruning the fruiting fan Pinch back growth buds on fruiting laterals to two leaves, leaving a replacement and, if wanted, a reserve lateral.

Next summer Pinch back replacement laterals to 10 leaves, and pinch back fruiting ones to five, unless required for framework.

After harvesting Cut back fruited lateral to the best replacement lateral unless required in framework. Cut out old or unwanted shoots, always maintaining a balance of young and fruiting wood.

Unless you want a real glut of these fruits for jam-making, bottling or freezing, one tree of each type should be ample.

Training and pruning
Damsons, gages and plums may be grown as open-centre bush trees, spindlebush trees, or as fans against a wall. As with other fruit trees, it is best to buy two- or three-year-old trees, in which the initial training has been done. The training for open-centre bush and spindlebush trees is the same as for apples (*see* page 117); train fan-shaped trees as described for apricots, opposite.

Once established, these fruits need very little pruning except to ensure that they do not become overcrowded. Also, remove very old, dead or badly placed wood.

Do all pruning in spring or summer to lessen the likelihood of attack by silver leaf (*see* page 149),

which enters the tree through open cuts and wounds and which is at its least active at this time of year.

Thinning and harvesting
Plums, in particular, should be thinned, as too heavy a crop could cause the branches to snap, leaving open wounds which provide entry points for disease. Thin in two stages – first in late spring and again within the month. At this point, the fruits should be about 5cm (2in) apart.

Pick plums, damsons and gages by the stalk to avoid bruising the fruit (the stalk should come away with the fruit as you pick). If you want plums for eating, leave them to ripen fully before picking. For cooking, plums, gages and damsons can all be picked before they are fully ripe. If there is a lot of rain at harvesting time, the skins of gages are liable to split before they are fully ripe.

Pests and diseases
Damsons, gages and plums are very attractive to hungry birds and the best protection against losing a lot of your crop is to cover the entire tree with close-mesh netting – this will also keep wasps away from the fruit.

Netting may not be pretty, but it is effective. The best way to fix and support the netting is to drive tall stakes into the ground around the tree – they must be a little taller than the tree itself – and drape the netting over and around them. Fix the netting to the stakes. Use a close mesh, as birds may get entangled in a wider mesh net.

Other commom problems to watch out for are aphids (*see* page 144) and silver leaf (page 149), which is common on plums.

Most fruit trees produce a wonderful display of blossom in summer, at a time when the vegetable garden can look a little bleak.

GROWING FRUIT · OTHER TREE FRUIT

PEACHES AND NECTARINES

These fruits originated around the Mediterranean, but may be grown successfully in cooler climates.

The nectarine is a type of peach, with smooth, rather than velvety, skin. It is also less hardy. Both are self-pollinating, although it will help if you brush over the flowers with a soft paint-brush around noon on sunny days.

Soil, position and cultivation

Both trees like well-cultivated, well-drained soil, which will retain moisture in summer. Growing fan-trained trees against a south-facing wall is the best way to success and it is the only place to grow nectarines. Peaches can also be grown as bush trees in sheltered, sunny gardens.

Plant as early as possible in the recommended planting period. Keep the ground around the roots free of weeds, but do not hoe too deeply in case you accidentally damage the roots. Water well in dry weather and apply a mulch of well-rotted farmyard manure in spring to help the moisture retention of the soil.

Pruning and training

Train as fans against a wall (*see* page 120). Once established, prune to get a constant, supply of one-year-old wood, as peaches and nectarines only produce fruit on the previous year's wood.

Thinning and harvesting

The crops of both fruits must be thinned to produce decent-sized fruits. Do this in two stages – when the fruits are marble-sized, reducing clusters to single fruits 10cm (4in) apart, and again when they are a little over walnut-sized. At this stage, reduce the crop by half so that they are about 25cm (9in) apart. Nectarines should be thinned to 15cm (6in). In both cases, at the first thinning remove all fruits that are growing towards the wall and will not have room to develop properly.

Test for ripeness by supporting the fruit in your hand and very gently pressing the flesh by the stalk. It should give and the fruit will come away easily from the tree as you lift it.

Nectarines (above) and peaches are grown in the same way; they are self-pollinating, so you will only need one tree.

Handle peaches and nectarines very carefully; they bruise easily.

SEASONAL GROWING GUIDE

FRUIT	SOIL AND POSITION	PRUNING	THINNING FRUIT
Damsons, gages and plums	Most well-drained soils. Avoid frost pockets	Very little required. Remove old, dead or badly-placed wood in spring or summer	Late spring and early summer to 5cm (2in) apart
Peaches and nectarines	Well-cultivated, well-drained soil. Best against a south-facing wall	Prune to maintain a fan shape and a good supply of one-year-old wood	Thin in two stages to 25cm (9in) apart
Cherries	Deeply-dug and well-drained. Any position	Prune to maintain shape and encourage a constant supply of new growth. Cut out old wood	No thinning required
Apricots	Well-drained, fertile loam in a warm and sheltered position	Prune into a fan shape, trained against a wall	Thin to 10–12.5cm (4–5in) apart

CHERRIES

There are two types of cherry: sweet and sour. Sweet cherries are rarely suitable for garden cultivation as they are not normally grown on dwarfing rootstocks and the full-sized trees are too large.

It is possible to fan-train sweet cherries against a south- or west-facing wall, but they will grow up to 6m (20ft) or more in all directions and, as very few varieties are self-pollinating, you will need more than one tree. Also, unless they are very closely netted, the birds will take the entire crop before you get a chance.

Sour cherries, of which 'Morello' is the most popular, are a better choice and may be grown as bushes, trees or against a wall. They are self-pollinating and are not subject to the same dedicated attack from hungry birds as sweet cherries are.

Soil, position and cultivation

As cherries send their roots way down into the soil, they like ground that has been deeply dug and is well-drained. Add lots of well-rotted organic matter when preparing the ground. If there is any danger of drying out, mulch round the roots well in early spring.

Pruning and training

Sour cherries can be grown as bush or fan-shaped trees, and trained as described on pages 117 and 120.

In subsequent years, prune to get a constant supply of new growth, as cherries fruit only on the previous year's wood. Limit size by cutting out a selection of old wood (three years old and more), back to a new shoot. Like plums, cherries should be pruned in spring to lessen possible infestation by silver leaf.

CITRUS FRUIT

In most parts of the UK an orange or lemon tree is generally little more than a novelty. Citrus fruit trees will need winter protection and, even then may not survive a prolonged period of harsh weather.

The most successful way of growing a citrus fruit tree is in a container of soil-based compost, such as John Innes No.2. Position this on a sunny, sheltered patio in summer and move indoors to a frost-free conservatory, traditional orangery or greenhouse for the colder months of the year. You could keep the plants indoors all year round, too, but make sure that you give them plenty of ventilation. Never allow the compost to dry out or the plant will progressively lose its flowers, fruit and then the leaves. Water regularly all year round.

The fruits take 12 months to mature, even longer for grapefruits, and for them to ripen, the trees need at least six months after flowering when the temperature stays continuously above 16°C (61°F), so even under glass the trees may need some extra heat. The heat is more important than actual sunshine for this process.

Oranges, lemons and grapefruits can all be bought at good garden centres, usually all year round. You might also find some more unusual crossed varieties, such as the orange and lime cross, bergamot.

GROWING FRUIT • OTHER TREE FRUIT

Harvesting

There is no need to thin cherries. Harvest when they are ripe by cutting off the stalks, using scissors. If you harvest sour cherries by pulling them off the trees (as you can with sweet cherries), disease may enter where the bark is torn.

APRICOTS

Apricots can be grown outside, but in very cold areas they will really only survive and produce decent yields of fruit if grown under glass. They are usually grown against a wall in a fan shape (*see* page 120).

Soil, position and cultivation

They like well-drained, fertile soil, preferably a fairly light loam. A warm, sunny position is essential, ideally against a sheltered, south-facing wall. Apricots may be planted in early or mid-winter. If planting early, wait until the following spring to begin pruning.

Apricots are self-pollinating, but as they can flower in late winter before insects are active, it is a good idea to pollinate them by hand. Protect flower buds from frost by covering the tree with a thick layer of fine mesh netting.

PESTS AND DISEASES

Peaches, nectarines, cherries and apricots are all susceptible to the same few pests and diseases.

Inspect trees regularly for signs of infection or infestation by pests and treat any problems promptly to minimise their effect. In particular, look out for die back (*see* page 148), bacterial canker (page 144), glasshouse red spider mites (page 146) and peach leaf curl (page 145).

Growing Figs and Grapes

Both these fruits originated in the sunny Mediterranean and will do best in a warm and sheltered site.

Grape vines will take a few years to get established, but, in time will produce enough grapes to make it worth trying your hand at brewing some wine (*see* pages 230–33).

FIGS

In colder districts, figs may need to be grown under glass, but in the milder south or the shelter of a walled garden there is no reason why a fig tree should not thrive.

Figs grow best in poor soils, ideally against a south-facing wall. Alternatively, they can be grown as a bush tree in a sheltered corner. Unlike other tree fruits, figs are not

Figs are ripe and ready to harvest when their skins have turned brown and started to split and the fruit feels soft to touch.

grafted onto a different root stock, so their roots must be confined to produce a good crop of fruit. Do this by lining the planting hole with stone, or concrete slabs, bricks or sheets of galvanised iron, or by planting a tree in a large tub with holes pierced in the bottom for drainage. Soil mixed with rubble and bonemeal is the ideal planting medium.

Plant trees in spring. If planting more than one tree, allow 4.5–5.5m (15–18ft) between them, although one tree is usually sufficient.

No mulching or manuring will be needed in the first few years as this will encourage over-vigorous growth. Once established, a mulch of well-rotted manure will be beneficial in dry conditions.

Training and pruning

A fan-shaped tree may be trained as shown on page 120 and a bush tree as on page 117. Once established, cut back side shoots in early summer to 10cm (4in), or so that about five leaves remain. Remove suckers and unwanted growth after one month, and tie in new shoots if necessary to keep the shape.

Harvesting

Fruits form in three layers along a fig branch. Those at the bottom of the branch will ripen; those in the middle will not have a chance to do so before the frost hits them, and the ones near the top of the branch will be next year's fruit, so must remain on the branches through the winter.

Harvest the larger fruits as they ripen (August to October) – the stem will soften, the fruits turn brown and the skins start to split. Discard the smaller fruits in the middle of the branch, and protect the following year's crop for winter by wrapping them in straw or dried foliage.

GRAPES

Grapes can be grown outdoors or in a greenhouse (*see* page 127). Both dessert and wine varieties – either white or black – are available.

You will only produce a really good crop if your vines have lots of warm summer sun. Choose early ripening grape varieties for colder districts. Ideally grape vines like sandy, stony or gravelly soil which is neutral or slightly alkaline. It must be well-drained.

Grapes need a sunny, sheltered position where there is no danger of frost lingering. A south-facing wall or fence is ideal. Prepare the site by digging in a little well-rotted compost. Buy one-year-old vines and plant them in spring, about 1.5m (5ft) apart. Keep the ground moist. The amount you grow is likely to be dictated by available space. An established cordon grown against a wall can produce up to 9kg (20lb) of fruit, or even more.

Training and pruning

The easiest way of training outdoor vines is to grow a single cordon on a wall. Vines should not bear fruit until they are three years old (remove the flowers as they form); they bear grapes on the current year's growth.

After planting, cut out all but the strongest shoot and tie this to a stake. Pinch out the flowers as they appear in summer, and cut back laterals to five leaves. Tie these laterals to wires. Rub out laterals that grow between the wires.

Repeat this process the following year. The next year, allow the vine to produce three bunches of grapes, and in the next year four or five bunches. Once established, prune the vine after the leaves have fallen, as below. Remove any rotting berries as you spot them and harvest ripe bunches cutting them with scissors.

PESTS AND DISEASES

Figs and grapes suffer from few problems. Fungal diseases are most common, especially under glass.

Be alert for signs of honey fungus (*see* page 148) and coral spot (*see* page 147) before they spread too far. Honey fungus can kill a vine; dig up and burn the plant and change or sterilise the soil before planting a replacement in the same place.

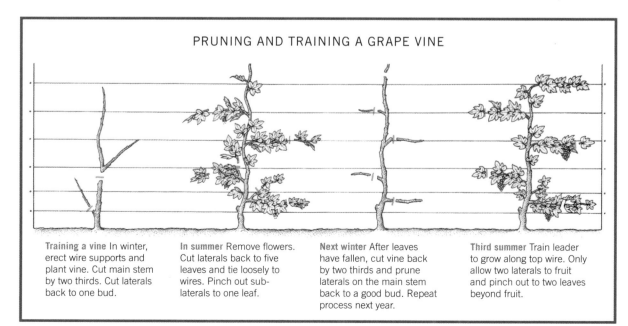

PRUNING AND TRAINING A GRAPE VINE

Training a vine In winter, erect wire supports and plant vine. Cut main stem by two thirds. Cut laterals back to one bud.

In summer Remove flowers. Cut laterals back to five leaves and tie loosely to wires. Pinch out sub-laterals to one leaf.

Next winter After leaves have fallen, cut vine back by two thirds and prune laterals on the main stem back to a good bud. Repeat process next year.

Third summer Train leader to grow along top wire. Only allow two laterals to fruit and pinch out to two leaves beyond fruit.

GROWING FRUIT • FIGS AND GRAPES

Greenhouse Fruit

A greenhouse can help you to get better and more reliable crops from tender fruits, such as melons, grapes, peaches and nectarines.

Most grand houses would once have had ranks of glasshouses for growing exotic fruits and grape vines. If you are aiming for variety it is worth including as much greenhouse space as you can to enable you to grow some of these delicious fruits.

MELONS

Melons can be grown in a cool greenhouse, but check regularly to ensure that they are not producing a mass of greenery and very little fruit.

Providing that you keep melons well-watered and pinch out the side shoots, there is no reason why you should not be able to grow your own fruit. Look for varieties recommended for growing in unheated greenhouse conditions.

Sowing and planting out
Raise the seed in a propagator, sowing in April or earlier if your greenhouse is heated. Prick out into small pots then plant seedlings in their permanent position in the border soil when they have four or five leaves. Plant 60cm (2ft) apart and construct a supporting framework similar to that for cucumbers (*see* page 102). Pinch out the growing tips – the main stem should have no more than about six large leaves – and train the side

shoots along the horizontal wires. Pinch out their growing tips when they are 30cm (1ft) long.

Melons will need pollinating by hand; transfer pollen from the male flowers (those with no embryo fruit behind the petals) to the female flowers using a fine paint brush or by pressing the male stamen into the female flowers.

Routine care
Keep the plants well-watered and feed regularly with liquid fertiliser as the fruits begin to develop. If the plant seems very heavily-loaded with fruit, pick out any that are either very small or very large so that the fruit

Figs and grapes, and other hot-weather fruits, will crop more reliably and in larger quantities when they are grown under glass.

left behind is a uniform size. Stop watering and feeding the plant when the melons have stopped swelling.

Support the melons during the ripening phase by placing them on a board or inside a string bag, suspended at an appropriate height. When they are ripe they will feel just soft when you push them gently by the stalk and will smell delicious.

Watermelons
You can grow watermelons in a heated greenhouse in the same way as for other melons. The fruits are around 95 per cent water, so regular, plentiful and even watering is critical for success – only stop watering while the fruit ripens.

The fruits are exceptionally heavy, but the plant grows by sprawling across the ground, not climbing up supports. Raise the ripening fruits on wooden boards, low stools or in a net suspended from a sturdy A-frame to keep them off wet ground that could cause them to rot. Water watermelons at the base, not from above, which can encourage mildew.

GRAPES

Vines grown in even a cold greenhouse are likely to yield more grapes than those grown outdoors, particularly if they are planted in a south-facing position.

If you have a lean-to greenhouse on a south-facing wall, you could grow vines on the greenhouse wall furthest from the house, reserving the house wall itself for tree fruits. Keep the vines' growth in check, so that they do not exclude too much light.

Planting and training
Vines can be planted either in the border soil of the greenhouse or just outside, trained in through a small hole in the wall. The simplest way to grow grapes in a greenhouse is on a single-stem cordon or rod – the same system as described for outdoor cultivation (*see* page 125).

Vines are usually bought as one-year-old plants, and planted in late October. Plant in fertile, damp soil, enriched with well-rotted compost. To train a single stem, tie it to a stake and pinch out laterals when they have five to six leaves. Train these along wires or strings.

Rub out any side shoots that grow from leaf axils and stop the lead shoot when it has reached the height you want or is level with the bottom of the greenhouse roof. Do not allow the plant to bear fruit until it is three years old. Even then, restrict cropping to two bunches for each lateral. Vines should be pruned hard each winter, taking the laterals back to a new bud close to the main stem.

Thinning out and feeding
As the grapes develop, cut out the small grapes from each bunch. This allows for bigger ones to develop and prevents the smaller ones turning mouldy as they get crushed by the larger ones.

Remember to water the vine over winter from time to time and top dress the soil with fertiliser and well-rotted compost in spring.

TREE FRUITS

Peaches, nectarines, apricots and figs will all thrive under glass and against a south-facing wall.

Although these fruits can all be grown outdoors (*see* pages 122–25) they will crop more reliably in a greenhouse. The general care and cultivation for growing tree fruits in a greenhouse is just the same as for growing out of doors, but they must be planted in very well-drained soil, which is fertile even at quite a depth – peaches extend their roots down for about 60cm (2ft). The trees must be kept well-watered throughout the year, even in winter, when there appears to be litle or no growth. Give them a good mulch of well-rotted farmyard manure each spring.

Balance warmth and fresh air
In winter, make sure that you shut all ventilation windows early in the afternoon to trap any warmth in the greenhouse. Open them in the morning to let in some fresh air. As the weather warms up, shade the greenhouse with blinds or shading paint to prevent scorching in sun.

Pollination is less likely to occur naturally in a greenhouse, since insects do not have free access to the blossoms, so you will need to do this by hand. Brush over the flowers with a soft paint brush, transferring the pollen from flower to flower. This is best done around midday.

Routine care
Indoor tree fruit needs spraying or syringing with water to ward off red spider mite and to encourage the flowers to set fruit. Spray once a day when the flowers are out and twice a day when the fruit buds have begun to emerge. Never spray the plants in direct sun and stop when the fruit begins to ripen.

Training and pruning are the same as for the same plants grown outside. Train trees as fan-shapes against a wall to be as efficient as possible with space and prune hard in spring so that the developing fruit is not obscured by foliage. If there is a lot of foliage, tie it back to allow sunlight to get to the ripening fruit.

Growing Rhubarb

Rhubarb is ready for picking from early spring onwards, earlier if it is forced, at a time when virtually no other fresh fruit is available in the garden. It can be used in a variety of puddings.

Only the stems of rhubarb are edible. Any flower stems should be removed as they emerge and leaves must be discarded.

Rhubarb will grow in just about all garden soils and sites, but does best in an open, sunny position. It is beset by very few pests or diseases.

Planting and routine care

As rhubarb is a perennial and can stay in the same place for five years or more, it is worth preparing the bed well. Dig it over and remove all perennial weeds, then incorporate some well-rotted organic matter, digging it deep, as rhubarb sends down long roots.

Plant rhubarb crowns in early spring so there is about 1m (3ft)

SEASONAL GROWING GUIDE

Planting	Early spring After preparing the ground in winter
Forcing	Late winter Outdoors Early winter Indoors
Harvesting	From early spring Plant out rhubarb forced indoors for another crop

between plants. The holes should be wide enough to take the entire rootstock and deep enough to allow only small shoots to protrude from the surface. Firm the soil around the rootstock and water if it is at all dry.

Water well in dry spells and mulch the plants each spring. Feed them in summer with liquid fertiliser. Cut out any flower stems and do not pick any rhubarb in the first year.

How many plants to grow

An established rhubarb plant should yield about 4.5kg (10lb) of fruit in a year, but remember this is spread over a period of nearly six months.

Harvesting

Pull stalks from the plant when they are turning pink. Hold them near the bottom and pull them from the plant with a gentle twisting movement. You should be able to gather rhubarb from late winter through summer, but do not pick too heavily in the second year and always leave a few good stems and leaves on the plant to help it gather its resources.

Raising new plants

New rhubarb plants can be obtained by digging up the old plant and

Forcing rhubarb

Rhubarb is generally ready for harvesting in spring, but it can be forced, so as to be ready for picking earlier. To do this, cover the emerging leaves with a bucket or large pot, making sure no light can enter. You can also use special clay or terracotta rhubarb forcers (below), which are an elegant shape and an attractive addition to the fruit and vegetable plot, but they are expensive when a bucket will do the job just as well.

Plants may also be dug up and brought indoors in early winter, so they are ready for harvesting in mid-winter. They are then planted out again and covered with a bucket or pot to encourage further growth. This will give you two harvests from one plant.

Forced rhubarb stems are pale and tender. Plants grow up fast to reach the light at the top of the forcing pot.

dividing up the roots into pieces that each have a growing bud. Do this in early spring using two- or three-year-old plants.

Growing Strawberries

Strawberries differ from other soft fruit in that they grow as small bedding plants, rather than on bushes or canes. Although considered to be one of the greatest fruit treats of all, they are not difficult to grow and it is possible to produce them in the garden from late spring through the summer right up to the first frosts.

SEASONAL GROWING GUIDE

VARIETY	PLANTING	HARVESTING MONTHS
Summer fruiting	Late summer – mid-autumn If you cannot plant until spring, pinch off flowers and delay fruiting for a year while the plants establish	Protect fruit with straw from late spring. Harvest through the summer months
Perpetual	Late summer Allow 45cm (18in) between plants	Protect fruit with straw from late spring. Harvest from early summer into autumn
Alpine	Autumn – mid-spring Sow seeds over winter. Transplant young plants later in spring, 30cm (12in) apart	Harvest summer to autumn

There are three types of strawberries: single crop varieties which produce one heavy crop – usually in early summer; the perpetual or *remontant* types which produce a number of crops from summer to autumn; and alpine strawberries, which bear their tiny, highly succulent fruits during the summer. They are all good sources of vitamin C.

Although strawberry plants are perennials, they should be pulled up and replaced after two or three years. Thereafter, they produce increasingly poor crops and are also more susceptible to disease.

Strawberries are very easy to propagate to get replacement plants without having to buy them. Alpines are best treated as annuals and reared from seed sown in the spring or grown from young nursery-bought plants.

Soil and position

Strawberries grow in all well-cultivated garden soils, but they do best in those that are well-drained and very rich in humus. Dig in lots of well-rotted organic matter about a month before planting. An open, sunny position will produce the heaviest crops, although they will grow successfully in some shade.

If space is a problem, strawberries can be grown in tubs, boxes, barrels, special strawberry pots or among the flowers in a border. Strawberry pots have holes in the bottom for good drainage and a layer of large pebbles should be put in the base before adding the potting compost.

Planting and routine care

If buying new strawberry plants, choose only those that are certified disease-free. They can be planted any time from mid-summer to late summer, to fruit the following summer, and the earlier in this time, the better.

If planting has to be delayed until the following spring, pinch off the flowers as they appear to allow the plant to direct its resources into becoming established before fruiting the following year.

Strawberries grow well in pots on a sunny patio, as long as they are well-watered, and being raised off the ground can help to protect them from some hungry garden pests.

RAISING NEW STRAWBERRY PLANTS

1 Select one or two healthy runners from each strawberry plant in June, and pinch out all the other runners where they join the parent plant. They will take up precious energy.

2 Sink a small pot of potting compost for each runner into the ground close to the parent plant and pin the runner into it. Pinch out any more growth to encourage the runner to root, rather than to grow.

3 Cut the runner from the parent plant when it is well-rooted and plant it out in its new site.

CULTIVATION OF STRAWBERRIES

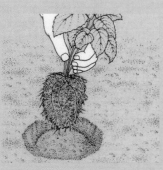

1 Make a hole in the soil deep and wide enough for the rootball. Make a low mound of soil at the bottom of the hole. Position the plant in the hole, spreading out the roots over the mound of soil.

2 Protect growing plants from wet mud, which will cause them to rot, by growing them on special strawberry mats (above) or over a mulch of straw.

3 When fruits begin to form on the plants, cover them with cages of netting to deter birds from eating the strawberries.

Water plants well immediately after planting and for the next few weeks. Thereafter make sure they do not dry out. Keep weeds under control by shallow hoeing, but take care not to disturb the plants' roots.

If you are growing strawberries in a greenhouse, you will need to pollinate the flowers by hand, daily, as soon as they open. Use a small, soft paint brush to transfer pollen from flower to flower.

Taking care of developing fruit
When the fruit begins to appear, put a 5cm (2in) layer of clean straw between rows and tuck it well under and around each plant. This helps to protect the fruit from soil splashing up in wet weather and rotting it. Alternative methods of protection are to use special strawberry mats sold at garden centres, to lay black polythene on the ground, or to slide empty jam jars over the fruits and rest them on the ground. Make sure the soil is moist if using polythene.

Protect developing fruit from attack by birds by covering the plants with netting supported on low stakes driven into the ground, and give feeds of liquid fertiliser to increase the size of the fruits once they begin to swell. Pinch off runners as they appear unless you want to raise new plants.

If you want early crops, protect the plant with polythene or glass cloches in late winter. If you want late crops from perpetual varieties, cover with cloches in early autumn. You should get crops at least until mid-autumn.

At the end of the season
After harvesting, strawberry plants may be treated in a number of ways. With single-crop plants, loosen the straw around the plants and burn it

Protecting strawberries

One of the best methods of protecting growing fruits is to raise them on beds of straw. Not only will it prevent the roots from rotting on soggy ground in wet weather, but when the season is over, the straw can be pulled up, taking any strawberry pests with it.

To lift fruits off the wet soil – keeping them clean and minimising the chance of rotting – put down a layer of straw beneath the plants.

(if the position of the plants makes this a safe operation). This burns off old leaves as well as destroying pests and other rubbish which has collected in the straw, but it does not kill the plant. An alternative, and the best solution for perpetual varieties that would be killed by the burning, is to cut off all the foliage to about 10cm (4in) above the crown of the plant, leaving the young growth to come through. Fork up the straw, cut stems and burn them.

A third way is to take one runner from each plant, and root them (*see* opposite) to form a new row. Then dig the old crop into the soil, or dig up the plants and burn them. This way you can produce a new row of strawberry plants every one or two years very easily.

To raise alpine strawberries, sow the seeds in potting compost indoors in late summer and prick out in early autumn, or raise under glass in mid-spring. Plant out the seedlings in late spring, setting them 30cm (12in) apart, with the same distance between each row. Thereafter, treat them as for other strawberries.

Harvesting
Pick strawberries on a dry day, when they are fully ripe, pinching them off by the stalk if you can to avoid

handling and bruising the delicate fruit. Pick alpine strawberries throughout the season to encourage the plants to continue fruiting.

Pests and diseases
Aphids can be a problem on strawberry plants (*see* page 144). Slugs and snails are partial to young fruits and are best protected against by putting down slug pellets before laying down the layer of straw or polythene to protect the fruit. Look out for signs of virus diseases (*see* page 146), mildew (page 146) and botrytis, or grey mould (page 146).

Good strawberry varieties

SUMMER FRUITING
• **Cambridge Favourite** Heavy cropper, scarlet, well-flavoured fruits
• **Red Gauntlet** Gives heavy yield of large, scarlet fruits. Will crop again in autumn if protected in spring

ALPINE
• **Alexandria** Sow early to crop from July to October. Large sweet fruits
• **Fraise des Bois** Excellent cropper giving small red fruits
• **Baron Solemacher** Masses of small dark fruits. Likes slight shade

GROWING FRUIT · STRAWBERRIES

Summer Berries

Most common soft fruits fall into one of two categories: those that are members of the rose family, such as blackberries, strawberries, and raspberries; and those that are members of the gooseberry family, including currants.

RASPBERRIES

Raspberries are very easy to grow and are among the most popular of all soft fruits. There are many different varieties – even yellow fruits – but they can be divided into two distinct types. Summer-fruiting raspberries usually crop in July and August, bearing their fruit on the canes produced in the previous year; autumn-fruiting varieties produce a smaller crop from September to November on growth that has been put on during the current season.

SEASONAL GROWING GUIDE

VARIETIES	PRUNING	HARVEST
Summer-fruiting Malling Leo; Glen Moy; Glen Ample	Cut fruiting canes down to ground level after harvesting. Leave the strongest new growth to bear fruit next year, cutting each cane back to a bud in early spring	July and August
Autumn-fruiting Autumn Bliss; Allgold	Cut canes back in February	September to November

Soil and position

Raspberries will grow in almost all well-cultivated soils, but they prefer those which are slightly acid and well-drained, but moisture-retentive. They will grow in partial shade, but do best in a sunny site that is sheltered from strong winds.

Planting and care

Dig lots of well-rotted manure into the ground a month or two before planting, and make sure that the site is completely free of perennial weeds. The canes can stay in the same site for eight years, so take care over the preparation of the ground. Plant, preferably in November, as described on page 112, leaving 45cm (18in) between plants and 1.5–1.8m (5–6ft) between rows. Buy only certified, disease-free stock – anything else may be harbouring virus diseases.

Water the canes well during summer and apply an annual spring mulch. Keep weeds under control by shallow hoeing, but be careful not to disturb the roots, which run close to the surface – a weedkiller or thick mulch may be a more effective solution to eliminate weeds. Protect the plants and the fruit from birds by covering them with netting or by growing them in a fruit cage.

Established canes bear approximately 450g (1lb) of fruit each year. Do not allow canes to fruit in their first season: cut out any flowers that appear to prevent them from producing berries.

For support, tie the canes to horizontal wires strung between sturdy posts hammered in at either end of the row or to single posts positioned at intervals along the row (*see panel,* right).

After harvesting in the second season, cut out the fruiting canes on summer-fruiting varieties just above the soil. Tie the eight strongest

Prune summer-fruiting canes that have borne fruit, cutting them back to ground level; select the strongest new growth and train it on wires for next year's harvest.

SUPPORTING RASPBERRY CANES

Raspberry canes cannot grow without support. The method you choose may depend on the size of your plot and the position of your canes; try one of these three tried-and-tested solutions.

• Drive stakes into the ground at either end of the row of canes and string parallel lengths of wire between the posts. Put the lowest wire around 30cm (12in) from the ground. As the canes grow, tie them to the wires.

• Drive stakes into the middle of each group of canes. Loosely tie the canes to the stakes as they grow. Use this method to support raspberry canes grown in pots.

• Make a box structure to support the canes by driving one stake into either end of each row. Attach two cross struts to each stake and string wire between these, enclosing the rows of canes within a wire 'box'.

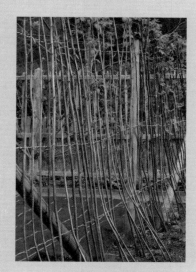
Horizontal wires strung between stakes are a simple way to support raspberry canes. Cut back new growth to just above the level of a supporting wire.

canes to the wires, and cut out all the weaker ones. Remove unwanted suckers which have sprung up between the rows at the same time. In very early spring, cut canes back to a bud that is no more than 15cm (6in) above the wire. Cut some canes a little shorter so that you have fruit at all levels. Cut autumn-fruiting varieties back the following February.

Harvesting
Pull the fruits off the canes gently as soon as they are ripe, leaving the stalk and core behind. They should be used immediately.

Raising new plants
New canes are easily produced from the suckers put out by existing plants, but only take these from canes that were certified virus-

free. Dig them up and transplant in November. It is generally best to buy in new stock every eight years or so.

Pests and diseases
Maggots of the raspberry beetle (*see* page 149), tunnel into the fruits, making them distorted and inedible. Look out for and pick off the beetles, which lay their eggs on the flowers, and the brown grubs that follow. Raspberries are also susceptible to various fungus diseases, including cane spot (*see* page 147), which causes purple spots to appear on the canes. These later turn to white and the cane eventually splits. Spur blight (*see* page 147) also causes purple spots on the canes, followed by withered leaves; in bad cases, the canes may snap. Cut out and burn infected canes to prevent the problem from spreading.

GROWING FRUIT • RASPBERRIES

BLUEBERRIES

Blueberries are a mountain and moorland fruit, widely grown in the USA. They are closely related to bilberries or whortleberries which grow wild in Britain. They are regarded as a superfruit and make good jams and jellies or fillings for pies and muffins.

Soil and position
Blueberries like an acid soil and will not grow on those which are alkaline. In these areas, you can still grow blueberries in large pots filled with an acid compost. Peaty soils which are moisture-retentive will produce the best crops. Although these bushes can withstand cold conditions, they need sheltering from strong, cold winds. An open, sunny site gives the best crops.

Planting and routine care
Dig some peaty compost into the site a month before planting if the soil is not peaty, and plant as described on page 111. Blueberry bushes are best started as three-year-old plants bought from a local nursery, and they should be planted 1.8m (6ft) apart. They will appreciate an annual mulch in early summer.

You should grow at least two bushes to ensure good cross-pollination. They will produce anything up to 4.5kg (10lb) of fruit per bush, depending on weather and growing conditions.

Blueberries need no pruning until they are four years old. After that, cut out old wood regularly each winter, taking it back to the ground or a strong new shoot. Cut out any suckers which emerge at the base of the plant.

Pests and diseases
Blueberries are remarkably free from problems and pests or diseases.

BLACKCURRANTS

Blackcurrants are rich in vitamin C and have wide culinary uses – for making drinks (including wine), puddings, jams and jellies. Again, there are several different varieties and these will produce varying yields. If buying new plants, get them from a reputable source and make sure they are two-year-old certified bushes. These are less likely to succumb to disease.

Soil, position and cultivation
Blackcurrants will flourish in most soils, but do best on those which are well-cultivated, rich and well-drained. Ideally, they like a sunny position, but although they will tolerate partial shade, they do need to be in a sheltered spot which is protected from cold winds and away from frost pockets.

Dig lots of well-rotted manure into the ground a month or so before planting – which is best done in the autumn. Follow instructions for

Blackcurrants need to ripen on the bush for at least a week after their berries turn black. Don't pick them too soon, or they will be sour.

planting outlined opposite and space plants about 1.5m (5ft) apart. Cut all stems down to 5cm (2in) from the ground straightaway and apply a mulch around the roots.

Water plants well in dry periods and apply an annual mulch each spring. Keep the ground around the plants free of weeds by shallow hoeing. If necessary, control weeds by mulching, rather than digging, which would disturb the root system.

The number of plants to grow depends on the variety you choose, but an average-sized mature bush yields approximately 4.5kg (10lb) of fruit a year.

Training and pruning
Blackcurrants fruit on new wood each year, but as the new wood grows on old wood, you must prune regularly to maintain a good balance of new wood, whilst keeping the plant bushy and allowing light to penetrate to all parts. In the autumn after planting, cut out the weakest shoots at ground level – the remainder will fruit the following summer. Thereafter, prune the bush by removing a quarter to a third of the old wood each year. Take the oldest wood first – it will be very dark. Cut back this wood to one or

SEASONAL GROWING GUIDE FOR BLUEBERRIES

Planting	Late autumn – early spring Space plants 1.8m (6ft) apart
Pruning	Late autumn – early spring Cut back old stems to the ground or a vigorous new shoot
Harvesting	Summer – autumn Pick over the bush several times, selecting the berries that are ripe

two growth buds from the ground so new shoots grow.

Harvesting

Pick blackcurrants when they are fully ripe – this is at least a week after they have turned from green to black. If clusters of fruit have both ripe and non-ripe fruit, the berries should be picked individually, which is a tedious task. Those picked on sprigs or trusses will keep marginally longer before use, but they should all be used or frozen fairly quickly after picking.

Raising new plants

Take cuttings in the autumn from healthy shoots of that year's growth. Cut off either end just beyond a bud so the cutting is about 25cm (10in) long. Push it into the soil. If the soil is very heavy, dig a trench about 15cm (6in) deep and sprinkle sand in the bottom. The cuttings should be about 15cm (6in) deep in the soil, with two growth buds showing above the surface, and there should be 25cm (9in) between cuttings. They will have rooted by the following autumn and may be transplanted to their permanent site.

Pests and diseases

The blackcurrant gall mite causes big bud (*see* page 149), a serious condition, in which the buds swell and fail to develop any further. Pick off any affected buds and treat the plant. Big bud can also lead to a virus called reversion (*see* page 145); the leaves become distorted and the crop is badly reduced or even eliminated. If this disease develops, the plants must be uprooted and destroyed. Always buy certified disease-free plants to minimise the chances of your harvest being wiped out by disease.

SEASONAL GROWING GUIDE FOR BLACKCURRANTS

VARIETIES	PRUNING	HARVEST
Ben varieties, including Ben Lomond and Ben Gairn. Modern blackcurrant varieties that are disease-resistant, compact and produce heavy yields **Wellington XXX** Mid-season, old-fashioned variety. Heavy cropper that produces lots of sweet fruits **Malling Jet** Late-season, traditional blackcurrant variety. Flowers late to escape frost damage	Pruning is the same for all varieties. Cut back the weakest shoots to ground level in the first autumn. Thereafter, prune in late summer to autumn, removing a quarter to a third of the old wood at the base of the bush each year to encourage new growth	Pick currants when they are ripe, in early to late summer. Pick individual currants if the whole truss does not ripen together

CULTIVATING BLACKCURRANTS

1 Plant canes in a sunny, sheltered position in autumn, while the soil is still warm. Blackcurrants are usually sold as bushes, in containers, not bare-root canes. Mulch well to retain moisture.

2 Cut back each shoot on a newly-planted bush to ground level, cutting just above an outward-pointing bud. The bushes will not fruit in their first year, but will grow strong and vigorous.

3 Take cuttings in autumn. Rub all buds from the lower end and push the canes into a v-shaped trench. Leave to root before moving to their permanent site.

GROWING FRUIT • BLUEBERRIES, BLACKCURRANTS

RED AND WHITE CURRANTS

Although related to the blackcurrant, these fruits are cultivated differently. Their training is more like that of the gooseberry (*see* page 138) and, like it, they may be grown on open-centre bushes or cordons.

White currants are a variety of red currant and may be eaten fresh as a dessert. Red currants are more often used for jam and jelly-making, although they too can be eaten

White currants have a delicate colour and flavour; their glossy red relatives are more robust, and a great accompaniment to meats, such as roast lamb and game.

fresh. Both plants grow best in well-drained, but moisture-retentive soils. A sunny position, sheltered from cold winds, and where there is no danger of frost collecting to damage the early flowers, is the ideal site.

The average yield from an established bush is 1.8–2.2kg (4–5lb). Some bushes will give twice this amount; cordons will yield less.

Planting and routine care

Dig plenty of well-rotted organic matter into the soil some weeks before planting and apply a general fertiliser containing potash. Buy two-year-old bushes and plant them as early as possible in the recommended planting period.

Drive stakes into the ground next to cordons to support them and secure horizontal wires between these. Branches on bush trees should be no more than 25cm (10in) above the ground.

Water in very dry weather and protect plants from birds. Pull out any suckers that appear from the roots or main stems. Control weeds by weedkiller or mulching rather than hoeing, which could damage the plants' roots. Apply annual winter mulches and feed with sulphate of potash at the same time.

Pruning and training

After planting, cut back branches so each has only four shoots. The second winter, cut each branch back by half to an outward-facing bud and cut lateral shoots back to two buds. The aim is to produce an open-centre bush where light can easily penetrate, and to produce spur

CULTIVATING RED AND WHITE CURRANTS

1 Plant bushes in a sunny, sheltered spot. Stake them for support and prune each year.

2 As fruit begins to form, protect the crop from birds by covering bushes with netting. Water in dry weather.

3 Pull out suckers as they appear near the roots of the main stems. Keep down weeds with gentle hoeing or pulling by hand.

wood which will bear the fruit. When established, cut the current year's growth back to about 2.5cm (1in) and cut out old wood to make room for new shoots. In summer, cut out lateral growths beyond five leaves.

Currants are trained and pruned in the same way as gooseberries (*see* page 138).

Harvesting

Pick the fruits as soon as they are ripe, harvesting whole trusses whenever possible. If they are not ripe, pick the currants individually.

Planting distances for red and white currants

Plant red and white currant bushes to the following suggested spacings. If more than one row of cordons is being grown, leave 1.2m (4ft) between them.

Bushes 1.5m (5ft)

Single cordons 40cm (15in)

Double cordons 75cm (2ft 6in)

Treble cordons 1m (3ft)

BLACKBERRIES AND LOGANBERRIES

Many people think of blackberries as hedgerow fruits, but cultivated blackberries are bigger, juicier and tastier than their wild cousins. They have such a wide use in cooking, jam or wine-making that it is worth finding space for a few canes.

Loganberries are the result of an accidental cross between a blackberry and a raspberry in the late nineteenth century, in California. The resulting berries are dark red and may be eaten raw or used for cooking. They are cultivated, trained and propagated in exactly the same way as blackberries.

Soil and position

Blackberries will grow in any soil, although those that are slightly acid and rich in humus will produce the largest crops. They will grow just about anywhere, even in a north-facing site, and can be trained over a shed or along a fence to form a hedge. For the largest yields, choose an open, sunny position.

Planting and routine care

Plant blackberry canes as outlined on page 112, in late autumn. Dig lots of well-rotted organic matter into the soil a month or so before planting. It is worth preparing the site well, because blackberries can remain in the same place for 10 years or more. Place canes about 2m (6ft) apart (slightly less for smaller canes; more for the more vigorous varieties) and stretch horizontal wires between them to provide support.

Water well in dry weather and keep the ground around the roots free of weeds. Mulch each spring with well-rotted manure or compost.

The number you grow depends on the varieties you choose – one cane of a vigorous variety can produce over 9kg (20lb) of fruit.

Training and pruning

As the canes grow, tie them into the supporting wires, using one of the methods illustrated below. The one-year-old canes produce the fruit, so try to keep new and old wood separate. After harvesting, cut out all that year's fruiting canes at ground level. If necessary, reposition and re-

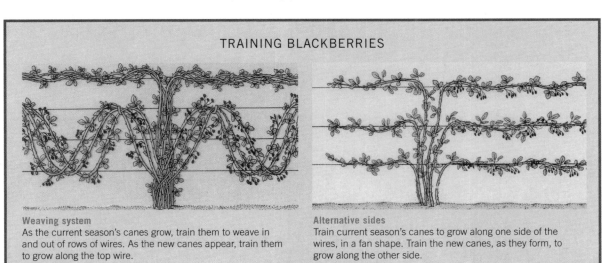

TRAINING BLACKBERRIES

Weaving system
As the current season's canes grow, train them to weave in and out of rows of wires. As the new canes appear, train them to grow along the top wire.

Alternative sides
Train current season's canes to grow along one side of the wires, in a fan shape. Train the new canes, as they form, to grow along the other side.

SEASONAL GROWING GUIDE FOR BLACKBERRIES

Planting	Late autumn – early spring Cut back each cane to 25cm (9in)
Training	Summer Keep tying in new growth throughout the growing season
Harvesting	Summer – early autumn Pick berries when ripe and use them straight away
Pruning	Autumn Cut back fruiting canes to ground level

tie that year's new growth, which will fruit next year.

Harvesting
Blackberries ripen any time from mid-summer to autumn, depending on the variety and, of course, the weather conditions. Pick them when they are ripe, handling them carefully so as not to crush them. Use them straight away, as they will quickly turn soft and mushy.

Raising new plants
Bend over a new shoot in mid-summer, and bury the tip in 10–15cm (4–6in) of soil, holding it in place with a stone. Cut it away from the parent plant in early winter, when it has rooted, and replant it in its permanent site the following spring.

Pests and diseases
Check your canes regularly for signs of the following common pests and diseases: raspberry beetle (page 149), cane spot (page 147) and spur blight (page 147).

GOOSEBERRIES

The different varieties of gooseberry make it possible to produce crops right through the summer from late spring. Dessert types can be eaten fresh; others are suitable only for cooking in some way.

Gooseberries are excellent for jams, chutneys and wine as well as many puddings. Although usually grown on a bush, they can be grown on single, double or treble cordons, which means they can be trained to grow against a wall or fence.

Soil and position
Gooseberries will grow in almost all soils, but prefer those which are well-drained but moist, and enriched by lots of well-rotted organic material. They like a sunny site, and should never be planted in a place where frost collects as they flower in early spring, and it will damage them.

Planting and routine care
Make sure the ground is completely free from all perennial weeds and apply a general fertiliser (preferably one that is rich in potash) to the site before planting. Plant two- or three-year-old bushes in the autumn, leaving 1.5m (5ft) between bushes. The lowest branches should be about 25cm (9in) above the ground. Single cordons should be 30cm (1ft) apart, double cordons 60cm (2ft) apart and triple cordons 1m (3ft) apart. They will need wire supports along which to train the branches.

Keep the ground free of weeds by shallow hoeing (so as not to disturb the roots), or with a weedkiller. Water the plants in very dry weather and apply an annual spring mulch of well-rotted compost, together with a sprinkling of sulphate of potash.

Protect plants from birds by covering them completely with netting or by weaving black cotton round the branches. Tear out any shoots that appear at ground level.

Mature bushes will yield an average of about 3.5kg (8lb) of fruit each year.

Training and pruning
The aim with gooseberry bushes is to keep a cup-shaped form to the bush with a good open centre. In the winter, cut summer growth shoots back by about half to two-thirds to a bud (leave the pruning until the buds start to swell if the bush has been attacked by birds – then you can be sure of pruning back to a healthy bud). If the bush is of a variety that has drooping growth, cut to an upward-pointing bud; cut upright varieties to an outward-pointing bud. Leave about eight branches well-spaced round the bush and cut the others to one bud from the base.

Thereafter, keep cutting the new growth back by half each winter and cut lateral shoots to about 7.5cm (3in) to encourage the formation of spurs. When the bush is really established, cut out old wood to maintain the shape and to allow light to penetrate evenly. Cut back leading shoots to about 2.5cm (1in) each year. Remove weak new shoots.

In summer, prune back side shoots to about five leaves (do this on all types of gooseberry bushes, cordons included). This encourages the fruit buds to form.

Cordons can be created from cuttings. For a single cordon, cut off all shoots close to the main stem, leaving the strongest one. Tie it to a stake and cut it back by half the current season's growth each year. Shorten side shoots to form fruiting spurs. Train and support double and

triple cordons in a similar way but select two or three shoots initially. In a double cordon, these should be trained horizontally and then cut off at an upward-pointing bud so they grow vertically. In a triple cordon, train two shoots as for a double cordon and treat the centre one like a single cordon.

Harvesting

If the crop is very heavy, thin the fruits when they are big enough to use, so they are about 2.5cm (1in) apart. If you like, you can thin them again to leave them 5–7.5cm (2–3in) apart, in which case you should

get large gooseberries for the final harvest. Gooseberries for cooking do not have to be completely ripe before harvesting – those wanted for eating fresh should be, if they are not to be too sharp.

Raising new plants

New plants can be raised from cuttings in the same way as blackcurrants (*see* page 135), but they do not root as easily. Take cuttings in the autumn, about 40cm (15in) long, from the current season's growth while there is still some leafy growth. Cut off the top 7.5cm (3in) of soft wood and rub

Although green is the traditionally accepted colour for gooseberries, many varieties are now available, including yellow and red fruits, too. Some varieties are too sharp to eat fresh, look for 'dessert' gooseberries if you don't want to have to cook them before eating.

out all the buds from the lower end, leaving three or four near the top. Thereafter, treat the same as blackcurrant cuttings.

Pests and diseases

There are two diseases specific to gooseberries: gooseberry mildew (*see* page 149) and gooseberry sawfly (page 144).

PRUNING GOOSEBERRIES

1 In the winter, cut summer shoots back to a bud, always maintaining a good cup shape to the bush.

2 In the summer, thin the fruits by removing every other one. Prune back side shoots to five leaves.

3 In winter, prune mature bushes to keep a cup shape. Cut leaders back by half and laterals to 7.5cm (3in).

DIRECTORY OF PESTS AND DISEASES

Preventing Pests and Diseases

It is inevitable that your fruit and vegetable crops will suffer attack from pests or succumb to disease at some point, but you can help to keep problems at bay with some commonsense and regular maintenance and this is far easier than getting rid of a problem once it has taken hold.

Being strict and careful about garden hygiene is the most important first step in keeping your plants healthy. Tidy up plant debris regularly, so that dead or infected leaves, fruit and twigs do not build up on the soil, infecting the other growing plants around them.

As you tidy in the fruit and vegetable beds, and whenever you water the plants, too, check your crops for any early signs of pest infestation or disease.

Always dig up and destroy plants affected by virus diseases to eradicate the problem quickly and weed your plot regularly to keep down weeds, where pests can live.

Choose plants wisely

Only buy plants, seeds, sets or tubers from reputable suppliers and always look for varieties specified 'certified disease-free'. Choose disease-resistant varieties if you know that a particular disease is prevalent in your area. If a nursery or garden centre looks messy, weedy and ill-cared-for, choose to buy your plants elsewhere.

Don't cramp plants

Just as with people, plant diseases will spread more easily in crowded places, so always follow the recommended spacings when planting out. Plants that are crowded will also often be too cramped for air to circulate freely and this can lead to problems with rotting, fungal diseases, mildew and more. They will also be competing with one another for water and nutrients and are likely to be weak and straggly as they race to grow up above their neighbours to reach the light. This makes them more vulnerable when pests and diseases do occur. What is more, it is harder for you to spot problems promptly if you cannot easily inspect plants because they are entwined with one another.

Greenhouse hygiene

It is particularly important to keep things scrupulously clean in the greenhouse, where the good growing conditions mean that pests and diseases will thrive just as readily as your plants.

Always scrub and disinfect pots and seed trays before and after use, clean up mess promptly and clean the greenhouse itself thoroughly

each autumn (*see page 38*). Open windows to allow air to circulate, to discourage mould and fungus.

NATURE'S PEST CONTROL

Many insects and creatures survive on a diet of the pests that would like to eat your crops. If you can encourage them into your garden and fruit and vegetable plot, then they will do much of your pest control for you.

It is easier to attract wildlife into a domestic garden than a vegetable plot, as the variety of plants is often greater there, but try to incorporate pollen-rich plants to attract hoverflies and other insect predators that will help to control aphids. Ground beetles will attack the eggs of damaging carrot fly and cabbage root fly if you provide them with some shelter in the form of ground cover to protect them during the day.

Bottom left *Ladybirds are voracious aphid-eaters; attract them with flowering plants.* Bottom centre *If you have a pond, its frogs will prey on a variety of garden bugs.* Bottom right *Beetles will prey on the eggs of many damaging pests, such as carrot fly.*

Treating Plant Problems

Vigilance and prompt action are the keys to successfully eradicating a pest or treating a disease. Inspect your crops regularly to spot signs of infection or infestation early.

Garden chemicals can be dangerous and should always be used as a last resort. Most insecticides will kill all insects, even the harmless or helpful ones, so only apply them to plants where a pest or disease is visible.

The following pages will help you to identify problems with your plants and suggest ways to treat or avoid them happening again, but it is a good idea to ask your local nursery or garden centre for advice on dealing with each particular pest or disease. They will be happy to recommend appropriate treatments or advise you on non-chemical methods where possible.

Using sprays safely

There will be times when the only practical solution is to use a proprietary spray insecticide, fungicide or other treatment. Always follow the instructions on the packet carefully and only use a treatment for its intended purpose. Use a small sprayer, targeting your treatment rather than spraying a wide area. Do not spray chemicals on a windy day, when they could be blown off course or even into your face.

Take care when treating fungal diseases, as too much fungicide can be as harmful to many plants as the fungus itself. Always check the bottle for any specific warnings or test the product on one or two leaves before treating a whole plant or entire crop. Although it is best to

Choosing insecticides

Systemic insecticides are absorbed by the plant and are used to treat sap-sucking insects, such as aphids and mealy bugs, which consume the insecticide-laced sap and die. Contact insecticides are sprayed onto the surface of leaves and stems and kill insect pests that come into contact with them, killing pests that eat the leaves, such as caterpillars. Ready-mixed sprays are the most expensive option, but the easiest to apply.

confine insecticide spraying to only the affected plants, fungal diseases spread from spores, so treat the affected plant and those around it.

Be thorough and careful, and be prepared to apply the treatment again a few weeks later to catch pests that have hatched out of eggs since the first spraying. Wear protective equipment and clothing: long sleeves and trousers, gloves, sturdy shoes and goggles and a mask if you wish.

Never leave left-over chemicals in your sprayer – you will forget what they are and could use them for the wrong thing next time you need the sprayer. Spray any unused chemical onto a patch of gravel then clean the sprayer before you put it away.

Always store all garden chemicals on a high shelf in a locked shed. Keep a note of their use-by dates and take care to rotate your stock so that you always use the oldest first. Take any part-full bottles you no longer need to your local recycling centre and ask their advice about disposing of them safely.

VISIBLE PESTS

PROBLEM	IDENTIFICATION	AFFECTED	TREATMENT
Aphids	Tiny insects, most prevalent in warm, dry spells, will settle in large numbers on leaves, shoots and young fruit, causing distorted growth	Many crops	Spray with proprietary mixtures either in winter to kill eggs or just before the blossom appears on fruit trees, to kill the insects
Asparagus beetle	Orangey coloured beetles and their grey grubs which feed voraciously on the foliage, turning it patchy brown and distorted	Asparagus	Cut foliage in autumn to destroy the eggs. Dust or spray with recommended proprietary mixtures
Blackfly	Infestations of tiny blackflies, which cling to the stems and suck the sap, causing the plant to wither and growth to become distorted. Eventually the plant dies	Broad beans, but also French and runner beans	Early crops usually escape, as the pods are harvested before blackflies are active. Pinch out growing tips of plants as soon as you notice blackfly and pick off and destroy any infected leaves. Spraying with proprietary mixtures will help to control them, or spraying with a jet of water from a hose can wash them off the plant
Glasshouse whiteflies	1.5mm-long whiteflies and scale-like larvae collect on the underside of leaves of plants grown under glass. The leaves become marked with sooty mould and honeydew	Tomatoes and cucumbers in greenhouse	Spray regularly with proprietary mixture
Greenfly	Clusters of tiny insects may attack lettuces in summer. They will be noticeable on the leaves and plants will eventually become stunted and will die	Lettuces and other salad crops	Good attention to garden hygiene and prompt destruction of any greenfly-carrying crops will help to control the pest. Attacks can be lessened by making sure that summer plants are kept well-watered
Mealy bugs	Small pink insects (4mm long) gather in patches on stems and leaves. They are covered with a white woolly wax	Crops grown in greenhouse	Spray with recommended proprietary mixture
Scale insects	Flat, scale-like insects, 1–6mm long, and brown, yellow or white. Found on the underside of leaves, clustered along leaf veins and on stems	Crops grown under glass	Brush off the scales with a soft toothbrush, or spray with recommended proprietary mixture

Other possible pests: **Cabbage white butterfly** (below), **Cutworms** page 147, **Flea beetles** (below)

LEAVES WITH HOLES

PROBLEM	IDENTIFICATION	AFFECTED	TREATMENT
Bacterial canker	Disease spots appear on branches and ooze a sticky substance. These branches produce small, withered, discoloured leaves and will eventually die back	Mostly plums, peaches, damsons and cherries	Cut out all infected wood and seal cut surfaces with protective paint. Spray with proprietary mixtures in late summer or early autumn
Cabbage white butterfly	Caterpillars eat through the leaves, making a mass of holes	Brassicas	Squash or pick off the clusters of yellow eggs from the leaves and remove and destroy any caterpillars
Capsid bugs	Ragged holes in young leaves, caused by adult bugs and nymphs feeding on the sap. Shoots may be deformed or destroyed. Raised brown patches may appear on the fruits, flowers or buds of apple trees	Apples, beans, currants and others	Spray with recommended proprietary mixture in spring, summer and early autumn to deter the bugs. Once symptoms are spotted, the bugs have usually gone. Clear up all garden debris in winter to prevent them overwintering near your plants
Flea beetles	Eats through seedlings in particular, leaving small, neat holes	Brassicas, radish and turnips	Evening, rather than daytime watering discourages the pest
Gooseberry sawflies	Leaves become stripped to their skeletons by caterpillars that are green with black spots	Gooseberries	Spray with proprietary mixture in late spring or when symptoms first appear. Pick off eggs and caterpillars from the undersides of leaves
Shothole	Leaves develop brown patches which turn into holes. Caused by leaf-spotting fungus or bacterial canker	Cherries, plums and peaches	Feed plants every year, mulch in spring and keep well-watered to guard against disease. Spray with a recommended fungicide in summer and autumn

Other possible causes: **Slugs and snails** page 147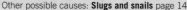

DISTORTED LEAVES

PROBLEM	IDENTIFICATION	AFFECTED	TREATMENT
Celery leaf fly	Maggots burrow into leaves, leaving trails of brown blisters. Growth becomes checked and plant will, ultimately, die	Celery, parsnips and other root crops	Check leaves and crush blisters as soon as you see them. Pick off badly infected leaves and burn them to prevent the pest spreading
Eelworms	Eelworms attack crops, causing the leaves to become swollen and distorted	Many vegetable crops and strawberries	Always buy good seed from a reputable dealer, as this is generally treated against eelworm attack
Frit fly	Larvae eat into the growing plant, causing stunted growth and distorted, ragged leaves. Attack generally occurs in early summer	Sweetcorn	Spray with a recommended proprietary mixture when the plants have produced just a few leaves. If attacks of this pest are common in your area, it is better to sow seed under glass, rather than sowing direct into the ground. This makes it harder for the pest to reach the young plants
Onion eelworms	Leaves become swollen and distorted and bulbs are soft	Chives, garlic, onions and shallots	Pull up and burn infected plants. Onions grown from seed are less likely to be affected than those grown from sets. Follow a strict crop rotation plan and do not grow onions on ground you know to be infested for at least three years
Peach leaf curl	Attacks peach leaves, showing up first as large, red blisters which turn white, then brown. The leaves become curled and crumpled before dying and falling off	Peaches	Spray with recommended proprietary mixtures in late winter, as the buds begin to swell, repeating 10–14 days later and again in the autumn, just before the leaves start to fall
Pear leaf blister mites	Tiny insects which feed on the leaves and produce tiny browny-pink blisters	Pears	Mites first appear in spring, so pick off and burn infected leaves after this time. Bad attacks can be controlled with proprietary mixtures
Petal blight fungus	Large, dark spots appear on the heads of globe artichokes	Globe artichokes	Spray with proprietary mixtures when buds develop and every two weeks thereafter
Reversion	A serious virus disease caused by big bud (see page 149). The leaves become distorted and there is a poor crop, if any	Blackcurrants	Pull up and burn infected plants. Avoid the disease by buying only certified disease-free plants
Whiptail	The leaves begin to shrink towards the central vein	Cauliflowers, broccoli, kohl rabi	Make sure the soil is not too acid and, if so, treat accordingly
White blister	Leaves become covered with white blisters	Brassicas, salsify and scorzonera	Remove and destroy leaves. Caught in its early stages, this should not affect plants adversely

Other possible causes: **Slugs and snails** page 147

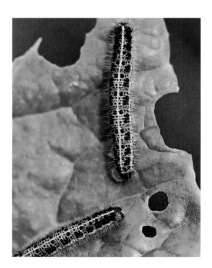

Left *The caterpillars of the cabbage white butterfly are bright and easy to spot: pick them off and destroy any clusters of eggs you find.*

Right *Aphids are among the most common pests on fruit and vegetable crops, and elsewhere in the ornamental garden. They will distort growth and ruin harvests. To reduce the problem and keep spraying to a minimum, try to encourage insect predators, like ladybirds, lacewings and hoverflies into your plot (see page 142).*

DIRECTORY OF PESTS AND DISEASES

DISCOLOURED LEAVES

PROBLEM	IDENTIFICATION	AFFECTED	TREATMENT
Celery leaf spot	Brown spots with black centres appear on the leaves	Celery	Spray with proprietary mixtures and buy only good seed from reputable suppliers, which will have been treated to safeguard against attack from this disease
Downy mildew	Sometimes attacks young plants under glass. Yellow spots appear on top surface of leaves and a furry, greyish-brown growth forms underneath	Brassicas, courgettes, onions	Keep the atmosphere dry and pay more attention to hygiene in the greenhouse
Fire blight	Causes flowers to blacken and shrivel, leaves to turn brown and wither, and shoots to die back	Apples and pears	Fire blight is currently a notifiable disease. If you have a case in your garden, inform Defra, who will advise you what to do
Glasshouse red spider mites	Tiny insects, which feed on the sap of plants, particularly tree fruits, causing the leaves to become mottled before turning a yellowish bronze and dying. They are active during the summer and early autumn	Greenhouse plants, including tree fruits grown under glass	Spray with recommended proprietary mixtures. Keep leaves syringed with water and dampen nearby paths
Grey mould (Botrytis)	Brown spots appear on leaves, and grey mould then forms on these. Fruits begin to rot and are covered with grey mould. The plants will wilt and die	Many crops, particularly lettuce grown through the winter and strawberries	Do not grow plants in cold, damp conditions; check plants under glass or cloches regularly and provide good ventilation. Choose disease-resistant varieties if growing crops in winter
Leek moth	Irregular white lines appear on the leaves. These are left by the maggots of the moth as they tunnel through the leaves	Leeks and onions	Spray with proprietary mixtures
Mildew	The whole plant becomes covered in mildew and the leaves curl	Many	Spray with recommended proprietary mixtures and increase watering. Ensure good air circulation around the plant
Mosaic virus	Leaves and fruits of plants turn yellow and mottled. Eventually growth becomes stunted and the fruits do not develop properly	Many, but particularly cucumber	Disease is spread by greenfly, so control these by paying attention to good garden hygiene
Red spider mites	Tiny creatures which feed on the leaves, turning them a dusty red colour. Spin very fine webs between the leaves	Pulses and fruit trees	These usually only attack plants in a very hot, dry atmosphere. Water regularly and mulch, to keep up the moisture levels
Rust	Brownish spots on leaves, that become twisted or distorted	Beetroot, spinach beet, leeks and sometimes mint	Pull off leaves and destroy them. Spray with recommended proprietary treatment
Virus diseases	Leaves become discoloured and often distorted	Many	Dig up and burn affected plants. Grow only certified disease-free plants to minimise the risk of disease

Other possible causes: **Bacterial canker** page 144 **Carrot flies** page 151

Far right *Red spider mite attacks pulses, such as peas and beans, the glasshouse red spider mite is a common problem on all kinds of plants grown under glass.*

Right *Rusty-looking brown spots on leaves are a sign of the disease, rust. Remove and destroy any affected leaves to halt the spread of the problem.*

DISTORTED OR WILTED SHOOTS

PROBLEM	IDENTIFICATION	AFFECTED	TREATMENT
Gall weevil	Makes hollow swellings on the roots, stunting the plant's growth	Brassicas	Pull up and burn affected plants
Mealy cabbage aphids	Masses of tiny round-bodied insects, which cluster on leaves and stems, causing distortion to the plant's growth	Brassicas	Spray with recommended insecticide and encourage insect predators to control the pest
Slugs and snails	Irregular shaped holes in leaves, slime trails on surrounding paths and stones, complete destruction of young plants	Many, particularly young seedlings	Remove plant debris regularly to avoid creating conditions where slugs and snails thrive. Pick off slugs and snails and destroy them and try to encourage wildlife into your garden to control these pests for you. Use slug pellets only where they cannot cause harm to other wildlife or animals

Other possible causes: **Pear leaf blister mites** page 145 **Root aphids** page 148

PROBLEMS WITH STEMS, BARK OR BRANCHES

PROBLEM	IDENTIFICATION	AFFECTED	TREATMENT
Cane spot	A fungus which causes purple spots to appear on the canes. These later change to white and the cane eventually splits	Blackberries, raspberries and loganberries	Cut out and burn badly infected canes and spray with recommended proprietary mixtures
Apple canker	Small hollows of dead-looking wood appear on the twigs and shoots. If left, they get larger until the whole branch dies	Apples	Cut out diseased wood and burn it. Seal the cuts with canker paint. Proprietary sprays are available for severe cases. Trees grown on waterlogged soil seem to be more susceptible to attack
Coral spot	A mass of red spots develops, usually on old wood	Tree fruits and currants	Cut back all affected areas to at least 15cm (6in) past the infection and burn. Seal all cuts with a wound-sealing paint
Cutworms	Worms eat through the stems at ground level. The greenish-grey caterpillars may be visible on the ground around the plants	Many root vegetables	Make sure weed growth is controlled, to make it hard for the pest to move from plant to plant
Spur blight	A fungus disease which, like cane spot, causes purple spots on canes. The leaves wither and canes snap in bad cases	Blackberries, raspberries and loganberries	Cut out and burn canes and spray others with recommended proprietary mixtures
Woolly aphids	Aphids leave tufts of waxy wool on branches and twigs. Some may develop into galls	Apples	This is difficult to control. Spray with a recommended proprietary mixture as soon as you spot the symptoms

Other possible causes: **Fire blight** page 146

Far left *Apple trees are particularly at risk from woolly aphids, which can lead to more serious disease.*

Left *Shredded leaves - even plants that disappear overnight - are often the result of slug attack. These slimy pests can destroy an entire crop.*

WILTING OR WITHERED PLANT

PROBLEM	IDENTIFICATION	AFFECTED	TREATMENT
Blackleg	A black rot develops at the base of stems, causing them to become soft; leaves turn yellow and the plant eventually dies	Potatoes	Use only certified disease-free seed potatoes
Cabbage root flies	Small white maggots feed on roots (particularly on recently transplanted seedlings), causing leaves to turn a blue-grey colour and plants to wilt and collapse	Cabbages and other brassicas	The cabbage root fly lays its eggs on the soil surface and the hatched maggots burrow into the ground, eating stems and roots. Prevent them doing so by fitting a plastic or rubber disc round the stem of the young plant and pushing it just below the surface to create a physical barrier
Club root	One of the most common diseases of brassicas. Unpleasant-smelling swellings form on the root, stunting the plant's growth. The leaves turn yellow and wilt	Brassicas, turnips and radishes	Always dig, rather than pull roots up to ensure that none are left in the ground. The disease can stay in the soil for years. Diseased plants must be burned. Alternatively, lime the soil. If possible, leave land entirely dormant, growing nothing on it for a year or two after an attack. Grow crops in raised beds on poorly drained soil to reduce attacks and look for the few disease-resistant varieties
Damping off	A fungus causes seedlings to rot at ground level and die	Seedlings under glass or grown in crowded, wet conditions. Plants only vulnerable until they develop their third pair of leaves	Destroy infected seedlings. Sow sparingly, water carefully and ensure good ventilation to avoid the disease. Always use clean seed trays, sterilised seed compost and only water with clean water, not that from a water butt
Die-back	Fungus which makes young branches and shoots wither and die suddenly	Mostly fruit trees	Prevent the fungus entering breaks or cuts in the wood by sealing any pruning cuts with wound-sealing paint. Cut off affected branches and seal the cuts
Foot rot	Root shrivels, causing foliage to turn yellow and stems to turn a browny red colour before rotting	Pulses and tomatoes	Follow strict crop rotation and avoid replanting on infected ground. Always use sterile compost for plants grown in containers
Honey fungus	Leaves wither and shoots die back and fungal growths appear. The plant will eventually die	Vines, figs	Dig up and burn dead plants and change or sterilise soil before attempting to replant in the same place
Leather-jackets	Fat, grey-brown grubs living in the soil attack the roots, causing plants to turn yellow and wilt. The plants may eventually die	Some vegetables, particularly brassicas	Fork the soil to turn it over and expose the grubs to birds. Alternatively, spread grass clippings on the soil, cover with sacking or cardboard overnight to draw the grubs to the surface then uncover and remove the now-infested grass clippings or leave the grubs for birds to pick out. Leatherjackets are crane fly larvae, so look out for adult flies and discourage or get rid of them
Onion flies	Maggots hatch from eggs laid on the surface of the soil and tunnel into the developing onion. It becomes soft and unpleasant. Attack can be detected by the purple-grey streaks that appear on the leaves	Onions	Onion sets are not usually attacked, and the pest is most prevalent on dry soils. Dig up and burn infected plants. Attacks are less likely if the plant is handled as little as possible during development. Handling increases the smell which attracts the onion fly
Root aphids	White or yellow-coloured aphids attack lettuce roots in summer. The plants become stunted and wilt	Lettuce	This is comparatively rare, but can generally be avoided altogether by growing disease-resistant varieties
Violet root rot	Foliage turns yellow and the roots become covered with a purple-coloured fungus. Although the attack usually starts on older plants, the disease will quickly spread to other crops	Mostly carrots, parsnips and asparagus plus some fruit crops	Dig up affected plants and burn them
Wire stem	The stems of young plants turn brown and begin to shrink	Brassicas	Raise seedlings in sterilised compost and treat the soil with a recommended top dressing

FRUIT DISORDERS

PROBLEM	IDENTIFICATION	AFFECTED	TREATMENT
Apple mildew	New spring shoots and leaves are covered with a powdery, grey-white coating	Apples	Spray with recommended proprietary mixtures to help keep the disease at bay, but cut out and burn badly affected growth. Remove all diseased shoots the following autumn. Make sure the tree is well watered in dry weather
Apple sawflies	Tiny ant-like flies lay eggs in spring blossom. Caterpillars hatch and burrow into the developing fruit, causing scarring on the skin and the fruit to fall before it is ripe	Apples and plums	Spray with recommended proprietary mixture weekly when the blossom starts to fall
Apple scab	Green, brown or black scabby blisters form on the skin of the apple, often making it distorted. Leaves and shoots can be similarly affected. Blisters on leaves and shoots will burst through the bark, causing cracks and scabs that can let in other infections	Apples	Remove and burn all infected growth. Spray the tree with recommended proprietary mixtures as soon as the flower buds appear
Big bud	A serious condition caused by the blackcurrant gall mite. It makes buds swell and fail to develop further, leaving you with a reduced crop or none at all	Blackcurrants	Pick off infected buds and spray bushes with recommended proprietary mixtures
Bitter pit	Brown spots develop on apples, running through the flesh	Apples	Prevent the soil beneath the tree from drying out by mulching. Spray with recommended proprietary treatment
Codling moths	Caterpillars burrow into the fruit of apples and pears. You may spot entry holes through the eye end of the fruit, but damage is rarely spotted before the fruit is cut open	Apples and pears	Spray with recommended proprietary treatment in early summer and again three weeks later to kill any developing caterpillars
Gooseberry mildew (American)	A white powdery coating forms on leaves, shoots and fruits. The growth at the tips of the shoots becomes distorted	Gooseberries	Cut out and destroy diseased shoots and spray with recommended proprietary mixtures or a weak solution of washing soda. Keep well pruned to ensure good light penetration to the bush. Grow disease-resistant varieties
Gooseberry mildew (European)	A white powdery coating develops on the upper surface of leaves and sometimes the underside and berries, too. Most common on old bushes	Gooseberries, blackcurrants and redcurrants	Cut out and destroy diseased shoots and spray with recommended proprietary mixtures or a weak solution of washing soda. Keep well pruned to ensure good light penetration to the bush. Not as damaging as American gooseberry mildew
Gooseberry sawfly	Caterpillars (green with black spots) eat the leaves, reducing them to skeletons	Gooseberries	From late spring onwards pick off and destroy any caterpillars. Spray with recommended proprietary mixture
Pear midges	Only occurs in certain places, but once it has attacked a tree, it will continue to do so until the tree has been thoroughly sprayed with a recommended proprietary mixture. The maggots of the pest bore through the skin and feed on the pears, slowing down the growth and making the fruit distorted. Infected pears will soon fall off the tree	Pears	Remove infected fruit and burn it. Keep the ground beneath the tree well-cultivated, so that predators have a chance to eat the pests, before they climb up the tree
Raspberry beetles	Maggots tunnel into the fruits, making them distorted and inedible	Raspberries	Spray with recommended proprietary mixtures as the fruits begin to change colour
Silver leaf	Leaves turn a silvery colour and the inner wood of branches turns purplish-brown. Eventually the branches will die	Many, including plums	Cut out all infected wood to about 15cm (6in) beyond the discoloured area and seal the wounds with protective paint. Make sure all pruning cuts are well sealed, because the disease enters through cut or open spots on the wood
Strawberry beetles	Fruit is eaten as it ripens, as if by birds, but glossy beetles up to 2cm long can be found beneath the plants	Strawberries	Keep the ground around plants free of plant debris and weeds to reduce the places for beetles to hide. Spray with recommended proprietary mixture when plants are not in bloom

Other possible causes: **Apple canker** page 147, **Capsid bugs** page 144

PROBLEMS WITH PULSES, TOMATOES AND LEAFY VEGETABLES

PROBLEM	IDENTIFICATION	AFFECTED	TREATMENT
Anthracnose of beans	Pods and stems develop sunken dark brown patches and brown spots develop on leaves.	Mostly dwarf and climbing French beans; sometimes runner beans	Dig up and destroy any infected plants and do not save and dry seed from them for replanting next year. Always follow a strict crop rotation plan to avoid growing beans on the same infected site the following year, as the disease will overwinter in the soil
Bean seed flies	Maggots in the soil eat freshly sown seeds	Beans and other pulses	Dress drills with proprietary mixtures
Blight	Brown-black blotches form on the upper side of leaves and a white furry coating underneath. Leaves eventually turn brown and rot. Fruits also develop a brown rot	Tomatoes and potatoes	Spray plants that are vulnerable to infection with a recommended proprietary treatment as soon as the fruits begin to set. Avoid growing tomatoes in the damp conditions that encourage blight and do not overcrowd them in the greenhouse. Cut off all affected foliage as soon as you notice signs of the problem
Blossom end rot	Brown or black circular discolorations, which appear on the bottom of the young, developing fruits	Tomatoes, peppers and aubergines	Keep plants evenly moist at all times – the problem is often a result of plants drying out and then being watered copiously. Pay particular attention to plants grown in growing bags, which can dry out quickly and may need watering several times a day
Blotchy ripening	Hard green or yellow patches appear on fruits, particularly on lower trusses	Tomatoes	Keep plants evenly moist and the temperature not too high. Try not to grow plants in poor soil or to let them grow too fast in poor light. Grow disease-resistant varieties to avoid the problem
Buck-eye rot	Brown rings appear on the tomatoes at the lower trusses	Tomatoes	Take care not to splash the fruit when watering the plant
Celery heart rot	Centres of celery clumps are wet, with a slimy brown rot	Celery	Slug damage or frost damage allow bacteria to enter plant, so protect from both to minimise attack. Follow a strict crop rotation plan to avoid growing celery again on infected soil
Cabbage whiteflies	Small whiteflies, which feed on the underside of leaves, leaving sticky discoloration. The growth of leaves is held back	Brassicas	Spray with proprietary insecticide
Chocolate spot	Dark brown spots appear on leaves	Broad beans, in particular, but also other crops	Disease is not usually serious, but prevent it by making sure the soil is well-limed and has had applications of potash. Pick off and destroy the affected leaves on nearby plants before sowing more seeds
Leaf mould	The upper surfaces of the leaves display yellow spots and mould appears on the under surfaces	Tomatoes grown under glass	A warm, humid atmosphere is the perfect situation for this disease to develop and spread. Maintain good ventilation in greenhouses and control the disease with copper-based sprays. Grow disease-resistant varieties. Remove and destroy affected foliage promptly
Pea and bean weevils	Small, light brown beetle, which is active at night, when it eats leaves. Only affects young plants	Peas, beans and other pulses	Hoe between rows to disturb sleeping insects and make them good prey for birds
Pea moths	Eggs laid on the leaves hatch into maggots, which tunnel into the pods to feed on the developing peas. Can often be detected by the tiny holes which appear in the pods	Peas	Eggs are laid in mid-summer, so early and late crops should escape attack. Control by spraying with proprietary mixtures
Pea thrips	Tiny, winged insects which eat pea leaves. If not controlled, they can cause stunted growth and poor flower development	Peas and other pulses	Keep plants well-watered and spray them well, too
Splitting	The skins of the developing fruit splits either down or around the fruit	Tomatoes	Water and feed the plant regularly. Maintain even moisture in the compost at all times – do not allow the plant to dry out and then water it generously

ROOT VEGETABLE DISORDERS

PROBLEM	IDENTIFICATION	AFFECTED	TREATMENT
Beet fly	Maggots hatch on beetroot leaves, tunnelling through them	Beetroot	Check leaves frequently and pick off and destroy damaged ones
Black leaf	Occurs in cold, wet soils. The bottom of the stem begins to rot, the roots shrivel, the whole stem softens and the plant becomes stunted, with yellow growth. The tubers are wet, soft and slimy	Potatoes	Follow a strict crop rotation to minimise the likelihood of disease. Destroy any affected plants immediately
Black slugs	Slugs eat into developing roots	Many, including root crops	Slugs are hard to control, as they live beneath the ground, so are difficult to detect until you harvest the crop and discover the damage. Try setting traps, as described for wireworms (below)
Carrot flies	Maggots eat into roots. Leaves turn a reddish colour then yellow, and wilt	Carrots, parsnips, celery and parsley	Sow seed as thinly as possible to keep later thinning to a minimum. Avoid handling plants and any thinnings as much as possible, as this releases a scent that attracts the flies. Sow early and late to avoid the time when adult flies are most active. Try erecting a barrier around the crop, growing in pots more than 45cm (18in) high, as this is above the level at which the adult flies fly, or growing under horticultural fleece. Companion planting with onions or dill is also said to deter the adult flies
Neck rot	Attacks onions in storage. It appears as a soft, brown rot, which will affect the whole onion and make it inedible	Onions	Make sure onions are completely dry before storing. If conditions are wet at harvest time, bring the onions indoors at once and dry them there. Crops can be treated with proprietary mixtures which help to discourage the disease. Do not overfeed crops – large roots are more susceptible
Parsnip canker	Attacks parsnips, causing rusty brown discolorations near the top	Parsnips	Sow disease-resistant varieties and follow strict crop rotation plans. Discourage carrot flies, as these help to spread the disease
Potato blight	Occurs in damp, autumn conditions, so early varieties should not be affected. Leaves become blotched with brown marks and the lower ones turn yellow. The tubers develop similar brown marks and turn rotten	Potatoes	Spray with proprietary mixtures
Potato cyst eelworms	Small cysts develop on roots. The crop is vastly reduced and plants may wilt and die. Earlies may escape attack as the eelworm is not usually active until mid-summer	Potatoes	Use certified disease-free seed potatoes and follow a strict crop rotation plan
Potato scab	Occurs in soil which has been heavily limed or does not contain sufficient organic matter. Scabby patches occur on the skin of the potatoes	Potatoes, but also found on beetroots, radishes, swedes and turnips	If caught in the early stages, scabs can be removed before cooking. Later, too much of the crop will be affected. Dig up and destroy if the attack is severe
Swift moths	Whitish caterpillars feed on plant roots. The caterpillars may be visible when digging or hoeing the soil	Carrots, parsnips and chicory	Pay close attention to garden hygiene. Pick out and destroy any caterpillars you see in the soil. Control may be necessary with proprietary mixtures
Wart disease	One of the most serious, but now less common diseases of potatoes, caused by a soil-borne fungus. Large, warty growths appear over the surface of the potato, which will eventually disintegrate	Potatoes	This is a notifiable disease; if your crop develops it, you must notify your local authority or Defra. Use only modern, disease-free seed potato varieties. Destroy all diseased potatoes
White rot	Attacks onions and leeks, turning the leaves yellow. They wither and die, revealing the base of the plant, which will be covered with a white mould	Onions, leeks and garlic	Dig up and burn infected plants. Follow a strict crop rotation and sow seed very thinly. Seed drills can be treated with proprietary mixtures to help to deter disease
Wireworms	Larvae eat into developing roots. The small worm-like creatures may be seen in abundance around the roots as you dig or hoe between rows	Root crops, potatoes and lettuces	Make traps by sticking a short length of stick into a potato and pushing it into the ground. The larvae will eat into this. Pull it out and destroy it

Possible other causes: **Cabbage root flies** page 148, **Leatherjackets** page 148

KEEPING ANIMALS

Keeping Animals
Pigs
Goats
Chickens
Ducks, Geese and Turkeys
Bees

Keeping Animals

Livestock can be a delight, that provides you with highly nutritious and tasty produce. Equally, it can cost you more money than any you might make or save. Try to remain business-like about your livestock – they are not pets.

The first and most important thing to remember is that keeping any livestock is a responsibility. The happiness and welfare of the animals is in your hands and even if you eventually mean to put them on the table in a tasty casserole, you have a duty to give them a happy existence while they are alive. Although many smallholders believe they are saving their animals from mass-production conditions, they may inadvertently be inflicting just as much cruelty through ignorance of their habits.

Food and shelter
Always ensure that you have housing ready before your birds or animals arrive. You don't have to buy new, purpose-built sties or hen houses: if you already have outbuildings or sheds, adapt and use these. Your animals will be happiest if you can keep them in conditions that emulate their natural life as closely as possible; and happy animals are healthy animals.

It is difficult to give rules about feeding, because animals have likes and dislikes and differences in appetite, just like people. Spend time watching your animals and get to know what they do and do not like.

Keeping healthy
This book does not aim to offer advice on treating animals that are ill – you will always need professional help from a vet – but animals kept on a small scale in clean, healthy surroundings should seldom succumb to disease. The rule is that if you notice anything wrong with your livestock isolate them to stop the problem spreading to the others and call the vet.

Balancing the books
Few people would claim that their eggs or honey cost them nothing, or that their pork was vastly cheaper than any they could buy. The point about home-produced food is that it is of an infinitely higher quality than any available in the shops.

It is a good idea to keep records – how much honey the bees produced and when; the amount of milk your goats give night and morning through the year; the eggs you get each day, and so on. By doing so

Keeping chickens is a good place to start if you are not used to livestock. With a secure hen house, they need little other attention.

you can spot irregularities when they occur and gain a more business-like view of your enterprise.

Start small
Do not try to become a poultry-keeper, bee-keeper, goat-keeper and pig-keeper all in one week. Do it slowly, one type of animal at a time, making sure you can fit them into your daily routine. If you try to do everything at once, you will be far more likely to fail and to give up.

Before keeping any of the animals discussed on the following pages, you should check with your local authorities and Defra to ensure you are not contravening any by-laws and to obtain all the necessary licences.

Keeping Pigs

If kept in the right conditions, pigs are fairly easy animals to keep and rear, but they demand daily hard work and are big, strong animals, so be prepared for the physical aspects of becoming a pig-keeper.

Mucking-out the pig house is at least a daily chore and heavy work. The pigs must be moved into the yard while you do it and may not always be cooperative when you try to guide them outside. An adult pig is strong enough to bowl you over.

If you keep pigs to sell – and if you breed from your sow, she will have eight or 10 piglets each time, so you

It is not a myth that pigs love to wallow in mud. Wherever you keep your pigs, you must allow them a muddy, wet spot where they can cool down in hot weather.

are unlikely to be able to keep them all. Also, consider that the price of pork fluctuates more than almost any other foodstuff, and to get the best price for your stock you may need to process the butchered meat into bacon, sausages or other goods that can be sold at a greater profit.

LIVING REQUIREMENTS

There are two main ways in which you can keep pigs: in a permanent yard with a sty or shed, or to allow them to live free-range within a large fenced-off area of your land.

Never consider keeping your pigs in a concrete sty. You may find this option suggested in old books, but pigs live by the snout – that is, their whole life consists of rootling through the ground – and most people would now agree that to deny them this by keeping them on concrete is cruel.

Licences and regulations

Before you can buy any pigs – even just one pig – you must first register your land as an agricultural holding. You must keep records of your livestock, tag your animals, comply with transport regulations and be able to produce a licence to transport livestock. Check with your local authority and Defra (there is good information on its website) about how to get started and what you need to know and to provide.

Space and fencing

To let pigs roam freely demands a lot of land – at least 2.4 hectares (6 acres) – but it is ideal for both you and the pigs. Pigs are the best cultivators of all; better by far than any mechanical equipment which

is subject to breakdown. They will hunt out all the roots – weeds and all – turning the ground over and fertilising it at the same time. You can be sure that yours will be the most delicious pork you have ever tasted if it is kept in this way.

Pigs will lean against the fences that confine them and rub against posts and rails, soon dislodging the stakes and weakening the whole structure, unless it is really strong and firm. At the bottom there should be at least one strand of barbed wire to stop them nosing their way through underneath. The fence should be at least 1m (3ft) high: pigs can jump, particularly if they are frightened, and could leap over a lower fence.

Should your pigs escape (and they almost certainly will from time to time), they are easy to retrieve.

Providing they know you and you have a bucket of their favourite food, they will follow you back to the yard.

Providing shelter

Housing for pigs can be as simple or as sophisticated as you wish to make it, as long as it is dry and draught-proof. Earth floors are fine, as pigs love mud. An alternative is a concrete floor, covered with wood – concrete on its own is rather cold. In either case, a layer of straw as bedding will be appreciated.

One of the simplest and best shelters is called the Roadnight shelter; they are also known as pig arks. These consist of one blocked wall, often made from wood, and one open wall, topped with an arched roof of corrugated iron.

Ideally you should be able to shut the pigs in, but if one side of the

shed is open, make sure it is not in the direction of the prevailing wind or driving rain.

Pigs rarely soil their living quarters during the day, preferring to do this outside, so the house should not get too mucky, but this area should still be cleaned out daily, because if they are shut in at night they will muck somewhere. It will make your job of cleaning out easier if the accommodation is tall enough for you to stand up inside.

Somewhere to wallow

Pigs love mud and, in hot weather in particular, it is important to provide them with a wet, muddy hollow in which they can wallow. The mud will help them to cool down and when it dries on their skin it will, like sunblock, also help to protect them from burning in the sun.

LIVING REQUIREMENTS

Your decision about how to keep your pigs could be made for you by the amount of land you have. To keep pigs free range you will need a large amount of fallow land that you can divide into areas for the pigs. They will need to move to a new area whenever each one is cleared, but cannot return to a patch of land for at least three years. In a permanent yard, you will need to provide food for the animals and you must provide water troughs in both situations.

OPTION	HOUSING	PROS	CONS	FEEDING AND OTHER REQUIREMENTS
Permanent yard	Yard surrounded by brick wall at least 1m (3ft) high or strong pig wire fixed to sturdy posts. Use common sense and make the yard large enough for pigs not to be overcrowded. Simple brick shed or pig ark for shelter, with deep bedding. Concrete yard sloping to a drain	Easily contained to stop pigs from eating your crops. Strong walls stop pigs escaping. Convenient for farrowing sows and looking after piglets	Fences must be very secure, as pigs can easily knock them over	Throw dried bracken or straw into the yard from time to time for pigs to rootle in. Feed with garden waste, potatoes, other root vegetables and comfrey plus turf for minerals
Free range	Area marked out with very strong fencing. Movable pig ark or shelter made from bales of straw with a corrugated iron roof. Provide deep bedding and encourage pigs in at night	Outstanding tasting meat; pigs will cultivate rough ground for you	Do not move pigs back to a patch for at least three years: parasites that attack them will remain in the soil for this long	About 10 pigs can be kept in 0.2 hectares (0.5 acres); move them to another patch when they have exhausted each one. If grass is plentiful, feed once a day with meal or concentrated food. Supplement with additional food (above) as necessary

ACQUIRING PIGS

As with all livestock, it is best to acquire your pigs from a local farmer or dealer, so the breed you buy will depend on what is available. Livestock markets are busy and intimidating places and not for the faint-hearted. A local breeder is a far better option for a smallholder.

Some of the most common breeds are shown on page 159. Bear in mind that some of the new breeds, developed specifically with meat production in mind, could be rather more highly-strung and susceptible to disease than some of the more old-fashioned types.

The Large White is a good and popular breed, as is the Landrace. Crosses between these two are also good pigs to keep, and all these breeds are renowned for being good-tempered. Keeping your own pigs is also a good opportunity to rear some of the traditional local breeds, such as the Gloucestershire Old Spot.

Buying weaners or breeding pigs

There are two possible systems for small-time pig-keepers to adopt. One is to buy eight-week-old weaners, keep them for 10–12 weeks (or longer if you prefer), and then slaughter them, and the other is to keep a sow and breed from her.

The first method is undoubtedly the most economic and also the least trouble. It also means you can keep just a couple of pigs to eat yourself, and you can sell the rest. If your sow has 8–10 piglets in a litter, you will need plenty of space to keep them comfortably until you can sell them on.

When buying weaners, look for piglets with long, lean backs and no signs of lameness. You will need a strong cage to get them home and a flat bed pick-up truck or trailer to transport the cage.

Moving pigs

Getting a pig to go where you want it to can be a challenge. A simple, but traditional aid is a long sheet of

Farrowing rails

These are essential at breeding times to prevent the sow from lying on her piglets. You can construct a frame by bolting or screwing wooden rails to some low, sturdy stakes. The piglets will naturally choose to huddle in the corners of the sty and will be protected by the rails when the sow lies there with them.

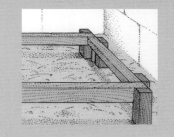

plywood, with hand holes cut in the top edge. Use this to direct your pigs in and out of a trailer and to and from the yard or pigsty when you get them home.

BUILDING A PIG PEN

You can build a sty for your pigs if you wish to improve their living conditions. This can easily be constructed from building blocks with a corrugated iron roof. Make it around 2.4 x 2.4m (8 x 8ft) and tall enough for you to stand up inside when cleaning it out. If you want to include windows, place them near the roof of the sty, opening outwards from the bottom, so that the pigs have ventilation without a draught. A concrete yard is easy to clean out and essential for giving the pigs somewhere to exercise and explore. Always include a sturdy drinking trough; pigs drink a lot of water, although they do not mind if it is not clean.

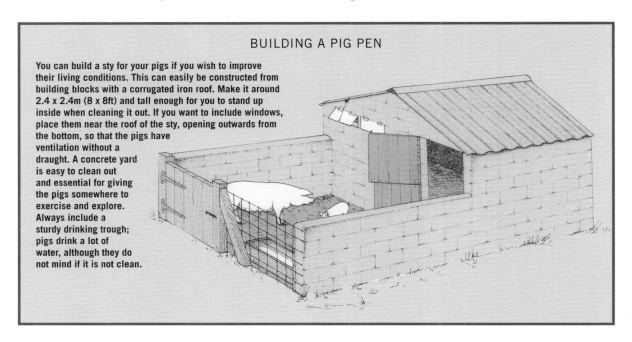

FEEDING

You are unlikely to be able to grow sufficient quantities of the root vegetables and potatoes on which pigs live, so you will almost certainly have to feed them some supplementary grain, as well.

Even if you do have a plentiful supply of root vegetables, if you are aiming to fatten pigs for slaughter, supplementary feeding is essential. The best form of concentrates are the commercially-prepared pig nuts, but these are not cheap. Eight-week-old weaners will need about 900g (2lb) of these per day, given in a morning and evening feed. This amount should gradually be increased to 1.8–2kg (4-4½lb) by the time they are about four months old.

A sow being used for breeding will want more and then still more food while she is pregnant and feeding her piglets. In addition she will need milk (preferably from goats if you keep them).

Although pigs naturally root about for food, it is a good idea to feed them pig nuts or other concentrated food in a trough, rather than scattering it on the ground. This will save it from being wasted by getting trampled into the mud or urinated on. Scatter vegetables and other larger foods (below) across their yard to give them something tasty to hunt around for.

Will pigs eat anything?

Besides their concentrates, pigs will enjoy a variety of other foodstuffs. Root vegetables are very important – Jerusalem artichokes, swedes, turnips, parsnips and so on – and these can be grown in their yard or on a patch of land where they are allowed to roam, so that they

can dig them out themselves. They like potatoes (although these are more digestible if boiled), and will appreciate some greens. You can provide this by giving them cuttings from hawthorn or beech trees for example, or nettles. Other things they like are apples (windfalls), comfrey, grass, clover and any of the brassica greens.

Traditionally, pigs are known for finishing off all the household scraps and kitchen waste, but new regulations following BSE outbreaks in the UK prohibit the feeding of cooked food waste to livestock or, in fact, any food that has been in the kitchen. You can still give them peelings or top-and-tailings from vegetables trimmed while still in the vegetable plot and they will happily consume any bruised or damaged fruit or vegetables that you do not want to keep for your own consumption.

If your pigs are free-range and still clearing the ground, they will really only need the supplementary corn –

Pigs will rootle for food on the ground, but pellets and small food are best given in a trough or bucket, so they don't get trampled underfoot and wasted.

the rest they should be able to forage for themselves.

Pigs drink lots of water, but unlike other animals such as goats, this does not have to be sparkling clean and clear. Give the water in troughs and make sure there is always enough in them.

MANAGEMENT AND BREEDING

Your pigs should give you remarkably little trouble and generally need very little attention.

In hot weather, throw a bucket of water over the pigs and another onto the ground in their pen. Pigs dig holes to sleep in and like these to be damp. Make sure your pigs have somewhere to shelter from hot sun, as they can suffer from sunburn.

If you do want to breed from a sow, let her have one season first (this will be at about six months old), and then breed from her when she is about a year old. It is possible to artificially inseminate pigs, although the timing is critical, and you must be sure of what you are doing, too.

The alternative is to take her to a local pig-breeder, providing they are willing to take her (some will not, because of the risk of infection). They will generally let her run with a boar for a few days until they think she has been served.

Taking care of piglets

The gestation period for pigs is 14–16 weeks, and a pig will usually have between 8–10 piglets, which she can rear easily without any additional help. Shut her in the shed or house to have her litter. It is always a good idea to construct a farrowing rail (see page 157) in the shed where the sow is to farrow, to stop her lying on her piglets and inadvertently crushing them.

A farrowing rail is an arrangement of very strong bars, which should be raised about 25cm (9in) from the ground and a similar distance away from the wall. It must be strong – old iron bed rails are ideal, or use sturdy wooden battens and rails – and should be firmly bracketed to the wall, or the pig will merely get her snout underneath and wrench it free.

The farrowing rails should be sited along the two walls of the sow's favourite corner of the shed, which is where she is most likely to have her piglets. It is a good idea too, to stack straw bales with gaps between them (like houses of cards) against the other two walls. Then, if the sow does move over there at any time, the piglets can escape into the straw. Lying on the piglets is no wilful act

on the part of the sow; it is merely that she is so big and they are so small that she can crush them all too easily.

If you have a power source at or near the pig shed, then it can be a good idea to install an infra-red lamp (with a red bulb) suspended in one corner, where the piglets can reach but the sow cannot. This provides the piglets with a warm corner to huddle and means that they are then only likely to bother the sow when they want feeding, since they do not need to seek warmth from her too. This is another way to help prevent them getting crushed by her lying on top of them.

The sow must be fed well throughout her pregnancy and while she is feeding her young, and the piglets should be weaned when they are four weeks old. Male piglets should also be castrated at this time, otherwise the pork will be tainted – a condition known as boar taint. This is a job best left for the vet.

Selling your pigs

Pigs can either be sold when they are about 12 weeks old, when they generally weigh about 40kg (90lb) and are known as porkers, or kept until they are about 72kg (160lb), when they are known as baconers.

You will soon discover that breeding pigs and fattening them are two different skills. It may be that you are good at both of them, but more usually you will find that you are better at one than the other and can decide to specialise.

If you keep your pigs to fatten them, you must take them to a local slaughterhouse to be killed and butchered. You can then keep any of the cuts of the animals that you want for your own consumption and freeze them, then sell the rest.

BREEDS OF PIGS

Every country and region has its own traditional local breeds of pig, such as the Gloucestershire Old Spot, Berkshires and Tamworths. Many of these are now considered rare breeds, but they are often hardier than the modern commercial breeds available and keeping your own animals can be a good opportunity to revive this aspect of your local farming tradition.

LARGE WHITE
Long-legged, large-boned pig which is a fast grower and an efficient converter of food into meat. Makes good, lean bacon.

GLOUCESTERSHIRE OLD SPOT
White pig with black spots. Good at grazing and will eat grass and vegetables. Although hardy, it produces small litters.

LANDRACE
Long and lean white breed with floppy ears and short legs (below). Very docile and makes an excellent mother. Good for lean bacon.

SADDLEBACK
Black pig with a band of white across the shoulders. Very hardy all-purpose pig. Sows give milk plentifully.

WELSH
A very old lop-eared breed of Western England, which makes a good mother. Being small, it eats less than the Large White.

LARGE BLACK
Black pig with deep sides. Easy to keep for a novice pig-keeper, as it is hardy, economical to feed and copes well in hot weather.

Keeping Goats

Goats are far better and more practical back-yard animals to keep for milk than cows. They are cheaper and easier to care for, more adaptable, require less space and, by and large, demand much less work and attention.

In return for your little time, goats give adequate milk yields for the average family. High-yielders will give up to 8 litres (14 pints) in summer, though this usually goes down to 1.2–1.8 litres (2–3 pints) in the winter. Providing they are properly fed and cared for, and milked in hygienic conditions, their milk will not be smelly or highly flavoured, as it is often reputed to be.

In fact, few people could tell goats' milk from cows' milk in a blind tasting, yet it has the advantage that it does not carry the tuberculosis bacillus and does not need to be pasteurised. Besides making excellent cheese and yoghurt, it can also help sufferers from eczema and asthma.

The claim that goats smell is really only applicable to male goats (billies) and it is not advisable to keep these anyway. They can be very temperamental and are not productive for the smallholder – only being useful to serve female goats (nannies).

If there is a branch of a goat society nearby, it is a good idea to join. They will give good advice about breeds as well as the practical aspect of goat-keeping.

LIVING REQUIREMENTS

Goats need a dry, draught-proof shed, where they can stand up, turn round and lie down. They are determined escapees, so any fences around their enclosure must be extremely strong and well-erected to withstand their efforts to get out.

The size of your goats' shed will depend on how much room you have and how many goats you intend to keep, but a shed 3 x 4.5m (10 x 15ft) will give ample space

Goats naturally forage on bushes and other greenery, and like to reach up for their food, so always provide hay for them in hay racks mounted on the wall of their shed, rather than in mangers at ground level.

LIVING REQUIREMENTS

The way you choose to keep your goats will be governed by the amount of space you have. If you allow them to graze outdoors, they will strip an area of land of its plant growth, making them useful ground clearers in the early days of your plot. In time, you will need several large areas to rotate if you choose this option. If you have access and grazing rights to an area of common land, you can walk your goat there in the morning and tether it on a long rope to graze for the day.

SYSTEM	HOUSING	FEEDING	OTHER REQUIREMENTS
Out of doors	Dry, draught-proof shed. Deep bedding to cut draughts. Should equal outside temperature to encourage growth of winter coat	Roughage available from grazing. Provide hay at night. Give concentrated feed when giving milk	Salt licks. Access to water. Frequent inspection and handling to keep tame
Strip grazing, rotational grazing	Provide shelter although undercoat will protect from rain. Shut in at night	Allows for fresh grass feeding. Strip grazed kale available in winter. Keep concentrates in dry bins and hay in airy shed	Electric fencing with three wires 40cm, 70cm and 100cm (15in, 28in, 40in) above ground. Salt licks
Tethering with shed (not for young goats)	Roomy shed for when not tethered. Platform for play and exercise	Move frequently to allow fresh grazing with bushes and branches available. Provide hay if there is a shortage of feed	Wide collar; tether-chain; swivel, harness and stake. Shade in sunny weather. Access to water and salt
Yarding with shed	Both shed and yard as large as possible. Fence or wall for looking out but keeping them in	Provide good variety, a garden for greens and grass from the edges	Take for walks for exercise and food. Salt licks and seaweed mineral supplements
Indoors	Roomy pen with light and air. Sleeping platform	Branches tied and suspended from ceiling. Scraps of bread and vegetables	Walks for exercise

Clipping goat hooves

Goats' feet must be trimmed every three weeks or so, or they will grow too long. The operation is best done by two people, with one to talk to and soothe the goat while the other does the cutting. Proper shears make the job easier – the horn is quite tough – although it can be done with a pruning knife and a steady hand. Always cut the hoof carefully.

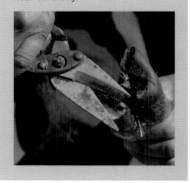

Make sure that any fences around your goat pen are very strong and securely fixed into the ground so that the goats cannot knock them down and escape.

for three grown-up goats to live and move around.

Goats hate cold, windy or wet weather and are best shut inside the shed on days like this, so a divided stable-type door, the bottom half of which should be about 1.2m (4ft) high, will offer some shelter, security and ventilation at the same time. If there is a window, it should be positioned high up and preferably hinged at the bottom to give ventilation without draughts.

The floor should be concrete, and slope slightly towards the back of the shed to aid drainage (there should be a couple of drainage holes in the wall for this, too).

There should be a hay rack on the wall; hang it quite high, as goats are browsers rather than grazers, and therefore naturally reach upwards for their food. They do not like to eat off the floor. The floor itself should be kept covered in straw; keep adding to this as it gets dirty and then clean it out when the floor level has raised by 30–45cm (12–18in). Stack the dirty straw neatly and let it rot – it makes excellent garden manure.

Keep your goats in one place

Goats should be shut in their shed at night, but during the day they can be kept in one of two ways: either in a well-fenced run, or tethered in places that provide suitable food.

If you choose to keep your goats in a run, the area will have to be rested from time to time to give it a chance to recover, so you must have at least a couple of such areas to devote to the goats. Fencing must be very strong: either erect solid, closely spaced paling fencing or drive thick wooden posts 60cm (2ft) into the ground and secure strong wire netting between them. Choose netting used for fencing sheep, not chickens, or goats will merely trample their way through it. Make sure that the fence is a good 1.5m (5ft) high.

If you have access to lots of hedgerow land, where goats can safely be tethered, or alternatively have a lot of spare, scrubby land you want grazed, you can lead your goats out from their shed and tether them in a different spot each day. Goats will usually accept wearing a collar and being walked on a lead, or length of rope.

Make sure there are no poisonous plants in reach where they are tethered, such as rhododendrons, privet, laurel, yew, ragwort or laburnum. Ivy is safe for them to eat, and they find oak leaves delicious. Goats will also make short work of flowers, vegetables and fruit trees, so keep them well away from any of these that you value.

In winter, it is often advisable to keep goats in a concrete yard, as muddy conditions can lead to foot troubles. Provide them with food and tether them out whenever the weather is good enough.

ACQUIRING GOATS

It is not fair to keep a single goat. They are sociable, gregarious and friendly, and one on its own will be miserable. Over two, have as many as you want, according to the land and time you have available and the amount of milk you need.

You can buy goats from any age – as young as four weeks, if you have lots of time to devote to looking after them and do not want milk for 18 months or so. If you want to be able to milk a goat straightaway, you will need to choose one that has kidded – she will go on producing milk for about two years after this.

The advantage of getting a young goat, apart from the cheaper outlay, is that she will get thoroughly used to

you, particularly if you give her the loving care and attention she likes to receive.

FEEDING

Another misconception about goats is that they will eat anything. In fact, it is when they are forced into a bad diet that they give smelly, bad-tasting milk.

Goats are actually very fussy eaters and will not, for example, eat anything that has dropped on the floor of their shed. They require a meal each night and morning of some sort of concentrated food, which could be a formulated dairy food or one mixed for you by your supplier. This should contain broad bran, crushed oats and flaked maize, and possibly any of the following – peas, beans, molasses, barley, linseed cake and salt. This feed should be mixed with some root vegetables and greens.

Use your vegetable trimmings and discards, though nothing that has

been taken into your own kitchen for preparation. Make friends with a local greengrocer and persuade him to let you have the offcuts from greens and any rotting dessert apples and mouldy oranges. Midday snacks of sugar beet are also appreciated. Always feed goats in a metal bucket or bowl – they can nibble at plastic.

How much to feed
The quantity of food to give a goat depends a lot on the age, size and temperament of each individual goat and what else she is eating during the day. Find out what her daily diet has been when you buy her, and gradually change or increase this as necessary.

Concentrates are important for milk production, but if you feed too much they will be wasted, because they will not increase milk production

If you buy goats as kids, you will need to spend a lot of time caring for them in their early weeks, but they will thrive on your love and attention and will learn to trust you.

over and above what is the normal average for that particular breed.

Clean drinking water must be readily available and the container will need frequent washing and cleaning. Goats will not drink from a slimy bucket.

Make sure hay is always provided in the hay rack in the shed, particularly if they are going out to eat on lush pastures during the day. Far from providing goodness, rich grass will just fill an empty belly with water and can cause bloating. It is unwise to let goats graze on really lush meadows for more than one hour a day. They also need a salt or mineral block to lick.

BREEDING AND MILKING

Although it is not uncommon for a maiden goat to come into milk, goats will not normally do so until they have kidded.

The first mating should generally be left until they are 15–18 months old. Some people claim goats can be mated as young as 7 months and, providing they are properly fed, will suffer no ill-effects thereafter; others say this will stunt their growth.

When they come into season – indicated by much wagging of the tail, loud bleating, general nervousness and unease, and maybe a slight mucus discharge from the vulva – they should be taken to a billy as soon as possible.

Take advice from other local goat owners and make sure you choose a good billy to mate her with. The highest success rate in matings occur if the nanny is serviced early in her season. They come into season every 21 days, usually from autumn to late winter.

MILKING A GOAT

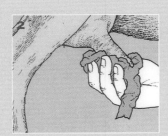

1 Before you take the goat to the milking shed, brush her coat to prevent any dirt falling into the milking bucket from her coat. Get her settled in the milking parlour and give her some food to distract her attention.

2 Wash the udders with a clean, sterilised cloth. Run your hands around the udders so that they are warm and the goat is used to your touch.

3 Collect the first milk from each teat in a small bowl or cup. This cleans and clears the flow. Discard this, as it will turn the rest of the milk sour very quickly.

4 Collect the milk you want to use in a clean, stainless steel bowl: a traditional milking pail for a cow will probably be too tall. Squeeze the teats unless they are small, when they should be pulled up and down.

Gestation is about 5 months (155 days); if you are already milking the goat, stop two months before she is due to kid. Goats generally manage the birth quite happily if left alone, and usually produce two kids. They are usually taken away from their mothers soon after birth and hand-reared so that you can keep milking the goat yourself.

If one kid (or both) is a billy, you will need to decide whether to get rid of him, or rear and fatten him for the table – billies do not make suitable goats to keep long term and, obviously, are no use for milk production. The goat should be killed at about four months old and will taste a bit like lamb.

Milking goats
Milking must be done night and morning, every day of the year: the loud bleatings will tell you when it is time. You should have a milking shed, separate from the goats' living quarters, though not necessarily far away. It is important that this milking shed should be kept immaculately clean at all times.

The breed you have is largely a matter of personal choice, although some are renowned for giving higher yields than others, such as Saanen and British Alpine. It is best to be guided by what is available locally and by the advice of knowledgeable goat owners in the district.

British Toggenburg
Large goat with long legs. Domesticated. Gives a high yield.

Saanen
Long legs, but baggy udder. Prefers good land. Quiet goat, which is easy to handle.

Anglo-Nubian
Lop-eared goat which gives good, low-fat milk yield. Flesh good for eating.

British Alpine
Big black and white goat which gives a high milk yield. Good for grazing.

A good procedure for milking is to brush the goat to remove all dust, wisps of hay, and other scraps or debris from her coat which might otherwise fall into the milk. Then take her to the milking shed. You will find it easier if you have a raised platform on which she stands for milking (goats are very low to the ground). Use a stainless steel bowl to collect the milk as you work – buckets are often too tall to fit under a goat.

The milking technique is to gently squeeze and release the teats – a bit like squeezing a sponge – rather than to pull them up and down. If your hands are big and the goat's teats are small, however, you will find you have to pull the teats up and down; squeezing them will be

Goats' milk is good enough to eat, but you can also make delicious soft goats' cheese, by separating the curds from the milk and straining them through muslin.

ineffective. As you get near the end of the supply, massage the udder and squeeze the teats hard to bring down the final drops. You will not hurt the goat, however hard you squeeze her teats.

Using the milk
The milk should be covered immediately with a clean tea towel, and then the goat taken to her day- or night-time quarters before she gets a chance to kick over the bowl. Strain the milk straight away through a sterilised milk filter (available from

goat suppliers) and cool it by placing it in its container in a large bowl of very cold water or in the fridge. Then put it into a churn or jugs: it will keep fresh for two or three days, but it must always be kept covered as it picks up other flavours very easily.

Alternatively you can freeze goats' milk as soon as it is cold – it will not separate and will keep for up to six months – or you can make cheese (*see* page 236).

Keeping Chickens

Chickens are possibly the easiest of all animals to keep and must be about the most productive. Not only do they provide you with lovely fresh eggs, but once they have outlived their egg-laying usefulness, they make excellent eating themselves.

A small group of chickens need not take up much room or much of your time and they can be quite economical to feed. However, be prepared for a fairly high initial outlay. Proper hen houses are extremely

LIVING REQUIREMENTS

Before your chickens arrive, you must decide how you are going to keep them and make sure that their new home is ready for them to settle in and start laying. There are many different ways of keeping chickens, and they all have their prosand cons; you just need to decide which is most convenient for you.

OPTION	HOUSING	PROS	CONS	FEEDING AND OTHER REQUIREMENTS
Free range	Chickens are allowed to roam freely during the day, but are shut in a house at night	This is undoubtedly the best way to ensure healthy, happy hens and will provide the best eggs. If hens are allowed to scratch and peck in the garden, your food bills will be lower	The hens will soon turn your garden into a meadow and will eat all the seedlings in any vegetable plot and many new shoots in the garden's borders, too. This is seldom a practical option for back-yard hen-keepers	Little additional feed required. Ensure a supply of clean, fresh water and make sure that shelter is available
Movable hen houses	Chickens are kept in movable "arks" – a hen house with a covered run attached. The house should be moved daily to give access to fresh ground	Less destructive than free range and safe from predators	You will need a large area to accommodate the moving run. An orchard is ideal, but a rare luxury	Ensure a fresh daily supply of green food, either fresh grass or supplementary feed. Make sure that the run is on level ground that does not leave gaps at the base for predators to get in
Permanent hen house with run	A wooden house with space for roosting and laying is attached to a permanent, fenced run littered with straw	Space-efficient and secure. Can be constructed by customising an old garden shed	The ground will become bare and unattractive and will need regular maintenance to prevent it from getting muddy	Feed the birds waste vegetables and scraps together with grass clippings or green shoots. Keep the food hopper in the house and provide a box filled with fine earth or sand for scratching

expensive to buy, chicken wire for fencing is very costly, and the hens themselves are by no means cheap.

There are ways to economise, though: it is easy to customise an old shed with perches and places for the chickens to lay, and if you let your birds roam freely you will not need the expensive fencing.

One of the great advantages of keeping chickens is that it is very easy for someone to look after them for you if you want to go away. Whilst people might be reluctant to come and milk goats or feed pigs, they are almost always willing to shut the hens in at night, let them out in the morning and feed them, in exchange for the eggs the hens lay while they are in charge.

A less pleasant aspect is that, even more so than with other livestock, chickens are prone to various diseases and ailments, so you must be prepared to wring a bird's neck when it is necessary. In addition, it is not uncommon to go to the hen house in the morning and

Chicks have instant appeal, but are not the best way to acquire hens, as they require a lot of care until they are old enough to lay.

find that a hen has died in the night for no apparent reason. Just remove it, but do not eat it, as it will not have been bled – the blood will not have drained from its veins as it does when you wring its neck and hang it (*see* pages 170–71).

ACQUIRING HENS

There are various ways of getting your hens. You can buy them as day-old chicks, point-of-lay pullets or older battery hens that have passed their peak of laying for a commercial egg-production operation but will still continue to lay eggs for some time.

Keep an eye on adverts in your local shop and spread the word around other local smallholders if you want to buy some chickens; there will often be someone nearby with chicks or pullets for sale.

Day-old chicks
These are the cheapest to buy, but they have to be fed for up to six months before they begin to lay. The mortality rate is often quite high and you do not know how disease-prone

BREEDS OF CHICKEN

Deciding which breed or breeds of chicken you choose is largely to do with whether you want brown or white eggs. The best advice is to buy locally whenever possible and choose a breed that is known to do well in your area.

RHODE ISLAND REDS
Fairly large birds able to stand tough winters. Prolific layers.

MARANS
Pretty, plump birds, good for eating. Lay dark brown eggs.

BUFF ROCKS
Fairly large, with yellow feathers. Lay tinted eggs.

WHITE LEGHORN
Small white birds which give white eggs. Less popular than other breeds.

LIGHT SUSSEX
Quite large, pale brown birds. Give brown eggs.

they are likely to be. They also need lots of care and attention. Some experts advise that they should be kept in some sort of incubator, although this is not necessary if you are prepared to keep them in a warm box in the kitchen, out of the way of cats and children.

Point-of-lay pullets
These are chickens that are about six months old and have just come into lay. They will lay for you as soon as they have settled down, which

can be up to two or three weeks, but is usually only a matter of days. By and large, they are the best option, particularly for novice chicken-keepers. They are likely to be healthy and, providing you keep them properly, should remain that way. They are the most expensive to buy.

Choosing your chickens

Modern breeds of chicken have been developed with maximum egg production in mind for commercial use. Many of them will not go broody, so if you do want to breed from your chickens, it is better to choose one of the old-fashioned pure breeds.

Unless you want a lot of surplus eggs, you can estimate how many chickens you need on the basis of two hens per egg-eating person in the family. Be prepared for your egg consumption to go up if you keep chickens, as your supplies will be replenished daily.

The only real reason for keeping a cockerel with hens is if you want to produce chicks, although it is a good idea with free-range hens, as a cock will keep his hens in order, bossing them around and apparently pecking them at random. A cockerel has a far more voracious appetite than his hens, so is much more expensive to keep, and if the hens will go broody, it is possible he will turn the whole pack so at one time. In addition, his early-morning crowing can quite often upset neighbours.

FEEDING AND DAILY ROUTINE

As with all livestock, keeping chickens has to become part of your own daily routine.

If the hens have a run, open up the hen house and let the hens out as

early as possible – dawn is best. If left too long, the birds may start to peck each other. Feed them and give them clean water.

Collect the eggs in the morning (most are laid between nine and noon and should be collected as soon as possible after laying to avoid breakages). Unless you are cleaning out the hen house or digging over the run, the chickens need no further attention until their next feed at three or four o'clock. Shut them into the hen house at about six o'clock to keep them safe overnight.

Feeding requirements

What you feed your hens depends on how you are keeping them and what they can forage for themselves. Those kept in a run will need some concentrated grain night and morning. This is easiest (and most expensively) supplied in the form of specially prepared layers' mash or pellets. Pellets are the most economical, as mash, even when dampened, tends to blow away in a strong breeze. Instead, you can feed them about 125g (4oz) of grain (mixed corn or wheat) divided between the night and morning,

A chicken feeder releases a little grain at a time, as the supply in the bottom tray is eaten. Alternatively, scatter feed over the ground and let the chickens peck for it.

and supplement this with a good supply of household scraps. To avoid contamination and disease, only give vegetable scraps, never meat, and only use vegetable trimmings and discards that you have prepared outside your household kitchen.

Concentrated feed can be scattered on the ground for the hens to scratch, or fed in a container. Clean water is essential and hens drink an enormous amount. You can buy special water containers, which are designed to help keep the water clean. A cheaper alternative can be made from a plastic bowl with an upturned flowerpot placed in it. This should stop the hens from getting into the bowl and making it dirty.

Grit and limestone

In addition, chickens need grit, which helps them to break up their food, and calcium or limestone to

Eggs

Hens lay most eggs in the summer when the days are longer and lighter. In their prime, you can generally expect to get eggs for five or six days a week from one chicken. This will drop off in winter, although from a flock of about 10 birds, it is usual to get one or two fresh eggs each week, even in mid-winter. Hens can be encouraged to lay in the winter if you light the hen house well, so they have, in effect, about 12 hours of daylight each day.

help them form egg shells. This can be crushed oyster shells (available from your local corn merchant) or recycled egg shells, dried off in a low oven and crushed. Each bird should have approximately 14g (½oz) of grit and limestone (or oyster shells) per week in the ratio of one to four grit to limestone.

BREEDING

If you have a broody hen and a cockerel, you might like to try to hatch some eggs. It is fun to do, lovely to watch and you may be able to add to your flock.

Broody hens are instantly recognisable – they refuse to move from the nesting boxes, sitting tight and clucking gently, they go off their food and they lay no eggs. Warm weather from April onwards is the time to watch for this. If you do not want a hen to be broody, put her in a cold box on her own, with no straw so she cannot make a nest, and place her where she can see the others. Let her out at feeding time and check a little later whether she has gone back to the laying box. If she has, put her back in the isolation box for a while longer.

When a hen goes broody and you want to breed some chicks, put her in a special box of her own, this time away from the others and with some straw so she can make a nest. She should not be able to get out of this, and ideally it should have a wire mesh bottom to allow damp and warmth to come up from the earth. Sit her on eight newly-laid eggs and leave her. Take her off the nest to feed and perhaps have a dust bath, but the eggs should not be left for more than about 15 minutes or they will get too cold. Providing all goes

well, the chicks will hatch exactly 21 days after the hen began sitting on them. There is nothing for you to do but wait until the tiny yellow chicks emerge.

Looking after chicks
The chicks need water but no feed for 24 hours. Put the water in a tiny container, otherwise they will fall in and drown. Thereafter they can be fed on chick pellets three times a day, or you can feed the mother grower's mash and watch her feed tiny crumbs to her babies.

You will be able to tell when the chicks are ready to leave the hen and become independent, because she will let you know she is clearly fed up with them. It is best to integrate them into the flock slowly, if you can, as they are likely to get pecked and victimised at first. Cock birds can be fattened for the table.

Hens are not always good mothers. If you get a good one, keep her for as long as possible to rear chickens for you. It is best, though, to change the cock each year. If you keep the same one, he will mate with his daughters and your flock will begin to be inbred.

Chicks will hatch three weeks after a broody hen starts sitting on the eggs. Introduce them to the rest of the flock little-by-little until they are accepted, so that they do not get pecked.

Clipping wings

Chickens should have the flight feathers on one of their wings clipped when they are six months old, or they will fly over fences and escape, perhaps into danger. Spread out one wing: you can clearly feel the meaty part of the wing and will be able to see the long flight feathers. Clip these off at the base, using very strong scissors, as the feathers are very tough. Although it seems a brutal operation when you do it, it will not hurt the bird or draw blood.

KEEPING ANIMALS • CHICKENS

PLUCKING AND PREPARING A CHICKEN

There are two processes in preparing a dead bird either for the table or to be kept or frozen before eating: first, it must be plucked to remove the feathers and then it must be 'drawn' to remove the innards.

Plucking is easiest done while the bird is still warm, as the feathers will come out more readily than when the carcass is cold. However, domestic hens and other poultry will have been toughened by a lifetime of pecking and scratching, and some people feel that the taste and tenderness of the meat is improved if it is hung for 24–48 hours first.

Hanging poultry
Hanging is usually done before the bird is plucked or drawn; if the feathers are left on, fewer flies are attracted to the carcass and the bird tends to keep better with the innards intact. You can hang poultry after plucking and before drawing if you do so in a cool, airy place where there are no flies.

If you want to hang the poultry for a day or so, you can make the subsequent plucking an easier job by pouring a kettle of boiling water over the bird – just to warm it very slightly on the surface and loosen the hold of the feathers a little.

Plucking a bird
Plucking is a messy job, so lay down plenty of newspaper or sheets to catch any flying feathers. When you are ready to pluck your bird, put it on a clean work surface and pull out the long tail and wing feathers first, jerking them sharply. Pluck systematically from the neck, back,

breast, wings and legs, taking a number of feathers between your thumb and fingers each time and tugging them sharply. The tiny pin feathers that remain are easiest to remove using tweezers or by grasping them between your thumb and the edge of a blunt knife.

Down feathers
All poultry is plucked in the same way, but ducks and geese are harder and take longer, as they have a covering of down beneath their main feathers. This down is removed in the same way, but is fluffy and will fly around as you work, settling in your hair and on your clothes. You can scald the feathers first, by pouring over some boiling water, and this will reduce the problem.

Collect the down, wash and dry it (in paper bags in a low oven or by hanging in a warm and airy place) and when you have enough, use it for stuffing pillows or cushions.

Plucking a goose is hard on your hands; a good tip is to wrap sticking plaster around the forefinger of your plucking hand to cushion it.

Drawing a chicken
With the breast side down, insert a knife at the bottom of the neck and

If you pluck a bird promptly after it has been killed, the job will be quicker and easier, as the feathers will come out more readily. Work methodically to do a good job.

slit the skin up to the head. Pull the skin away from the neck, then cut through the neckbone as close to the shoulder as you can, inside the skin.

Remove the crop and the windpipe, which go to make up the giblets, pull out the neckbone and cut round the skin close to the head to separate it from the body. This way you leave a large flap of skin which can be folded over the bird's back and will help to prevent the meat from drying out as you roast it. The neckbone and head are discarded.

Turn the bird round, insert the knife into the vent and cut up to the parson's nose. Loosen the innards by putting a couple of fingers into this opening and then into the opening at the neck end and gently working them round against the inside of the carcass. This job will be less unpleasant if you have starved the bird for 24 hours before killing it.

When you feel the innards are loose, gently pull them out through the opening at the vent. If you keep them all together and work carefully, you should not break the gall bladder. If this does break, it will give the bird a bitter taste.

Run cold water through the bird to clean it inside and out and dab it dry with kitchen paper. Remove the feet by slitting the skin round the knee joints and twisting the lower legs. Cut through the white sinews. Tuck the flap of skin at the neck under the wing joints.

Separate the heart and liver from the rest of the innards, taking care not to damage the gall bladder attached to the liver. Cut open the gizzard and wash it. This, with the heart and neck, forms the giblets and can be used to make stock or soup. Use the liver separately.

Killing birds

The most economical way to keep chickens in terms of getting the maximum egg production is to keep them for two laying seasons (until they are about 18 months old) and then kill them and start the flock again. They will go on laying for some years to come, but although the eggs get larger, they will also become fewer.

The best way to kill a bird is by wringing its neck. Stun it with a blow to the head then hold the legs with your left hand, letting the body hang down. Hold the neck close to the head with your right hand. Pull the neck down and twist firmly so that the head is bent backwards, towards the back. You will feel the neck break. If you pull too hard you will pull the head off. Hang the bird with its head down so the blood drains out of its veins before plucking and preparing (opposite).

Ducks, Geese and Turkeys

If anything, ducks are even easier to keep than hens, although they are less common. Geese and turkeys can also be accommodated, although you may not keep more than 50 birds in total without registering your flock with Defra.

DUCKS

Although some people say that ducks will be content with just enough water to immerse their heads and necks, you really need a pond or stream to keep these birds happy.

Ducks' living requirements are far more primitive and straightforward than hens. All that is necessary in addition to a pond is a dry house containing some straw, in which they can be shut up at night to protect them from foxes. It needs no nesting box or roosting perch – in fact, a packing case can be turned into an excellent duck house. A couple of large holes punched in the back will give adequate ventilation.

Keeping ducks for eggs or meat
Duck eggs are often considered to contain impurities, which is one of the reasons why ducks are less frequently kept than other poultry. In fact, the shells are porous, so if laid in the mud around a stagnant pond, dirty water could get into the egg. Laid in clean surroundings, they are perfectly good, clean and quite safe to eat. The best way to ensure this is to keep the ducks shut in their house until about ten o'clock in the morning. They lay their eggs before this time and therefore will do so in the clean house.

The eggs are larger and richer than hens' eggs, but will not keep as long and should be used within a week.

If keeping birds for the table, buy them when they are very young and keep them for 10 weeks. Fatten

Don't attempt to keep ducks unless you have a large enough pond for them to swim in, or have a stream running through or alongside your property.

them with barley meal and kill them when they are exactly 10 weeks old, at which point they are at their best. They are also easiest to pluck at this stage; thereafter, they begin to moult and the new feathers, which will be starting to come through, are much more difficult to pull out.

If keeping them for eggs you can get ducks as day-old chicks or point-of-lay pullets, just like chickens (*see* page 167).

Feeding

Ducks are voracious eaters, but will thrive on little more than plain grass and will help you in the garden by keeping down slugs and snails. They will also keep down the vegetable patch, by eating your crops, so make sure they cannot get to it. They will need some grain in the night and morning. Feed it in a container rather than scattering it and if there is any left after an hour, feed them less next time. They will also appreciate their share of greens and vegetable trimmings. Ducks need as much clean drinking water, grit and limestone for their shells as you would give to chickens.

Breeding

In general, ducks do not make good mothers. It is much better to give a clutch of eggs to a broody chicken and let her hatch them. This will take 28 days, but dampen the eggs each day in the final week, as ducks would do.

Do not let the chicks into the water to paddle or swim until they are four weeks old – before this, their feathers will not repel the water and they could easily drown.

If your ducks are an egg-laying breed and you have extra drakes, kill them at 10 weeks old and eat them. Ducks have their necks wrung in the same way as hens (*see* page 171).

GEESE

If you have a large orchard or patch of grass where they can graze, or if you have access to unlimited greens, geese are probably the cheapest of all poultry to keep.

Although they have become less popular, geese still make excellent eating and many people prefer them to turkeys at Christmas. Goose eggs are larger and richer still than duck eggs, and you can expect to get about 100 eggs a year from each of your birds.

An important point to consider before buying some geese is that they are extremely noisy and aggressive and will chase after people they do not know. This can be both an advantage and a disadvantage, but they are well known as excellent guards against intruders.

If you keep geese, you must establish from the start that you are the boss, particularly with the gander. Look him fairly and squarely in the face and let him know you will brook no nonsense. The way to deal with a goose if it does attack you is to grab it by its neck. This is

A duck house does not need much fitting-out – a box will be quite adequate – but a ramp sloping down to the pond will be appreciated, both as a slide and an exit from the water.

easier than it sounds, as long as you are bold, as the bird advances with its neck forward, squawking at you as it approaches. It is unable to do anything if you grab it firmly, but not tightly enough that you will hurt it, around the neck.

Living requirements

Like ducks, geese have very simple housing requirements and only need somewhere with four walls, a roof and a floor, in which they can be shut up at night to keep them safe from foxes. Alternatively they can be shut in a well-wired run (wire the top as well as the sides, for extra protection).

Feeding

Their staple diet is grass, but they cannot cope if it is really long; it needs to be of medium length, which they will crop as neatly as a lawn. If you want to fatten them, give them some grain too, and if you put this in their night-time accommodation, it will help to lure them inside. In addition, like all poultry, they need grit and limestone, and access to clean water. They drink great quantities of water, in fact, and as they immerse their entire heads as they drink, it should be given in a fairly deep container. Clean it as soon as it gets dirty.

Breeding

You can breed from your geese if you want to. They sometimes take a while to select a mate, but once done, they have paired for life. You can expect the geese to produce 10–20 eggs, but these will seldom all hatch in a single clutch. Beware of the male, particularly during breeding time; he usually gets very protective and aggressive and it is best to try to stay well away from the

Geese will peck at grass on the ground, but can also be fed supplementary grain if necessary. They are noisy birds, so do not keep them too close to your neighbours.

mother goose's nest.

Geese make dreadful mothers, and so if you want to breed some goslings, put the eggs under a large broody hen, who will be able to hatch 4–6 at a time. They take upwards of four weeks to hatch, and if being hatched by a hen, must be turned each day in order to stop the contents settling. Sprinkle them with water, making particularly sure they are kept wet in the final week before hatching. Feed goslings on bread and milk to begin with and then on chick feed.

Killing geese

Geese cannot be killed in the same way as chickens and ducks: they are too big and strong. There are two ways of killing them, but for both, you must stun the bird first by giving it a hefty blow to the head with a heavy instrument. Then, either cut its throat at the bottom of the neck to sever the jugular vein, or hold the bird by the feet, with its chin resting on the ground. Get a helper to lay a pole or metal bar across its neck and tread on either end of this to keep it in place. Then pull the legs up towards you to break the neck.

TURKEYS

These are the birds least frequently kept on a small scale, mostly because they have a reputation for being hard to rear. They are usually bred solely for their meat, although their eggs are actually very similar in taste to those of chickens. One turkey egg is approximately the equivalent in size to two hen's eggs.

Turkeys are prone to get a disease called blackhead if they come into contact with chickens, so they cannot be kept together in the same run. In fact, this contact can even be as remote as you dealing with the turkeys after having been in the hen house. However, modern turkey feeds contain the antibiotic which combats this disease, so providing you feed proper turkey pellets, you should encounter no problem.

A turkey house is similar to a hen house in design, although the birds are much larger. The turkeys like to have perches, but make sure these are strong and solid enough to bear their weight. If you are able to keep the turkeys free-range, so much the better – they will wander around all day constantly pecking and eating.

Breeding turkeys

Turkey eggs can be difficult to hatch; they are large birds for the size of eggs they lay and they are apt to break them inadvertently in the nest. It is better to use a broody hen if possible, and she can hatch from 6–8 eggs. She will then rear the chicks, teaching them to eat and caring for them.

Using an incubator

An alternative is to hatch turkey eggs in an incubator, kept at about 38°C (101°F). Keep the incubator where the temperature is constant – in the house is better than in a shed, where the temperature will fluctuate. The trouble with hatching turkeys in this way is that young chicks are very difficult to rear as they are reluctant to begin eating without a mother bird to teach them. To overcome this, chop up onion tops and put them on top of their food.

Fattening chicks for Christmas

Besides there being a market for turkey eggs, the chicks can easily be sold as one-day-old birds, or you can keep them, fatten them and sell them at Christmas.

Turkeys are best kept as free-range birds, if possible. They will still need to be shut in a shed at night, though, to keep them safe from predators.

BREEDS OF DUCKS AND GEESE

There are some traditional local breeds, which make a good choice if you just want a handful of birds. Contact local suppliers to find out which breeds do best in your area and which are most widely available.

EMBDEN
Large pure white bird – the most popular breed of goose.

CHINESE
White bird, which is considerably smaller than the Embden.

TOULOUSE
Slightly smaller than Embden, with mostly grey feathers.

KHAKI CAMPBELLS
Prime layers, which give over 300 eggs a year. Go off laying early in the year.

AYLESBURY
Very popular duck, which is kept for eating. White feathers.

WHITE PEKIN
Long-necked bird which is also kept for the table. White feathers.

Keeping Bees

Bees cannot truly be 'kept', but if you can persuade a colony to take up residence on your property, it is well worth doing so. Even one hive will provide you with all the honey you can eat.

Take advice from bee-keepers in your area if you are a complete novice. It is a good idea to join a local bee-keeping society: most run courses for beginners.

Can you keep bees?

Before deciding definitely to keep bees, it is important to discover how you react to being stung. Some people react very badly and keeping bees could be too dangerous. Accompany a local bee-keeper on an inspection of his hives; you will probably get stung and you can then judge your reaction.

EQUIPMENT

Certain equipment is essential, and it can be expensive. Try to borrow or buy things second-hand when you are starting out – you can always upgrade later.

The most essential piece of equipment for yourself is a bee-veil to protect your face from stings. You will also need gloves (you may dispense with these later, but wearing them helps to give confidence to a beginner) and wellington boots, into which you tuck your trousers, which are, themselves, tucked into long socks, so the bees cannot get inside.

You might prefer a bee-suit, which offers complete head-to-toe protection, but these are expensive unless improvised out of a pair of overalls. Remember that bees climb upwards, and so will climb up sleeves but not down trousers, and protect yourself accordingly.

For the bees, you need a hive, a hive tool to lever out the frames and a smoker. This is used whenever you want to open up the hive; in it you burn anything which smoulders, such as dried grass, fir cones or insulation board. The smoke subdues the bees, as their reaction to it is to gorge themselves with honey, making them dozy and therefore less likely to sting when you disturb them.

A complete bee suit (below) offers head-to-toe protection against stings. Using a smoker (above) will subdue the bees before you open up the hive to work inside, making them less likely to panic and sting you.

To start a colony of your own, you need a nucleus of bees, including a queen bee that is laying. Introduce this to your hive and the colony will build up to around 40,000 bees.

THE HIVE

This is the most expensive item of equipment, but may often be acquired second-hand. Scrub and disinfect it before use, and check whether it needs any repairs.

The two most common types of hive used are the WBC and the modified National. The WBC is the traditional pyramid shape, but the National is usually recommended for beginners.

Positioning hives
Do not site hives near a footpath or road, where people could be bothered by the flight of the bees, nor under heavy trees where the spot is likely to be damp, or a frost pocket. Ideally, they need a place that is shaded from the rest of the garden by a fairly tall screen (though not right up against the hives).

ACQUIRING BEES

It is always best to acquire bees from a local bee-keeper: the bees are adapted to a particular region and its climatic conditions, so bees from another district are unlikely to do as well.

The easiest way to start a new colony is to acquire a nucleus from another bee-keeper. This is a mini-colony, consisting of about five frames of drawn comb with 5,000–8,000 bees and a laying queen. A bee-keeper should not let you have this nucleus until it is certain that the queen is laying – early summer is most likely.

Getting started
The nucleus is put into the centre of the lowest box, which is filled on either side with frames of foundation. Another box of foundation is placed above this. The initial aim is to build up the colony, but the queen will lay according to the food coming in and as there will not be many spare bees to go out to collect nectar, you will need to give supplementary feed. Make a syrup from 900g (2lb) of sugar dissolved in 550ml (1 pint) of hot water, cooled to room temperature. The amount of feeding will depend on the weather, but aim to feed them up to about 18kg (40lb) of sugar in the first year.

It is unlikely that you will get any honey in the first year, but if the weather is right in July (hot, sunny, sultry days with rain at night to encourage plant growth) you can replace the feeder with a super (a box of eleven frames) full of foundation frames. At the end of the season, you could get between 4.5–9kg (10–20lb) of honey.

As the colony builds up over the first few weeks, move the frames

Dealing with stings

If you keep bees, you will get stung sooner or later. Scratch out the sting straight away, using a hive tool or fingernail. The bee leaves a poison sac with the sting, plus the mechanism that continues to pump the poison from the sac, so if you squeeze the sting, it will only send the poison shooting into you, causing more irritation and swelling. Generally, the pain stops in a few minutes and the swelling subsides in a few hours. If it is really painful, bathe the sting with witch hazel or soak with diluted Epsom salts.

around every fortnight or so, being careful not to split the brood. By winter you will have two full boxes of drawn comb which is ideal for over-wintering the bees inside.

Managing the colony
Inspect the hive every fortnight from early to mid-summer to make sure the queen is laying and to see if there are any queen cells. These are much larger than ordinary cells and will protrude out from the comb. If you allow a new queen to hatch out, the colony will swarm.

Either remove the frame and destroy the queen cells, or make an artificial swarm. Find the old queen in the hive and put her and the frame of eggs she is on in another box with some frames of drawn comb. Leave these on the current site and put all the brood frames, including the queen cells together with the drones, on another site. When the foraging bees return, they will automatically go into the old

hive; this will house the queen and all the foraging bees, and is known as an artificial swarm.

Meanwhile, in the adjacent site, with the nurse bees and the queen cells, panic will set in as there is no food coming into the colony and the bees will tear down all the queen cells except for one. The new queen will emerge, leave the hive, get mated and come back to start laying, beginning a new colony. If you only want one colony, find the original queen and destroy her or give her away. Put the new queen into the old hive and the bees will follow her.

Renew the queen in a colony every two years.

REMOVING HONEY

Honey may be taken from the hive from mid- to late summer, depending on the nectar flow in the area.

Put a board with a one-way bee-valve under the supers and, when the bees have gone down to the lower boxes (after about 48 hours), remove the top frames. To extract the honey you must first scrape the wax cappings on the cells off with a large uncapping knife. The frames are then put into a special centrifuge or honey extractor. It spins the frames round at speed so the honey falls into the bottom of the drum. From there it is filtered into the honey tank, from where it can be drawn off into jars. The maximum amount of honey you could expect from a single frame is 2.2kg (5lb); the maximum in a super is 22.5kg (50lb).

Extract honey from all the boxes above the queen excluder. This leaves some honey in the lower boxes, but not enough to feed the bees through the winter, so give them a syrup feed from autumn.

SWARMING

If you inspect your bees regularly and follow the procedure outlined above, experienced bee-keepers would claim that there is no reason for bees swarming.

Bees will only swarm if the hive becomes overcrowded, or if a new queen hatches. If the bees do swarm, about half of them will leave the hive, with the queen. They will cluster nearby and unless they are

Your honey will have some of the flavour of the flowers the bees fed on, although in a domestic plot, they will have flitted from plant to plant, giving no one particular taste.

collected by a bee-keeper, will move off a day or two later. The swarm only remains yours for as long as it is within your sight. If you lose sight of the bees, another bee-keeper is entitled to collect and claim them.

Collecting a swarm

Place a white sheet on the ground beneath the swarm. Hold a strong cardboard box or straw basket directly under the largest part of the swarm and shake the branch of bush where the bees are resting. This will cause most of the bees to fall into the box. Invert the box over the sheet and prop up one side with a small stone. After an hour or so, all the bees should be in the box.

Return at dusk and wrap the box in the sheet, then take the swarm to a new hive. Place a board in front of the hive, sloping up to the entrance. Spread the sheet over the board and shake the bees out of the box. Bees run uphill when they are frightened, so they will run up into the hive.

FOOD FROM THE COUNTRYSIDE

Gathering from the Wild
Herbs and Plants
Fruit and Nuts
Fungi
Fishing
Food from the Seashore
Hunting and Shooting
Gathering Firewood

Gathering from the Wild

The countryside, hedgerows, inland rivers and lakes, and the shoreline with its coastal waters, all harbour rich crops of edible plants, animals and fish, and yet few of these are exploited to their full potential.

Always treat any produce gathered from the wild with respect and caution, but this does not mean they need to be neglected altogether. The countryside is home to all manner of fungi, fruit, nuts, herbs, plants and flowers, many of which will augment and enliven your homegrown food and cost nothing more than the time needed to find and pick them.

Fungi are probably the most neglected of all free food: millions of edible fungi go uncollected each year in woodlands, but amateur foragers are understandably reluctant to try them. Some species are deadly poisonous and unless you are able to identify them for certain, there is no foolproof test that will tell you whether a particular fungus is safe to eat or not.

It is worthwhile learning to identify the poisonous ones, so that you can gather and eat the others. A good field guide will help you, or you could join one of the many 'fungus forays' organised around the country in autumn, where an expert will show you the ones that are safe – and tastiest – to eat.

Harvest from verge and hedge

There are many edible wild plants and herbs that grow in abundance. Be on the look-out as you explore your surrounding countryside, and ask people who have lived in the district for a long time whether they know of anything that grows in any nearby woods or moorlands that is particularly good to eat.

Many of the plants that abound along the grass verges of our roads today were attributed with great healing powers by country folk not so long ago and can still make delicious additions to soups and salads. When picking plants from the wild, there are a few simple rules that everyone should observe in order to ensure their own survival, as well as that of the countryside.

Make sure that you know that what you are picking to eat is edible and not poisonous; even with the aid of a field guide, if you are a beginner and cannot find someone who is definitely able to confirm this for you, leave the plant alone. Most produce is best gathered on a sunny, not rainy day, as the wetness is likely to encourage it to deteriorate faster.

Place your gatherings into an open shallow basket, rather than a polythene bag (in which they will be crushed), and pick only

Only gather edible produce from places that are free from pollution, such as busy passing traffic, and only pick what you can identify.

Herbs and Plants

The list given below of edible roots, leaves and flowers is by no means complete, but illustrates the most widely available and commonly used plants. In addition to these, look out for wild vegetables, because nearly all those cultivated in gardens and vegetable plots have their wild counterparts.

Cabbage, carrots, celery, parsnip, radish, salsify, turnip and watercress are all found growing wild, although probably not all in the same area. You may also find wild garlic (Ransoms) growing abundantly in woods in spring – unmistakable with its pungent smell.

the quantities you know you can deal with at any one time. Try to gather only from the places that are relatively unpolluted. Most plants are best if gathered young.

Proper respect for the countryside and its wildlife is of paramount importance. It is illegal to pull up wild plants by the roots in many places and, in any event, it is unnecessary for your purposes. Likewise, do not strip plants completely of their leaves and flowers – this could easily kill them. Nor should you take all the flowers or seeds from annual plants or they have no hope of being able to re-seed and grow again.

Meat and fish

The countryside is home, too, for a number of wild animals and birds which can be caught and eaten. There are extensive and complicated rules and regulations that govern all aspects of hunting, shooting, fishing and trapping, so make sure you are

Fishing might not be a practical everyday way to obtain food, but a day fishing off the beach or for freshwater fish can be fun, rewarding and productive, too.

aware of what you must comply with and obtain all the necessary permits or licences before you start.

Rivers and inland lakes or reservoirs can be fished to provide food, although this practice is now regarded more as a sport than a way of obtaining food. The equipment used is sophisticated and can be expensive – far from the stick-and-bent-pin image of one-time streamside fishing.

The seashore and its immediate coastal waters is another rich source of edible goods. Around the shoreline you can find a number of plants, as well as various edible seaweeds and the many sea creatures that bury themselves in the sand or live among the rocks. Or you can try your luck with sea fishing.

Beech
Pick leaves when they are very young and tender. They make a lovely addition to salads.

Broom
Grows abundantly in open country. Pick the flowers when they are still in bud and pickle them in vinegar or salt. Alternatively, sprinkle them over salads as a decorative and tasty garnish.

Burdock
Grows in abundance in thickets, roadsides and along the edges of woods. Eat the young leaves as a salad vegetable; chop the leaf stems raw into salads, or simmer them gently and serve with butter as a vegetable. Scrape and boil the root to eat like salsify.

Chickweed
Grows as a weed in most gardens as well as on wasteland everywhere.

Strip off the tiny leaves by running a fork down the stems and cook them like spinach or use raw as a sandwich filling.

Chicory
Grows particularly where the soil is chalky. The leaves can be used raw in salads and the root can be ground to make a drink that is often used as a substitute for coffee.

To make chicory coffee, clean the roots thoroughly and cook them in a moderate oven until they are dry and crisp, then grind them in a coffee grinder. Let them steep for some minutes in boiling water before straining and drinking the liquid.

Comfrey
A much-neglected and under-used plant that grows commonly in ditches or damp ground near river banks. It makes a pleasant alternative to spinach and is cooked in the same way.

Cowslip
Found in thickets and along roadsides, and particularly noticeable in spring with its umbrella-like clusters of tiny white flowers. These can be infused to make a refreshing drink, or the liquid can be used as a delicate flavouring for puddings. The young leaves can be used as a salad vegetable and the adventurous might like to use the root to give a different aroma to their home-made beer.

Dandelion
One of the commonest, yet most useful of all wild plants. Found growing abundantly in all wasteland and open grassy spaces, it is generally considered to be a weed, but it is not so long ago that the plant was cultivated in many vegetable gardens. The leaves make a tasty and nutritious salad vegetable, but should be picked young – in springtime before the well-known

An abundance of chickweed makes a vibrant green carpet over this woodland floor – a marvellous haul for a forager.

Dandelion, below, grows like a weed in many garden lawns and beds, as well as in the wild. The leaves, in particular, are good to eat, when they are young.

yellow flowers appear – as this is when they are at their least bitter and most tender. They can also be cooked like spinach, and many people recommend mixing them with the leaves of spinach or sorrel (*see* page 184), both raw and cooked, in order to reduce the rather bitter taste. The roots can be dried in the sun, then roasted and ground to make a coffee substitute. They can also be cooked as a root vegetable or used to make wine or cordial.

Dead nettles
Pick young leaves and cook like spinach. The flowers can be used to make a drink.

Dog rose
The flowers have a pleasant, if not very substantial, culinary use. They can be used to flavour jams, jellies or honey. Painted with egg white and sprinkled with caster sugar, the crystallised petals make a pretty decoration for light puddings. Try them as an unusual sandwich filling or as a delicate garnish to a light salad. For rose hips, *see* page 187.

Fat hen
One of the common garden weeds, it will also be found growing on wasteland. It is rich in iron and is another substitute for spinach.

Hawthorn
One of the most useful and versatile of all wild crops – the young leaves are delicious eaten raw as a salad vegetable; the flowers can be made into a fresh-tasting liquor by packing them into bottles with brandy and caster sugar (pick the flowers before

Bright red hawthorn berries make a good jelly to accompany roast, red meats or pick the flowers in spring to flavour brandy liqueur.

noon on a sunny day and use only the petals); and the berries can be made into jelly.

Horseradish
Grows in abundance on waste ground. Peel the roots and grate them to make horseradish sauce or cream.

Jack-by-the-hedge
Grows in abundance on the outskirts of woods and in hedges. The leaves can be chopped over salads (they have a slightly garlicky flavour), or they can be made into a sauce to accompany various meats.

Lime
The healing properties of this tree were such that many years ago they were planted by royal command along roadsides in the United Kingdom. The leaves make a good salad vegetable or sandwich filling. The flowers, picked while they are in full bloom, and dried, make a

refreshing tea that is renowned for being extremely soothing.

Marsh samphire
Found on salt marshes. The young leaves can be cooked like any leafy green vegetable.

Plantain
Widely found growing on waste land, the young leaves can be used raw in salads or cooked like spinach.

Poppy
Another plant whose contribution to the family larder cannot be claimed as a great money-saver. However, the seeds contained in the brown seed heads that follow the red, papery flowers, can be used to flavour cakes, biscuits and bread, or sprinkled over salads.

Primrose
The flowers of this spring plant can be used to make a refreshing drink or they may be crystallised

in the same way as rose petals to make edible cake decorations. Gather them sparingly though: primroses were over-picked in the past and their numbers are only just recovering.

Salad burnet

Commonly found in grassland, particularly on chalky soil. Crush the leaves slightly and use them in salads, or add them to cool long summer drinks.

Sorrel

Throughout the spring, wood sorrel may be found in woodland and shady places; common sorrel is found on grassland and open country. Both are widely neglected. Use sorrel raw in salads, or cooked in soups, soufflés, omelettes, stuffings and sauces for meat and fish, or as a vegetable accompaniment. It does contain a lot of oxalic acid, so do not eat it every day of the week.

Sorrel has myriad uses in the kitchen, in soups, salads, stuffings and sauces. Look for it in spring, when it is most abundant.

Stinging nettle

Another much-neglected plant that is widespread and grows in great abundance. Pick it when very young – ideally no more than 15–20cm (6–8in) high – as you are less likely to get stung by these young stalks, and cook them like spinach (the stinging formic acid is destroyed in cooking), use them as a flavouring for soufflés and omelettes, or make them into soup.

HERBS

Only the herbs most easily found are listed here. If you are lucky you will find balm, borage, parsley, fenugreek, basil and lovage too. If you find a large patch of borage, you can use it as a salad vegetable, cook it like spinach or as a base for soups. If you have enough herbs, you can preserve them (*see* page 219) by drying or freezing.

Angelica

May be found in damp places around the outskirts of woods or near streams. Although classified as a herb, its main culinary use is as a decoration for puddings or flavouring for cakes. For this, the stems are candied by simmering and steeping them in heavy syrup over a period of a few days.

Fennel

Needs seeking out but may be found on waste and damp ground and often likes coastal locations. The leaves may be used fresh or dried – chopped, to impart the characteristic aniseed taste to a variety of dishes. The seeds which are gathered in the late autumn can be dried and ground like peppercorns.

Marjoram

Grows in grassy wastelands, and particularly on dry, chalky soil. Use the leaves fresh or dried in the same way you would cultivated marjoram.

Meadowsweet

Grows abundantly in most locations, but particularly in damp, shady ground and near marshes. Both

Wild herbs
1 Angelica
2 Fennel
3 Meadowsweet
4 Marjoram
5 Mint
6 Thyme

leaves and flowers may be dried and
used for flavouring, or to make a
refreshing, soothing drink.

Mint

Various types of mint grow wild,
and in abundance. The most
common varieties are corn mint,
which appears on open ground and
woodland clearings, and water mint,
which likes damp locations.

Use wild mint in the same ways
as you use the mint you grow in your
garden or make a good supply of
mint sauce to last you through the
winter. Mint makes a most refreshing
ice cream, too – with or without
chocolate chips.

Thyme

One of the most widespread of all
wild herbs, it grows in grassland and
open ground. It can be used just like
cultivated thyme, although some say
the flavour is milder.

Woodruff

Found in woodland and thickets.
The leaves may be picked and dried
and are described as smelling like
vanilla, new mown hay and honey.
Woodruff can be used to flavour
sausages and hamburgers and gives
a pleasant flavour to wine or long,
cool, summer drinks.

*Hang meadowsweet flowerheads upside
down in a cool, airy place to dry, then you can
crumble them into sweet dishes or preserves
to add a subtle flavour.*

*Thyme is one of the most popular garden
herbs, but also one of the most abundant
found in the wild. There are many different
varieties, all with their own distinctive flavour.*

Fruit and Nuts

The wild fruits of the hedges can be use in a variety of ways: eaten raw as a dessert or as the principal ingredient for a pudding, to make jams and jellies, in chutneys or pickles, as garnishes to a meat course, and for wine or soft drinks.

Nuts have just as many culinary uses and can often be the main protein source in a meal. They also make superb additions to stuffings and sauces.

SOFT FRUIT

Pick and transport soft fruits carefully to avoid damaging them, unless you plan to make jam, in which case a little bruising will not matter. A plastic, lidded tub makes a good container for foraging, or line a basket or trug with a plastic bag.

Barberry

Once common, disease has made this shrub a rarity now, but you may still be lucky enough to find one. The bright red berries appear in mid-summer. Beware of the thorns when picking. Use berries for jelly or as a sauce to go with meat.

Bilberry

Also known as the blueberry and whortleberry, these bushes are generally found on open countryside, nestling among the heather. They often grow singly some distance apart from one another, so you will need time and patience to gather more than a handful of berries.

The berries are small, round and blue-black in colour, and they appear from mid-summer to early autumn. They make excellent jelly and wine or can be used in all types of fruit pudding.

Blackberry

Blackberries are widespread in hedges, waste land and woodland outskirts. The familiar fruits appear from late summer onwards, but they should not be picked after the early autumn, when they will have become soft and mushy. Blackberries can be used in jams, jellies, chutneys and for all manner of puddings and sauces, or in wine-making.

Cloudberry

Found where the ground and atmosphere are damp. The fruits are similar to blackberries in shape but a pale, pinky colour. They grow on very low shrubs. If you can gather enough ripe ones, they can be eaten raw as a dessert. Otherwise, use them in any way you would blackberries.

Cranberry

Another fairly rare shrub in Britain, found in marshy and boggy land. The principal, or traditional, use for the hard, dark red, shiny berries is as a sauce to accompany roast turkey. They also make a good stuffing for all sorts of meat, or can be used in puddings.

Elder

Both the flowers, which appear from early summer, and the berries, which

Wild berries make rich and delicious compôtes to serve with yoghurt or ice cream, or jams and jellies to enjoy all year round.

follow them later in the season, are valuable crops. The elder tree grows in forests and waste land. The clusters of white flowers can be made into a drink by pouring boiling water on them (let it cool and chill it before drinking) or into wine. They impart a subtle flavour to gooseberry puddings, jams or jellies, and can also be dipped in batter and deep fried to make fritters.

The berries are ready for picking when they are black and hanging heavily from the branches. They can be mixed with other fruit in jams, jellies or puddings, made into sauces and chutneys, used to flavour spiced vinegar, or made into superb wine. Dried, they can be substituted for currants in cakes and biscuits.

Gooseberry
Careful searching in forests and thickets will often yield wild gooseberry plants. The familiar green bomb-shaped fruits appear from mid-summer onwards. Use them in any of the ways you would use their cultivated cousins; such as in tarts, fools, jams and wines.

Raspberry
Wild raspberries and mulberries grow in thickets and on heathlands. The berries are ripe during summer. They can be used in all the ways suitable for cultivated fruit, but if you only find a few, use them to flavour vinegar for a salad dressing, or mix them with other fruit.

Red currant
This grows naturally as a wild plant, and is also found scattered in wild locations, having been seeded by birds after eating from cultivated specimens. Look for it particularly along thickets or at the edge of a wood, near a stream. The round, bright red fruits appear in summer and may be used in the same way as cultivated ones.

Rose hips steeped in boiling water make a soothing tea, or you can make them into a syrup rich in vitamin C (see below).

Rose hips
The orangey-red berries appear on the wild rose or dog rose from late summer until late autumn. They can be made into a syrup which is very rich in vitamin C and, besides making a fruity drink this can be used to flavour puddings, ice creams, milk shakes and more. Cut the hips in half, or put them through a mincer, and then boil them for about 30 minutes. Let the contents of the pan drip through muslin or a jelly bag overnight. To each 600ml (1pint) of liquid, add 450g (1lb) of sugar and boil again.

Rowan
This tree may be found anywhere, particularly in cool woods. The heavy clusters of orange berries appear from summer to autumn and can be

used with crab apples to make a jelly to accompany meat. They can also be made into wine.

Strawberry

Wild strawberries grow in open forest and on heaths and need careful seeking out. The tiny fruits, similar to those of the alpine strawberry, ripen during summer and have a far sweeter flavour than any cultivated variety. They are also rich in vitamin C. Ideally, eat them raw, with ice cream to make them go further or, better still, with champagne poured over them.

HARD FRUITS

These fruits must all be cooked in some way before they can be eaten. They are not as sweet as most soft fruits, although a frost will reduce the sharpness of some, including sloes and bullaces.

Bullace

The typical, small plum-shaped fruits of the tree may be red, purple, yellow or green, and the tree is actually the ancestor of all cultivated plums. It is found in thickets and often in a neglected corner of a cottage garden. The fruits are similar to the sloe (*see* below) in that they are very tart, but this will diminish if they are left until after the first frost. They can then be used in fruit pies, or perhaps more wisely in chutneys or wines.

Crab apple

This is the ancestor of all cultivated apples and can be found growing singly in thickets and occasionally in woods and on heaths. The crab apple has been widely crossed with cultivated varieties of apples, and many of these have found their way back into the thickets, so the

Crab apples cannot be eaten raw, like larger apples, but have many uses in preserves, jellies and stewed puddings.

crab apples you find might well be variable in colour, size and taste (true wild crab apples are incredibly sour). Pick them as you find them in summer and autumn and use them to make jellies, sauces, puddings, chutneys or pickles, according to their sweetness.

Medlar

Although a Mediterranean species, it is not uncommon to find a wild medlar tree. The brown fruits are roughly pear-shaped with a five-leaved calyx at the top. They are not ready for picking until at least mid-autumn, or when they look as if they are turning rotten. If you pick them any earlier, they must be stored in a dark place and 'bletted' until they are soft and appearing to start to rot. They make a delicious alternative to apple sauce to eat with pork, or may be roasted in the oven and eaten as an accompaniment to meat, or as a pudding (with honey and cream). They also make a delicious jelly.

Quince

Like the medlar, these trees grow large and contorted and may be

found in hedgerows. The hard, yellow, apple or pear-shaped fruits are ready for picking in early autumn. They cannot be eaten raw and are most frequently used in jelly.

Sloe

The small, bluish-black berries are the fruit of the thorny blackthorn which still makes up some of the densest thickets. The berries eaten raw are extremely sour, although they can be mixed with apples to make a jelly, or even a fruit pie. If you are going to do this, pick them after the first frost, which takes away a little of the tartness and makes the skins a little softer.

The more usual (and luxurious) use of sloes is to make sloe gin: prick the skins with a pin, mix with an equal quantity of sugar – less if you do not want the gin too syrupy – and pack into bottles. Top up with gin and leave for two or three months. Strain off the liquor and either eat the berries or add them to an apple pie. An alternative to pricking each berry when making sloe gin is to freeze your fruits to split the skins and then use them once they are defrosted.

Scour the hedgerows for sloes in autumn – they are a popular wild crop and the bushes are often stripped by other foragers.

NUTS

Nuts fall from the tree when they are ready, but are protected from damage by their hard shells. If you find a nut tree, gather what you can from the surrounding ground.

Beech

Trees are widely spread and the nuts appear in early autumn, although only once every three or four years. Four nuts are usually contained in the brown husk. They can be eaten but are more usually made into oil. Grind them in a coffee grinder, put them into a muslin bag and press it with a heavy weight, letting the oil fall into a bowl.

Hazel

Known also as cobnuts, these trees are found in woods and thickets and yield their tasty harvest mainly in early autumn.

Sweet chestnut

The prickly green cases, each containing up to three nuts, begin to fall off these tall trees in autumn. Like beech nuts, they must be shelled and peeled, and they also have an inner skin which makes them very bitter unless it is removed (which is not easy). It is more usual to cook them before eating them, either by roasting in the embers of the fire, or to make soups, stuffings or additions to casseroles. Puréed, they can be used in a number of puddings or made into *marrons glacés*, which are costly to buy. This is done by repeatedly boiling the peeled nuts with sugar and glucose, letting them steep in the syrup between boilings.

Walnut

Only a very few of these trees exist in the wild, but they are worth looking for. The nuts ripen in mid-autumn, although you can pick them earlier for pickling to go with cheese or cold meats. The ripe nuts can be used in many dishes, both sweet and savoury.

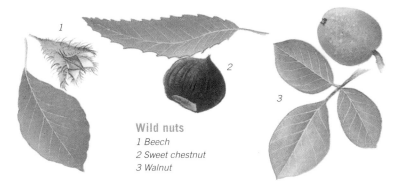

Wild nuts
1 Beech
2 Sweet chestnut
3 Walnut

Walnuts are delicious to eat as a snack, but also make wonderful additions to cakes, breads, stuffings and salads.

FOOD FROM THE COUNTRYSIDE • FRUIT AND NUTS

Fungi

It is imperative to be able to identify fungi if you intend to gather them for eating, and the best way to learn to do this is to spend time collecting with someone already experienced. Look out for organised fungi collections run by natural history societies or other local groups.

Most fungi are found in their greatest numbers in forests – particularly those of beech and oak – where the ground is rich in leafmould and, therefore, humus. In general, they like warm and damp, but not water-logged, conditions. Although some of the edible species appear in the spring, most are found in the autumn and grow in greatest profusion if the summer was good and the autumn is wet, but not cold.

Field fungi

The most important exceptions to the forest habitat are the field mushroom and the horse mushroom, and these are probably the most coveted and sought-after of all wild, edible fungi. They have more taste than their cultivated cousins.

Both field and horse mushrooms are found in meadows and pastures. The horse mushroom, as its name suggests, likes fields frequented by horses, but also cattle. Look for it near cowsheds or horses' shelters in fields and along gallops used by racehorses when they are out on exercise. In a good year they will start springing up towards the end of the summer and continue through until late autumn. They often, although not always, appear year after year in the same spot.

Safety tips and rules for picking

There are some simple, but essential, points to remember when collecting fungi. Always follow these rules to keep yourself safe and healthy – and above all, never pick or eat anything you cannot confidently identify.

Harvest fungi by twisting them by the stalk so they break free at the base. Pulling them out of the ground is selfish as it destroys the whole plant and stops it growing back; cutting them with a knife will hamper your identification, as the base of the stem is often a guiding feature.

Collect them on a fine day, not when it is raining, as fungi will deteriorate quickly if picked when they are wet. Put them into an open container – a shallow basket is ideal; a polythene bag is not, as it provides the perfect conditions for very quick decomposition.

The fungi you collect should be mature, but not so old that they are beginning to decay. Do not pick young mushrooms, the tops of which are still bunched or buttoned. Their identification characteristics will not have developed and a poisonous species could easily be mistaken for an edible one.

Pick only perfect specimens (or as near perfect as possible); not those that are ragged, torn or slimy. Go through them again when you get home, and discard any that you feel are suspect. All wild fungi must be cooked before eating – never eat them raw. Also, they should be cooked or dried (*see* page 209) as soon as possible after collecting – and washed very thoroughly first.

A cluster of edible parasol mushrooms this large on the forest floor is a lucky find. Mushrooms are most plentiful in a wet autumn following a good summer.

EDIBLE FUNGI

The texture and flavour of all these edible fungi vary widely. In most cases, it is best to pick a medley of different sorts to use together.

Field mushroom (*Agaricus campestris*)
Found in damp grassland, often growing in a ring.

Horse mushroom (*Agaricus arvensis*)
Found in pastures grazed by horses, cattle and sheep, especially near cattlesheds and hayricks or along paths where horses are exercised.

Wood mushroom (*Agaricus silvicola*)
Found in damp woods.

Parasol mushroom (*Lepiota procera*)
Found at the edges of woods and in grassy clearings in woods or by roadsides. Pick as cap is beginning to open, and discard the stem.

Oyster mushroom (*Pleurotus ostreatus*)
Found growing on dead tree trunks, branches or stumps, particularly beech. Found throughout the year, but is commonest in autumn and winter. Pick when young and stew slowly, or dry.

Chanterelle (*Cantharellus cibarius*)
Found in forests, particularly those of beech and oak. Stew in milk; needs slow cooking.

Morel (*Morchella esculenta*)
Found in thickets, woods, grassy banks. Also likes rich, bare soil.

Cep (*Boletus edulis*)
Found in forests, beech in particular. Good for drying.

Bay boletus or bay sponge cap (*Boletus basius*)
Found in forests, particularly of conifers or where the soil is poor or chalky.

Boletus erythropus
Found in forests, particularly conifers, or on poor soil. Do not

Ceps are found mostly in beech forests, where they can be hard to spot among the autumn leaves. They are good mushrooms for drying.

worry about the blue colour to the flesh when cut or broken.

Shaggy ink cap (*Coprinus comatus*)
Found on roadside verges, rubbish tips and other places where organic rubbish is buried. Gather while gills

are still white, discard stems and scrape scales from caps.

Giant puffball (*Lycoperdon giganteum*)
Found in forests and grassland. Eat when young and the flesh is white,

Edible fungi
1 Field mushroom
2 Horse mushroom
3 Parasol mushroom
4 Oyster mushroom
5 Morel
6 Cep
7 Shaggy ink cap
8 Cauliflower fungus
9 Common puffball

Safety essentials

It is important to stress that you should never eat any fungus unless you are absolutely certain it is an edible species. Never test by tasting; a remarkably small amount of a deadly species could kill you. And never risk an uncertain identification; if you are not completely confident, leave the fungus behind. Similarly, even when you know a species to be edible, if you are trying it for the first time, eat only a little; it might disagree with you even though other people can eat it with no ill effects.

The common puffball (left) springs up from forest floors, through layers of decomposing leaves, but can also be found in grassland. It is edible, and best picked when the flesh is white.

194

not yellow.

Common puffball (*Lycoperdon perlatum*)
Found in forests and grassland. Pick when flesh is white.

Cauliflower fungus (*Sparassis crispa*)
Found near pine trees, sometimes growing on the stumps. Eat when young, or dry.

Hedgehog fungus or wood hedgehog (*Hydnum repandum*)
Found in forests. Needs boiling for 20 minutes or so to prevent it from tasting bitter.

Blewit (*Tricholoma saevum*)
Found in pastures and other grassland, often in gardens, as well as in forests and thickets.

Wood blewit (Tricholoma nudum)
As for blewit. Pick when underneath and stems are tinged violet.

Yellow swamp russula (*Russula claroflave*)
In wet ground under birch trees.

Bare-toothed russula (*Russula vesca*)
Found in forests, particularly of beech and oak.

Blackish-purple russula (*Russula atropurpurea*)
Found in forests, particularly under oak trees.

As sinister as its name, the death cap is one of the most deadly fungi and is found beneath oak and beech trees.

POISONOUS FUNGI

Get to know these, so that you can be quite certain to avoid them.

Death cap (*Amanita phalloides*)
Found in forests, particularly oak and beech. It is deadly.

Destroying angel (*Amanita virosa*)
Found in forests; rarer than above.

Fly agaric (*Amanita muscaria*)
Found in forests or near coniferous and birch trees.

Panther cap (*Amanita pantherina*)
Found in forests, particularly beech, as well as on heathland and grassland.

Fool's mushroom (*Amanita verna*)
Found in forests, usually beech.

Paxillus involutus
Brown roll-rim found in forests.

Inocybe fastigiata
Found in forests, particularly beech.

Red-staining inocybe (*Inocybe patouillardii*)
Found in forests, particularly of beech, and grows near paths or near the outskirts of woods.

Clitocybe dealbata and ***Clitocybe cerrussata***
Found in coniferous woods.

Livid entoloma (*Entoloma simuatum*)
Found in forests, parkland and some gardens, favouring clay soils.

Sulphur tuft (*Hypholoma fasciculare*)
Found in large groups round the base of trees. Can be found at any time, but usually during summer and autumn.

Devil's boletus (*Boletus satanas*)
Found under beech trees in particular, but look under all trees that grow on calcareous soils.

Yellow-staining mushroom (*Agaricus xanthodermus*)
Found in pastureland.

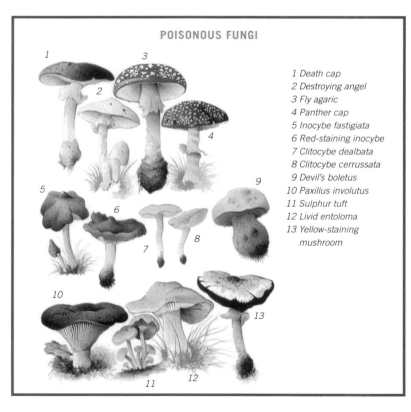

POISONOUS FUNGI

1 Death cap
2 Destroying angel
3 Fly agaric
4 Panther cap
5 Inocybe fastigiata
6 Red-staining inocybe
7 Clitocybe dealbata
8 Clitocybe cerrussata
9 Devil's boletus
10 Paxillus involutus
11 Sulphur tuft
12 Livid entoloma
13 Yellow-staining mushroom

Fishing

Sea and freshwater fishing in rivers and lakes are a fun way to boost your food supplies, though seldom a reliable source of fish throughout the year.

Always make sure you have the appropriate licences and permits for wherever you want to fish. Most waterways are controlled in some way, and you cannot set up just anywhere with your rod and line. Ask the advice of locals or look for signs along the bank, indicating what restrictions are in place and who to contact for permission to fish.

SEA FISHING

For sea fishing, you can fish from the shore or go out in a boat. Take care to follow the advice of the coastguard if bad weather is expected; small boats are very vulnerable in rough seas.

Fishing from the beach

You don't need to set to sea to fish from it. If you are patient, you can catch plenty of fish and shellfish without even leaving the shore and barely even getting your feet wet.

On a rocky beach try searching the rock pools at low tide, turning over the rocks one by one. If you are lucky you can get bucketfuls of prawns (shrimps) and Belmain bugs.

Another way of catching prawns (which are mainly found on rocky coastlines) is by suspending a wide necked net from the rocks into water that is about 1.2–1.5m (4–5ft) deep. Lower the net into the water so the net is just covered and leave it for 5–10 minutes. Pull it up and check inside for your catch. Bait the net

with old fish to raise your chances of a good catch.

Using a long line

This is a line laid down the beach at low tide, the ends secured through a wooden board which is buried into the sand to anchor it. All the way along the line are short traces – 15–25cm (6–9in) long – which have baited hooks on the ends of them. As the tide comes in, it will bring a number of fish in with it and they,

You may not be able to guarantee a catch, but fishing from a beach early in the morning on a fine day will always bring you pleasure.

hopefully, will take the bait. When you go back at the next low tide, there should be a line full of fish. If you live in an area where there are a lot of crabs, which will take your bait, put little corks on the traces. This will lift them as the water flows over them, taking them out of reach of the crabs.

Bait

All sorts of fish can be used for bait; an oily piece of mackerel, for example. The traditional bait is the lugworm, for which you need to get up early and go and dig at low tide. Look for the worm-like casts they throw up in the sand; either locate the blow-hole a little way off and dig under that or, better still, find a patch of beach that is riddled with casts and just dig. There are two types of lugworm: the blow lug and the black lug. The latter is better – it is bigger and more favoured by fish – but it is also harder to find. Be prepared to grab hold of them as you dig, as they disappear from you as fast as you can find them.

Using a rod and line

If you have plenty of time to spare, try fishing with a rod and line from the beach, casting into the water at high tide. The length of line needed will depend on the sea bed and whether it drops away quickly, but on a normal beach you will need a line of at least 64m (70 yards), so you will need to be an experienced angler. Bait the line with up to about 30 hooks on small traces – any more than this and you will need a mechanical winch to haul in the line.

Lobster-pots

These basket-type pots are specially designed so that lobsters and crabs can swim into them, but cannot swim out. Although they are often put in 10m (30ft) of water or so from a boat, you can wade in and position them closer to shore around wrecks or rocks, or in estuaries where lobsters and crabs are known to be found. They should be weighted to keep them on the bottom and their position marked with buoys. Visit them periodically to remove anything you have caught.

Fishing from a boat

If you have a small boat, other possibilities will open up to you, but remember that it is unwise to go more than about 1 mile (1.6km) offshore, as you may not get back to safety if the weather deteriorates quickly. You should only venture that far out in good weather conditions.

When considering offshore fishing, try to determine where the

Commercial lobster fishermen will drop large numbers of pots into deep water from a boat, but you can still catch crabs and maybe a lobster if you are lucky, with just a handful of pots positioned in much shallower water, closer to the shore.

fish are going to be, so that you keep the chances of a fruitless mission to a minimum. Ask more experienced fishermen or learn by examining the sea bed at low tide. If there are gulleys or outcrops of rocks for example, these are the places where the fish will gather when they come in, so position your boat above them.

There are various techniques for fishing from a boat, and what you do will depend on the equipment you have and whether you are going for bottom-living fish such as plaice, sole, dab or flounder, or those that mainly frequent the mid-water, such as bass, mackerel and pollack.

Offshore rod and line

If you are fishing with a rod and line, you will do better with bait than flies. If looking for bottom-living fish, anchor the boat and weight the line so the bait remains on the bottom. If you are going for the mid-water fish, let the boat drift, gently moving down the tide. You should play the line through the water: this means gently pulling it so the fish are attracted by the moving lures.

Your line can have several traces with hooks running off it, to maximise your chances of a catch. As soon as you feel a bite, haul the line in; if you have gone through a shoal of mackerel, for example, you may have a fish on each hook and if you are quick and have a small outboard motor, you may have time to wheel the boat round and go through the shoal again.

Fishermen fishing the bottom often help the size of their catch by attaching what is known as a 'rubby-dubby' bag to the anchor. This gory item is a bag crammed full of fish guts, which exudes a highly alluring juice into the water, thereby attracting the fish to it.

FRESHWATER FISH

How often freshwater fish will supplement your diet depends on where you live and whether you are likely to fish often enough to make it worthwhile obtaining a rod licence.

Most rivers, lakes and reservoirs cannot be fished officially unless you obtain a rod licence and a licence to fish. In most instances these are issued by the local water authority, except in the case of privately-owned lakes, reservoirs and stretches of river, in which case, permission has to be sought from the owner. In addition, there is a closed season for coarse fishing.

There are countless different species of freshwater fish, many of which are edible. The chief ones – and those most coveted by sporting anglers – are salmon, sea trout and other types of trout. In addition there are bream, carp, perch, pike, roach, char, barbel, chub, gudgeon, trench, grayling and eel – all of which can be eaten.

Tickling trout

Experienced trout ticklers can pull fish after fish out of the water without any kind of rod or net. The technique is to put your hand gently into the water (in a known trout river) and wiggle your fingers. As the trout drifts over your hand you continue the wiggling movement, tickling the belly, until, with one quick movement, you get your hand round it and flick it out onto the riverbank.

Finding the best spots

You can increase your chances of catching fish by learning to recognise where they are. Bream, for example, tend to swim in shoals, and can be spotted by areas of muddied water in an otherwise clear stretch of river, while pike are lazy fish that often lie quietly in wait for their prey in the deepish water of a reed bed. If you do catch a pike, you can reduce its rather muddy taste by soaking it in vinegar and water.

Fish will be attracted to all sorts of bait – worms, maggots, garden slugs, and even bits of cheese, bread and potatoes. Always check with the authorities or water-owners where you plan to fish: some do not allow the use of live bait at all and you have to fish with artificial flies or lures.

Using a net

If you are fishing with rod and line, it pays to have a net, too, to help you land big fish. You will also need a keep net, a long net that you tether to a stake on the bank and where you can keep the fish you have caught while you continue fishing.

If you are fishing with rod and line, it pays to have a landing net, too, to help you land big fish without injuring them. You will also need a keep net, a long net that you tether to a stake on the bank and where you can keep the fish you have caught while you continue fishing.

What will you catch?

This depends on where you are fishing and the time of year, as well as the day-to-day weather conditions, the temperature of the water, and so on. You can catch whiting all the year round, although they are most plentiful in the winter. Dab, flounder and sole are also year-round catches, although sole feed mainly at night, so are difficult to catch during the day. Not all the fish you catch may be to your liking, but they are worth tasting, at least once.

Food from the Seashore

The shellfish, and the molluscs in particular, that live on the rocks or in the sand or rock pools at the water's edge are easy to gather, with no special equipment. You will also find many edible plants living close to the sea, which make the perfect accompaniment.

Pick your time and place for seaside foraging. Most shellfish are best looked for in rock pools as low tide approaches. Once the water has ebbed away, they cling tightly to their rocks and are almost impossible to prise away.

Molluscs

Shellfish, and molluscs in particular, should always be treated with caution but, by and large, they do not deserve the reputation they have for causing food-poisoning. They feed by pumping water through their shells, filtering out the food particles as they do so, and any bacteria contained in the water tends to be retained. For this reason, molluscs found near sewage outlets should always be left well alone, and it is wise to do the same with those living on piers, jetties or other possible sources of pollution. Collect them only from clean, unpolluted stretches of water.

Some people advise against collecting molluscs during the warmer summer months. This is their breeding season, so they will necessarily not be in prime condition, and the warmer temperatures of the water can increase the chances of dangerous bacteria multiplying.

The other important point about shellfish of all kinds is that they decompose very quickly. Never collect any that are already dead (if the shell is open, or if they do not hold fast to their rocky stronghold, this is a sure sign). They should be alive at the moment of cooking, which should be done as quickly as possible after collection. Wash them very well first.

Cockles

These small molluscs are also found in tidal mud or sand, often in the mouths of rivers. They generally live just under the surface and are visible either by the narrow veins of mud showing up against the sand or from the fact that the area looks a little darker or muddier than the rest.

You can usually find a good number of cockles all together. Scoop them out with your hands or dig with a blunt-pointed rake and put them carefully in a bucket or bag. Soak the cockles for several hours in a bowl of clean, salted water, having first washed off any clinging mud and sand. They will filter the water through their shells, getting rid of sand and waste matter.

Then put them into a large pan with a small amount of water over a gentle heat and shake until the shells open. Pick out the fleshy meat and add to fish salads, soups, stews, sauces or pies.

Clams

A great favourite in America, clams are most frequently found in the muddy sands exposed between tides. They are among the largest of the molluscs, and usually live quite deep beneath the surface, so you will have to dig for them.

Clams can be eaten raw, but they are often difficult to prise open.

Insert a sharp knife (preferably a special oyster-shucking knife) between the shells at the hinge and twist it. Cut off and discard the fleshy siphon. Alternatively, they can be persuaded to open by shaking the shells in a saucepan over a medium heat for a few minutes.

To cook them, boil for 5–10 minutes, then remove from the shell. You can eat them like this, fry them, or add them to soups, stews or sauces, in which case they generally need a little more gentle boiling to ensure that they are tender.

Limpets

These single-shelled molluscs cling to rocks, jetties, piers and other structures, but should be gathered only from clean rocks which are washed daily by the incoming tides. Prise them free with a knife and treat them like cockles, soaking before cooking. They are much tougher than either clams or cockles and will need long, gentle simmering if they are not to be rather chewy.

Mussels

These bi-valves are found on rocks close to estuaries and the shoreline. Because they are so susceptible to pollution, be particularly sure that you only gather them from clean places. Take them only from the low rocks that are washed by each tide. Discard any with broken shells, or those that do not close immediately the shell is tapped.

Scrub the shells and soak them for five or six hours in cold water, preferably with a handful of oatmeal added. The mussels will feed on this, excreting the dirt in their shells. Discard any that open or float to the surface in this time then cook by steaming over a gentle heat, like cockles, or by baking them.

Only gather mussels from places that are free from pollution. Discard any that are open or that open when soaked in water before cooking, as they are likely to be bad.

a pin not worth the effort. However, they are free food and may be gathered from among the seaweed found on the rocks on the middle or lower shores. Rinse them and then leave them to soak in cold water. Cook for about 10 minutes in boiling water then let them cool before taking them out of their shells.

COASTAL PLANTS AND SEAWEEDS

Some coastal plants and seaweeds are edible and delicious. They are particularly well-suited to eating with the fish and shellfish found living alongside them.

Seaweeds are rich sources of iron and minerals. They are often treated with the same suspicion as fungi, but, like them, they can provide a tasty, free meal. Always wash seaweeds very thoroughly in cold running water before cooking them; they are likely to be salty and gritty.

Rock samphire
This delicious plant takes some effort to collect, as it grows on cliff faces, but it is worth the work. You may also find it among the shingle and rocky outcrops of many coastlines without the need for rock climbing. Pick the leaves and cook like other greens or fry them gently in a little butter.

Sea beet
Known also as sea spinach, sea beet grows widely on sea shores, even on shingle. The leaves can be picked and treated just like cultivated spinach.

Oysters
These are increasingly difficult to find wild, and most are reared in commercial beds. If you do find them, do not let your enthusiasm mar your judgement – if they are in polluted waters, leave them alone.

Oysters live in shallow waters, often near or attached to rocks or stones. To eat them raw; prise the shell open by inserting a sharp, strong knife at the hinge, twist it, then use it to free the oyster from the outer shell. Add a squeeze of lemon juice and swallow. Oysters can also be used in recipes for other shellfish.

Winkles
Many people consider winkling these tiny animals out of their shells with

Sea kale
Another plant that grows on sandy or shingle shores. Pick off the big leaves, strip them to leave the stems, boil these and serve with melted butter.

Sea purslane
This plant likes the salty marshes found near the coast. The leaves may be used in salads.

Carragheen or Irish moss
The reddish-purple fronds (which may turn green in very strong sunlight) of this seaweed can be found in shallow pools, clinging to rocks and stones. Gather it when young, wash it well and simmer it slowly in the ratio of one part seaweed to three parts milk or water, adding sugar to taste. The seaweed will dissolve, at which point it can be strained and flavoured to make a blancmange or jelly, for the mixture will set firm when cold. You can dry it by washing it and putting it in the sun. Use as gelatine.

Dulse
The fan-like fronds of dulse may be found in shallow waters or hanging onto rocks on lower shores. Discard the older parts, once gathered, as these tend to be tough; the younger parts are more tender and can be used raw in salads or cooked like a green vegetable.

Kelp
Found round the low-tide mark on seashores, particularly those that are rocky. Kelp may be treated in the same way as carragheen to provide vegetable gelatine. It may also be used raw in salad.

Laver
This is one of the most commonly-used seaweeds and its purply-green fronds, which turn black when dry, grow on all manner of stones and rocks. It particularly likes those that become covered with sand. It is most often used to make laverbread, which in fact is a sort of purée, traditional in Wales as a breakfast delicacy when rolled in oatmeal and fried with bacon. To make the purée, wash the seaweed thoroughly, then simmer it, changing the water as it begins to stick, until it is thoroughly mushy. It is also used as a sauce to go with lamb or mutton.

Sea lettuce
The translucent green fronds of this seaweed will be found on all parts of the shoreline, sometimes floating in shallow water, sometimes in rock pools and sometimes hanging onto stones or rocks. It can be washed and cooked like a green vegetable.

Low tide often reveals a rich harvest of coastal plants, such as sea lettuce (left) and other seaweeds. Always wash them well to remove salt and grit before use.

Hunting and Shooting

There are many laws governing the killing of any wild bird or animal beyond the boundaries of your own property. Always ensure that you comply with all legal restrictions as well as making certain that you and any other land users are safe at all times.

It is illegal to shoot or kill any wild animal or bird anywhere except within your own property, unless you have permission from the owner of the land. There are also strict laws protecting native birds. Even then, you can only kill the animal within the permitted open season and only if you hold a game licence.

This also applies to any wild game that stray on to your property, in search of your tastiest vegetables: you can kill them, providing they are in season, and providing you have paid sporting rights to the local council. Also, of course, if you intend to shoot wild animals or birds, you must hold the relevant firearms licence. In addition, there are extremely strict and complicated laws relating to the sale of wild game.

Rabbits are 'ground game' and may be taken throughout the year. Game birds include pheasant, partridge, quail, woodcock, wild duck and geese, grouse and pigeon. All except for pigeons have a closed season to protect them while they are breeding. Game bird shoots are often organised and quite social occasions and to shoot larger game, such as deer, you will almost certainly need to join an official shoot. Rabbits and birds can be hunted on a small scale, too.

Rabbits

You will find rabbits in all wild habitats. There are still incidences of the disease myxomatosis, so if you catch a rabbit, check to see it is healthy before considering eating it. The eyes are the tell-tale feature: in a diseased rabbit, they will be swollen and runny. Rabbits should be paunched (de-gutted) as soon as possible after killing, or the meat will be tainted. Some people say they should not be hung like other game, but you may well find that the meat has a better flavour if you do hang it for a few days before cooking.

Game birds

Modern farming methods, with chemical sprays, have depleted the

Pheasants are easy to shoot. Organised day shoots – during the open season – are a good way to get some for the pot.

supply of many game birds' favourite foods, so these birds are often now raised by landowners, rather than existing in large numbers in the wild.

To tenderise the meat, game birds should be hung by the neck for about a week in a cool, well-ventilated place. In cold conditions they can safely be hung for longer. Although they are often hung with their feathers still on, they are best plucked as soon as possible after killing, as a warm bird is the easiest to pluck (*see* page 170 for instructions). The insides are left in during the hanging.

Gathering Firewood

Unfortunately, very little good firewood is free for the taking. All forest belongs to somebody and, theoretically, you should ask the owner – whoever it might be – before you even pick up kindling from the forest floor.

If you are able to gather kindling, remember that it really means small bits of dead twigs and branches that have fallen to the ground. It does not mean snapping branches from the parent tree.

These small dead branches will start a fire quicker and better than firewood that has been chopped up small for kindling. If you have a local source, it is much quicker to go and gather an armful of twigs than to start chopping up old packing cases or splitting down large logs.

Felling trees for firewood

The only trees that you can chop down for firewood are those growing in your own garden. Even then, you should check with your local authority that you are free to do so without contravening any tree protection order or other local byelaw.

If you are lucky enough to own a patch of forest, there could be a legal limit on the amount of timber you are allowed to cut down in each quarter of the year. Also you must have a felling licence, although if you are felling fruit trees, or trees that are less than 1.5 metres (5ft) tall and with a trunk of less than 7.5cm (3in) in diameter, this is not necessary. There are a few other categories of tree that are also exempted from the licence regulation so check with the local authority or the Forestry Commission before you begin.

FELLING A TREE

Felling a tree is simple if you know how and extremely dangerous if you do not. Seek the advice of experts and watch them at work before attempting it yourself.

The ideal situation is a perfectly erect tree standing somewhere where there is nothing to obstruct it as it falls. Before you start, it is vital that you plan which way you want the tree to fall and that you have planned an escape route from the site if the tree falls in the opposite direction.

Always stack firewood in a dry, but airy place. Freshly felled wood should be allowed to dry, or 'season' for up to a year before burning.

Even if you know what you are doing, it is sensible to seek advice if the tree is in anything but perfectly straight-forward circumstances. This would include if it is very large, leaning heavily, close to a deep ditch, telegraph poles or other trees, or is growing on very uneven ground.

Never attempt to use a chainsaw or other power saw without first having had proper training; they are extremely dangerous in inexperienced hands. The Forestry Commission runs courses and it is well worth trying to attend one of these if you have a lot of potential felling on your land. Failing that, stick to the axe and hand saw. They may take longer, but they are generally safer.

If you cut down trees, you should also plant new ones to ensure future generations do not inherit a landscape denuded of trees. Plant young trees – the younger they are, the better they are likely to take and establish themselves. If you are planting hardwood, it will be 20 years before you can chop it down for firewood. Ash is better: it should be ready for cutting again within about 12 years.

HOW DO THEY BURN?

Different woods burn at different speeds and with varying amounts of heat and smoke.

Ash is generally regarded as being the best wood for burning. Beech and oak are good, but slower-burning, and they do not give out the same heat. Oak, in particular, needs to be mature to be at its best. Elm must be thoroughly dry.

Old fruit trees, such as apple, plum and pear make good burning, but most conifers should be treated with respect; they burn well, but spit badly, so are best used in an enclosed wood-burning stove.

All logs should be left to dry, or 'season' before burning, otherwise they soot up the chimney with a black, gooey resin, which will soon close up the chimney altogether. The best way to do this is to stack them neatly in a covered log store or inside a dry shed.

HOW TO FELL A TREE

1 Chop a large wedge in the tree on the side that you want it to fall towards.

2 Chop a similar-sized wedge slightly above the first, but on the opposite side of the tree.

3 Exert pressure on the same side of the tree to make it fall in the direction you planned.

4 Once the tree is felled, trim off the branches and chop the trunk into logs.

SPLITTING LOGS

1 Drive a wedge into the end of a log using a sledgehammer.

2 Drive the wedge in carefully so as not to splinter the wood.

3 Continue driving more wedges down the log until it splits in half.

4 Once the log is split, it can be chopped into smaller pieces as required.

PRESERVING YOUR PRODUCE

Preserving Your Produce

Instead of buying out-of-season produce from the supermarket, the gardener can enjoy his or her own produce, which has been preserved in some way, all year round.

All foods taste best if they are harvested and eaten immediately, but there are few places with a climate temperate enough to provide such extended growing seasons, so food must often be preserved.

In all preserving, it is crucial that you follow any instructions – especially the cooking temperatures and times – very carefully and, in most cases, use only perfect produce at the start. If there is any question of the safety and reliability of a preserved food, throw it away.

It is a good idea to keep a record of each batch of produce preserved, recording what it was, how much it weighed, how long it took, the shelf life, and so on. You will soon develop a rhythm of planting, harvesting and preserving which will fit the flow of the seasons and the produce from your own land.

Fruit and vegetables

The methods of storing and preserving depend on the individual fruit or vegetable. Many can be frozen, but root vegetables are the easiest of all, being stored in sheds, in the ground or in boxes of sand. One popular method of preserving vegetables is to keep them in vinegar to create pickles, chutneys, relishes, sauces and ketchups.

Freezing fruit – soft fruit in particular – will alter its texture; raspberries are often mushy when defrosted, but still delicious made into a sauce or filling. Some fruit and vegetables can be dried and used in that form or after being soaked in water to rehydrate. Apples dry particularly well when cut into thin

Some crops are prone to ripen in gluts – too many to eat all at once, but perfect to preserve for later in the year, by turning them into wines or chutneys, or storing in a cool, dry place.

rings. Fruit is sometimes better preserved in syrups or purées.

Making wine, beer and cider at home is another good way to use up a glut of produce, but requires patience if the results are to be anywhere near palatable.

Meat and fish

If you keep goats, pigs or chickens, you may wish to preserve the flesh rather than give it away or sell it. Salting and smoking are useful techniques, but the meat will not keep for very long. You can also preserve the produce that comes from your goats and chickens if you cannot consume it all fresh. Eggs can be pickled and goats' milk turned into a range of dairy products, particularly yoghurt and soft cheeses.

Preserving Vegetables

Vegetables can be stored and preserved in a number of ways. Some leave the vegetable in its natural state so that it can be used as if it had just been harvested; others change its nature, but still allow you to enjoy your home-grown produce, whatever the season.

Root vegetables store most successfully in their natural state, and they can also be frozen. Freezing is probably the most successful method of preserving most other types of vegetables in order to keep them as close as possible to their natural state.

A few vegetables, such as the salad crops like lettuce and endive which have too high a water content for successful freezing, can really only be stored when they are turned into a cooked dish, such as soup, which is then frozen.

LEAVING IN THE GROUND

All root vegetables, and some others such as leeks which have a very long harvesting season, can be left in the ground through the winter and dug up as you want them.

There are three main objections to this as a storage method: you are unable to use the ground for anything else; the ground may be so hard that you cannot get a fork into it; and it can be very cold work – picking Brussels sprouts when they are frozen to the plant and the frost or snow is thick on the ground is few

people's idea of fun. A compromise to storing them in the ground is to dig up the root vegetables and bury them again in large pots of damp compost. Store the container in a frost-free greenhouse over winter, keeping the compost just moist.

CLAMPING

This old-fashioned way of storing potatoes and root vegetables is still effective and requires less space than storing them in the ground.

Select a spare patch of ground. Cover this with a layer of straw, then pile the root vegetables (take off all leafy tops first) on top in the shape of a pyramid. Cover with more straw, then dig a ditch around the heap, throwing the soil over the top. Ensure some straw protrudes through at the bottom to allow for ventilation, and

pat the earth hard and flat with the back of the spade.

The advantage of clamping is that vegetables keep freer of disease than when stored in a shed. The disadvantage is that in a very cold winter, it does not give adequate protection against a heavy frost.

STORING IN A SHED

It is often easier to store root vegetables in a dry, cool, frost-proof, gloomy shed. There are various ways of keeping them there, but always remember not to wash them before storing, or they will rot.

You can make a sort of mini-clamp by piling the vegetables in a corner

Root vegetables will keep well if you re-bury them in large pots of damp compost, stored in a frost-free greenhouse.

of the shed, separating the layers with straw and protecting them with some sacking. Or you can layer them in containers, separated by sand or peat which prevents the vegetables from drying out or shrivelling.

Use wooden boxes – old-fashioned fruit trays are ideal if you have a friendly greengrocer who is willing to donate some to you – or pile the vegetables in dustbins and put a 5cm (2in) layer of sand in the bottom. Put a single layer of the root vegetable (carrots, parsnips, beetroot, salsify, winter radish) on top, arranged neatly and close together. Top with another layer of sand, and then continue layering in this way. The containers must be kept in the dry, cool shed.

The option that requires least effort is to try piling up swedes in a corner of the shed and using them from here as required. Of course, they are vulnerable like this to any mice or other rodents that can get into the shed. Beware of storing vegetables in a garage, particularly one in regular use for storing a car or petrol-operated machine, as they could easily take up the taste of petrol fumes.

Storing in sacks

Most root vegetables can be stored in heavy paper or hessian sacks, but not polythene, which holds in the moisture and will make them rot. Storing in sacks is a good way of keeping potatoes; pile them into the sack, leave it open for a couple of days, then close it up and store in a shed as above. Potatoes must be kept away from the light or they will turn green.

Stacking in boxes

Onions and garlic can be stored in shallow slatted wooden fruit boxes,

Loosely pack root vegetables, such as these beetroots, into wooden trays and cover with sand to keep them dry and fresh until you are ready to use them.

but always make sure that the vegetables are thoroughly ripe before laying them down. Then just put them into the boxes in single layers and stack the boxes one on top of another.

Tying onions in strings

The other traditional way of storing onions is in strings or ropes, and these should again be kept somewhere cool and frost-free. There are various methods of stringing the onions together, but always check first that the onions have been dried ready for storage and have long stalks.

A simple method of tying onions in strings is to knot the stalks of four onions together and plait a strong piece of string around them, so that they hang neatly. As you add each new onion to the collection, knot the stalks around the string, making sure that the bunch always hangs evenly. When you have strung enough onions, hang up the bunch in a cool, dry place.

Using nets

Onions can also be hung up in nets, but check them frequently to make sure none are rotting and infecting others. This is also a way of storing ripe marrows or pumpkins; they will keep for several weeks.

Pumpkins can be stored on a shelf in the shed, as can marrows, but they will not keep very long. Cauliflowers can be kept for a few weeks if hung upside down by their roots in a cool shed.

DRYING

A few vegetables can be dried, although this is more frequently done with herbs (*see* page 219) or fruit.

Runner, French and haricot beans, peas, mushrooms and onions can all be dried. However, they will lose all their valuable vitamins if stored this way, so always make freezing your first choice if possible.

Runner and French beans

Pick beans when young, and top, tail and string them if necessary. Wash the vegetables and slice the runners. Plunge into boiling water for about three minutes, rinse quickly in cold water, then spread them out on a clean tea towel or a thick wad of kitchen paper.

When they have dried a little, spread them out on oven trays and leave in the coolest possible oven until they are dry and crisp. This takes a few hours. Pack into jars with air-tight lids and keep in a cool, dark place. They should be soaked for several hours in cold water before being cooked in the usual way.

Haricot beans

Leave the pods on the plants until autumn when they have turned white. Pick the whole plant and hang up in a dry, cool place which has good air circulation. When they feel quite dry, either shell the beans or put them in a sack and beat and shake it to separate the beans from the pods. Spread the beans on sheets of paper or trays until they are hard and dry. Store in jars and use as recipes dictate.

Peas

Either pick them young, pod them and follow the method for runner and French beans, or leave them on the pod and follow that for haricot beans. Drying on the plant is usually less successful unless you grow a variety specifically bred for this.

Mushrooms

You can dry those you collect from the countryside, but they must be absolutely fresh and the very best specimens. Peel them if they look dirty, otherwise wipe them clean with a damp cloth. Remove the stalks and either thread the caps onto a piece of string (making sure they do not touch each other), or put them in a single layer on a wire cooking tray. Hang strings in a warm place (such as above a boiler or in an airing cupboard) and put the trays in the coolest possible oven.

Leave until they are dry and crisp and can easily be crumbled, then store in an air-tight jar. For frying or grilling, boil them in a little water for about 15 minutes, or soak for an hour or two. They can be added as they are to soups and stews to cook with the other ingredients.

Onions

Peel and cut into 0.5cm (¼in) slices. Separate into rings and plunge into boiling water for half a minute. Drain and rinse quickly under cold water.

Drain on a tea towel and then follow the procedure for drying beans. Soak the onions for 30 minutes before using them.

SALTING

This is the old-fashioned way of preserving runner beans, although freezing is now more common. Cucumbers, which will not freeze, can also be preserved in salt.

Runner beans

Pick the beans when young, top and tail them, then string, wash and slice them. Put a 1cm (½in) layer of salt in a jar, which can be plastic, glass or earthenware, then cover this with a layer of beans.

Continue alternating beans and salt until you have used up all the beans, or filled the jar. Cover the jar and leave it for a few days. You will find that as the beans shrivel, they reduce in size. Top up the jar with more beans and salt. Finally, seal the top and store it until you want the beans. Take out as many as you require at a time, wash them well in cold water and then cook in the usual way.

Cucumbers

Salt cucumbers as soon as they are picked, while they are still fresh and crisp. Slice them fairly thinly and place in a shallow container. Sprinkle heavily with salt, press a plate on top and leave overnight. The next day, drain the cucumber and pat it dry with kitchen paper or a tea towel. Layer with salt in a jar in the same way as for runner beans, finishing with a layer of salt. Seal the jar and store it. When they are needed, wash the slices well under cold water and leave them to soak for an hour in cold water.

Stringing onions and hanging them is the traditional way to store this vegetable. Keep long stalks on the onions when you lift them.

Storing tomatoes

Tomatoes can be frozen once they are ripe, although they can only be used for sauces, soups or stews thereafter; frozen tomatoes are no good for salads because they are too mushy once defrosted. You can also store green tomatoes harvested at the end of the season by wrapping them individually in newspaper and keeping them indoors in a drawer or box. They should keep from autumn until Christmas.

FREEZING

This is probably the most successful method of storing vegetables, but it can be tempting to keep more than you could ever use. Freeze only as much as you need to last you until the next fresh harvest: frozen food does not last indefinitely.

Vegetables should be frozen as soon as possible after picking, so only pick at one time the amount you can reasonably process straightaway. If you intend to freeze a sizeable proportion of any one type of vegetable, it is sensible to grow one of the varieties that have been specially developed for freezing. Only freeze vegetables which are in prime condition; discard any that are bruised or damaged.

Pack vegetables for the freezer in meal-size quantities. This is less important for those vegetables that you 'open-freeze', laying them out individually on trays and freezing before packing into bags and containers, as they remain separate when frozen and may be tipped individually from the bag. Open-freezing takes a little more time, but produce treated this way is easier to handle than solid blocks of vegetables in ice. It is suitable for peas, beans, courgettes, baby carrots and other vegetables that grow in small individual pieces.

Blanching

It is usual to blanch vegetables before freezing them, as this helps to retain the colour, flavour and texture of the vegetable and also preserves the vitamin content. A special blanching basket is a worthwhile investment and the prepared vegetables are then plunged into boiling water for the prescribed time (*see* opposite). After this they are plunged into ice-cold water for the same length of time to stop the cooking process.

Use a large pan of water when blanching, as it is essential that the water returns to the boil within one minute when the vegetables are immersed in it. The recommended amount is 2.8 litres of water to 450g of vegetables (6 pints to 1lb). Don't try to put more than this amount of vegetables into the blanching basket at any one time.

The same water can be used to blanch about six batches of vegetables, but replace the cooling water each time, as it will have warmed up slightly. Fill a bowl with cold water and tip some ice cubes into it. Drain the vegetables well after cooling, patting them dry with some kitchen paper, before packing, labelling and freezing.

Frozen food safety

Follow the normal freezer rules of packing vegetables into rigid plastic containers or polythene bags, excluding as much air as possible in both cases. Label them with their name and the date on which they were frozen and then keep a freezer log so you can use produce in rotation.

What can you freeze?

The chart opposite gives instructions for preparing vegetables for freezing, and the length of time they should be blanched in boiling salted water, unless otherwise stated. Not all those vegetables included in the growing section of this book will be found on the chart, because some are not worth freezing.

Most salad vegetables have too high a water content and some root vegetables, such as Jerusalem artichokes or swedes can only be frozen as a purée or a soup.

The exception to this is if you want to freeze a small selection of mixed vegetables – including a variety of roots – to add to stews or casseroles. In this case, prepare and blanch all the different vegetables individually and then freeze them together in a bag.

Beetroot and red cabbage can be frozen, but are more usually preserved by pickling (or, in the case of beetroot, in boxes of sand); the results of freezing these are not really worthy of the freezer space they would occupy.

Freeze vegetables in meal-sized portions, in bags or boxes, or open-freeze them on trays and put into bags once they are frozen.

FREEZING VEGETABLES

VEGETABLE	PREPARATION	BLANCHING TIME
Artichokes, globe	Cut off stems and coarse outer leaves. Remove the choke if you wish; wash thoroughly in cold water.	7 minutes in water with lemon juice added. Blanch 5 at a time
Asparagus	Cut off the woody, lower stems and wash spears well. Sort into various thicknesses	2 minutes for thin stems / 4 minutes for thick stems
Aubergine	Wash and cut into 0.5cm (1.4in) slices. Drop these into water with lemon juice added to avoid discoloration. Can be open-frozen	4 minutes
Beans, broad	Choose young beans and shell them. Can be open frozen	2 minutes
Beans, French	Wash and cut off the ends. Choose young ones and leave them whole	2 minutes
Beans, runner	Wash, trim off ends and slice or cut into 2.5cm (1in) lengths	2 minutes
Broccoli, purple sprouting and calabrese	Choose small, tender shoots. Cut off tough stalks and leaves, wash thoroughly in salted water and grade into thick and thin stems	3 minutes for thin stems / 4 minutes for thick stems
Brussels sprouts	Choose small, firm sprouts; remove outer leaves and wash in salted water. Grade into sizes if they vary. Can be open-frozen	3 minutes (4 if they are big)
Cabbage, white	Choose a firm-headed variety which is young and crisp. Shred and wash thoroughly in salted water	2 minutes
Carrot	Young carrots are best. Wash (rub off the skins after blanching) and cut off tops. Leave whole and open-freeze. Wash, scrape and cut larger carrots into slices	4 minutes for whole carrots / 3 minutes for sliced carrots
Cauliflower	Choose compact, white cauliflowers and cut into small florets. Wash well. Can be open-frozen	3 minutes in water with lemon juice added
Celeriac	(If wanted for cooking, not for eating raw.) Peel and cut into cubes	4 minutes
Celery	(If wanted for cooking, not for eating raw.) Choose crisp young stalks. Cut off roots and leaves, wash thoroughly and cut into even-sized lengths	3 minutes in water with lemon juice added
Courgette (small zucchini)	Choose young, firm courgettes. Cut off ends, wash and cut in half lengthwise or into slices. Can be open-frozen	1 minute
Kale	Choose young shoots, trim off thick stalks and older leaves. Wash thoroughly	3 minutes, but not essential
Kohl rabi	(If wanted for cooking) Choose young ones, peel and cut into even-sized chunks	6 minutes, until almost tender
Leek	Cut off roots and green top. Remove outer leaves. Wash thoroughly; leave thin ones whole and split thicker ones into even-sized lengths. Can be open-frozen	3 minutes
Marrow (large zucchini)	Choose young, firm ones. Peel, discard seeds and cut the flesh into even-sized, fairly large chunks	2 minutes
Parsnip	Choose young, unblemished parsnips. Top and tail, peel and cut into chunks	2 minutes
Peas	Choose young ones. Pod and grade into sizes if they vary. Can be open-frozen	1 minute
Pepper	Wash, slice and remove seeds and white membrane. Can be open-frozen	6 minutes, until almost tender
Potato (new)	Choose small, even-sized potatoes and scrape or scrub them	6 minutes, until almost tender
Potato (old)	Raw, they are only worth freezing for chips. Blanch and freeze or partly fry until just tender, but not turning brown. Cool quickly and freeze. Can be open-frozen	3 minutes
Salsify	Choose young roots, peel and cut into even-sized lengths	2 minutes in water with lemon juice added
Seakale beet	Choose those with tender midribs. Remove leaves (and use or freeze like spinach – see below) and cut ribs into even-sized lengths	3 minutes
Spinach	Use young, unblemished leaves and process immediately after picking. Strip leaves from the stalks and wash thoroughly	2 minutes. Drain well and squeeze out excess water
Sweetcorn	Choose young cobs. Remove the green husks and silky tassels and sort into sizes. If you like you can cut the kernels from the cobs and freeze them	4 minutes for small cobs / 6-8 minutes for larger ones / 3 minutes for kernels only
Tomato	(For use in stews, soups, etc.) Choose firm tomatoes and wash and dry them. Freeze whole	No blanching
Turnip	Choose young, small turnips. Cut off the ends, peel and cut into chunks. Small ones can be left whole	3 minutes (4 if freezing whole)

Equipment for Making Preserves

Most of the things you will need for making sweet or savoury preserves will probably be already in your kitchen, but they must all be a material that will not react with the acids in fruits and vinegars, such as stainless steel, plastic, nylon or wood.

You can buy special jam pans, called maslins, which are very large and have a sturdy carrying handle and a lip for pouring, but a standard large saucepan will also suffice, as long as it has a heavy bottom and is stainless steel or has a non-stick or enamel lining. When cooking sweetened mixtures, keep the pan no more than half full – the mixture will spit when boiled – so adjust the quantities of a recipe to suit the size of your pan. You will also need the following:

Scales Most preserves can be made without accurately measuring the ingredients, but some scales can also be helpful. For making large quantities, you may find bathroom scales a better choice.

Knives Always use sharp, stainless steel knives to make clean cuts and minimise the discoloration of fruit.

Spice bag A small square of muslin can be tied around a collection of spices, or you could use a paper from a coffee machine, but special drawstring bags or metal spice balls are also available.

Wooden spoon A long-handled wooden spoon is essential for frequent stirring without burning yourself.

Slotted spoon Scum is often produced when making jams and jellies; skim this off with a slotted spoon to prevent the finished preserve from turning cloudy. You can also use a slotted spoon for removing fruit pips and stones during cooking.

Thermometer You can test whether jams and jellies have reached their setting point by dropping a little onto a cooled saucer, but a sugar thermometer designed for measuring high temperatures is more precise.

Sieves and **colanders** Make sure that they are either stainless steel or nylon.

Bowls and **measuring spoons** or **cups** You will need a selection of bowls, jugs and measuring equipment.

Funnel These make it easier and safer to decant hot preserves into jars and bottles. Wide-necked funnels are available for jars and standard narrow ones for bottles.

Ladle For transferring the preserves into their jars, a ladle is far easier than trying to tip the heavy pan.

Jelly bag and stand Jellies must be strained through a muslin bag part-way through cooking. These can be improvised, but a shop-bought bag and strainer stand is a good investment.

Pressure cooker This is not essential, but will save a lot of time for recipes where you need to pre-cook vegetables to soften them.

JARS AND BOTTLES

You can buy jars new in standard sizes or save used jars and wash them for your own preserves. You will need to buy new lids, or improvise with cling film. Wide-mouthed jars are most useful for pickles, as they are easier to fill.

Always inspect jars carefully before use to make sure that there are no cracks, chips or other damage. If you pour hot jam into a flawed jar it will shatter; even if it does not, the cracks will harbour bacteria that could spoil your preserve.

Sterilising jars
Wash jars in hot soapy water then rinse in hot water and stand them, upright, in a large, deep pan. Fill the pan and the jars with boiling water and boil rapidly for 10 minutes. Use tongs to lift the jars out of the water and drain them upside down. Use the jars warm if the preserve you are putting in them is also warm, but allow them to cool before filling with a cold preserve.

Always fill jars to just below the rim; if you leave a lot of room at the top, the air trapped inside the jar can contain microscopic organisms that will spoil the preserve.

Covers and lids
Acid-proof lids can be used for sweet preserves, but vinegary chutneys and pickles must be sealed with a vinegar-proof lining. If you only have metal lids, which are not vinegar proof, cover the jar with cling film before putting on the lid.

You don't need much special equipment, but may find it useful to buy a jam thermometer (top left), jelly-straining bag (top right) or piece of muslin (below right) and a ladle (below left).

Pickles, Chutney and Relishes

Many vegetables can be preserved in vinegar, by making them into pickles, chutneys, relishes, sauces or ketchups. Spices add a tangy and often sharp flavour, and the resulting preserves are delicious as garnishes to many cooked or raw dishes, or stirred into soups, stews, casseroles and more during cooking.

The most important thing to remember in the preparation of all these preserves is that any cooking must be done in an aluminum, stainless steel, or enamel-lined pan, as vinegar will react with copper or brass and taint the taste of the preserve. Use wooden spoons and

Preserving will help to prevent produce that tend to ripen in a glut – like courgettes and tomatoes – from going to waste.

THE SELF-SUFFICIENCY MANUAL

CHOOSING A PRESERVING METHOD

PRESERVE	METHOD	SUITABLE VEGETABLES
Pickles	Pickling retains the shape, colour, and texture of the vegetable, while preserving it in spiced vinegar. Many fruits can also be pickled, as well as hard-boiled eggs	Beans (runner or French), beetroot, cabbage (red or white), carrot, cauliflower, celery, courgette, cucumber, marrow, mushroom, onion, pepper, and tomato (red or green)
Chutneys	Chutneys are preserves in which vegetables are chopped and cooked slowly with vinegar, spices and sugar, and often with fruits such as apple, dates and sultanas. They have a jam-like consistency	Beetroot, marrow, pepper (red and green), pumpkin, tomato (red and green). Good fruits for making chutney include apple, apricot, blackberry, damson, gooseberry, orange, pear, and rhubarb
Relishes	Relishes retain the crispness of the ingredients by chopping the vegetables coarsely and cooking them quickly or not at all. Most relishes should be kept for around two months before using	Tomato, pepper and celery; sweetcorn, pepper and onion; cucumber and onion; beetroot and cabbage; other combinations according to what is available
Sauces and ketchups	Sauces and ketchups are made by cooking vegetables with vinegar then straining and cooking again to give a concentrated flavour and smooth consistency. Sauces may be made from several different vegetables, but ketchups are usually made from only one	Mushroom, onion, tomato

Above left Make sweet pickles, such as figs and lavender, by adding sugar to the vinegar. *Above centre* Pickled cucumber makes a tangy accompaniment to cold meats. *Above right* Add lemon or herbs to give a fresh flavour that will complement summer vegetables, such as these pickled artichokes.

stainless steel knives, rather than metal ones, and nylon or stainless steel sieves. Vinegar will corrode metal jar tops unless you buy specially-treated vinegar-proof ones. Jars with air-tight plastic screw-tops or clip-on lids with thick rubber gaskets are good alternatives, but always ensure that jars are air-tight to prevent the vinegar from evaporating.

MAKING SPICED VINEGAR

You can buy ready-spiced pickling vinegar, but it is fun to make your own from a good basic malt vinegar so you can tailor the flavours and level of spice to suit your taste.

The most common spices used are cinnamon, allspice, cloves, mace, and peppercorns. Always use whole

PICKLING VEGETABLES

Choose young, unblemished vegetables for pickling and make sure that they are crisp and fresh, as they will be preserved just as they start. Save less-than-perfect specimens for chutneys. If the vegetables are cooked before pickling, pack them into warm jars while they are still hot; raw vegetables should be packed into cold jars.

1 Wash and chop the vegetables if necessary (some, such as onions, are best pickled whole). Steep the vegetables in coarse salt or salt water for 24 hours to draw out any water they contain, which would dilute the vinegar.

2 Wash the vegetables well then drain them thoroughly. Pack them into clean jars up to 2.5cm (1in) from the top.

3 Drain off any water that collects in the jar then fill with the strained spiced vinegar to 1cm (½in) from the top. Seal the jars immediately with air-tight lids.

Unopened jars can be stored for 18 months in a cool, dark place. Once opened, keep in the fridge and use within a month.

spices, as powdered ones will make the vinegar cloudy, and add around 6g (¼oz) of each per 1 litre (2 pints) of vinegar. Use more spices for a stronger flavour and add bruised root ginger, mustard seeds and crushed dried chillies for heat or sugar for a sweet pickle. Leave the spices to steep for at least one month. If you want a light-coloured pickle, start with a white, distilled vinegar.

CHUTNEYS

For a chutney, the vegetables are prepared by chopping them finely or mincing them to ensure the finished chutney has a smooth, even texture – how finely you chop will depend on your personal taste.

The vegetables are cooked slowly with vinegar, spices, sugar and any other additions (such as fruit or sultanas) for a long time. Malt vinegar is usually used, although white, distilled vinegar can also be used. It may be spiced as for pickles or the spices may be added during the cooking – ground spices can be added direct, whole spices should be tied in a muslin bag, suspended in the mixture throughout cooking and then removed.

The spices used are similar to those used to spice the vinegar in pickle making. Individual recipes will specify their own combinations. Most recipes include sugar, and brown sugar generally gives the best colour.

Achieving a soft texture

If vegetables are particularly tough (onions for example) it is often advisable to soften them first by cooking them in a small amount of water or vinegar in a covered pan. Once they are soft, add the rest of the ingredients and the remaining vinegar and continue the cooking with the pan uncovered: the liquid must be able to evaporate to produce the desired pulpy texture.

Chutneys generally require a good one or two hours' cooking, by which time there should be no liquid left on the top of the vegetables or round the edges of the pan. If you think the mixture has become too solid (and remember it will thicken still further as it cools), add a little more vinegar.

The hot chutney should be poured into warm, clean jars and covered immediately with screw-top or clip-on, air-tight lids. The flavour will mature and mellow during storage, and all chutneys should be kept for a few months before they are used.

MAKING CHUTNEY

It is not so important to choose crisp, young vegetables as it is when pickling produce, but make sure all blemished parts of those used are cut away and discarded.

1 Cut the vegetables and fruit into small pieces. Salt watery vegetables, such as courgettes, and leave them to drain in a colander overnight or for several hours at least before rinsing ready for use.

2 Put all the prepared fruit and vegetables into a large pan together with the vinegar and spices. Bring to the boil and simmer, without a lid, for between 30 minutes and 1½ hours, or until the mixture is soft, but not mushy. Stir occasionally to prevent sticking.

3 Turn the heat to low and stir in the sugar. Once it has dissolved, return the pan to the boil and cook until the chutney is thick, stirring regularly to prevent sticking. The chutney is ready when no liquid appears when you drag a spoon across the bottom of the pan. It will thicken more as it cools.

4 Spoon carefully into jars and seal them promptly.

Making relishes

As with pickles, vegetables should be fresh, crisp and young. Wash and chop them into small, coarse pieces and cook as directed in the recipe, although for many relishes the vegetables are left raw. Add spiced vinegar and, usually, sugar and allow the relish to mature for around two months before use.

SAUCES AND KETCHUPS

These are prepared in the same way, but ketchups usually only have one vegetable ingredient, while sauces may include several.

Only use vegetables that are ripe and well-flavoured, and discard any bruised or damaged parts. The vegetables should then be washed, and chopped finely or minced, before being cooked together with the vinegar and spices as stipulated in the individual recipe. When the vegetables are soft and pulpy, push them through a sieve and return to a clean pan to continue cooking.

If sugar is to be used in the recipe, it is generally added after the vegetables have been sieved, and additional vinegar may be added at this time too.

If using corks to seal your bottles, let them steep in boiling water for about 15 minutes first. This sterilises and also softens them, making it easier to push them into the bottles.

Sterilising the sauce

Sauces and ketchups made from vegetables which have a low acid content – tomatoes and mushrooms in particular – may ferment during storage, so they have to be sterilised.

MAKING TOMATO KETCHUP

Once you have tasted home-made ketchup, you will never go back to the sweet, but bland, commercial varieties in the shops. Add a couple of teaspoons of sun-dried tomato paste to boost the flavour if your tomatoes are not quite ripe. This makes enough for one bottle, about 2½ cups.

INGREDIENTS
1.3kg (3lbs) ripe tomatoes
2 red onions
2 celery stalks
2 cloves garlic
220g (7½oz) light brown sugar
175ml (6floz) cup cider vinegar
½ teaspoon cayenne pepper
1½ teaspoons paprika
½ teaspoon salt
2 teaspoons sun-dried tomato purée if wished

1 Chop the tomatoes, red onions, celery stalks and cloves of garlic and put them all in a large pan. Cook over a very low heat until the tomatoes are pulpy.

2 Increase the heat and boil rapidly until the mixture thickens, stirring frequently to prevent it sticking or burning on the bottom of the pan.

3 Press the mixture through a sieve and return it to the cleaned-out pan or a fresh one. Over a low heat, stir in the remaining ingredients.

4 Stir continuously until the sugar has dissolved then simmer the ketchup, stirring frequently, until the mixture has thickened to the right consistency.

5 Bottle and then sterilise the ketchup (*see* below). Store in a cool, dark, dry place for one month before using, but do not keep for longer than one year.

Screw the caps loosely, or tie down the corks, otherwise they will blow out during the sterilising process.

Put a false bottom in a pan which is deep enough to take the bottles, so that water can be added to come up to the bottom of the screw tops or corks. The false bottom can be made from thickly folded newspaper or by using a piece of slatted wood or a wooden or metal trivet. Put the bottles on top of this, making sure they do not touch each other or the sides of the pan.

Pour in sufficient warm water to come up to the bottom of the corks or bottle caps and heat the water to a temperature of 77°C (170°F).

Maintain the temperature of the water for 30 minutes, then remove the bottles, using tongs, and screw them up tightly. These sauces and ketchups should be used quickly once they have been opened. Those that do not require sterilising will keep for several months once opened, as will pickles, chutneys and relishes.

STORING AND PRESERVING VEGETABLES

The most successful and usual methods of preserving or storing vegetables are given in the chart below.

VEGETABLE	METHOD OF STORING OR PRESERVING	VEGETABLE	METHOD OF STORING OR PRESERVING
Artichoke, globe	Freeze	**Radish** (winter only)	Boxes of sand
Artichoke, Jerusalem	Leave in the ground or freeze as a soup or purée	**Salsify**	Freeze
Asparagus	Freeze	**Scorzonera**	In boxes of sand
Aubergine (eggplant)	Will keep for a fortnight in a cool place, or freeze immediately	**Seakale beet**	Freeze
Beans, broad	Freeze	**Shallot**	Hang in strings or nets, or pickle
Beans, French	Dry or freeze	**Spinach** (all sorts)	Freeze
Beans, haricot	Dry	**Swede** (rutabaga)	Stacked in a cool, frost-free shed
Beans, runner	Dry, freeze or salt	**Sweetcorn**	Freeze
Beetroot	In boxes of sand or peat, or pickled	**Tomato**	If green, in dark drawers until ripe, or freeze
Broccoli	Freeze	**Turnip**	In boxes of sand
Brussels sprouts	Freeze		
Cabbage, white	Freeze. (Savoys can remain in the ground until wanted)		
Cabbage, red	Pickle		
Calabrese	Freeze		
Carrot	In boxes of sand, clamps or freeze		
Cauliflower	Will keep for three weeks if hung upside down in a cool shed, or freeze		
Celeriac	In boxes of damp sand		
Celery	Freeze		
Chicory	Freeze in made-up, cooked dishes		
Courgette (small zucchini)	Freeze		
Cucumber	Salt or freeze as a soup		
Garlic	In slatted wooden boxes or tied in strings		
Kale	Freeze		
Kohl rabi	In boxes of sand		
Leek	Leave in the ground or freeze		
Marrow (large zucchini)	Hang in nets in a cool, airy place or freeze		
Okra	Freeze		
Onion	Hang in strings, or in slatted wooden boxes		
Parsnip	In boxes of sand or clamps		
Peas	Freeze or dry		
Pepper	Freeze		
Potato	Clamps, or in hessian or paper sacks		
Pumpkin	On shelves or hang in nets in frost-free shed		

A cool shed or outbuliding is an excellent place to store fresh produce in sacks, boxes of sand, strings or baskets. Make it as rodent-proof as possible. If the building has power to it, install a large chest freezer, too, so that you can store all your produce in one place. Always keep records to ensure that you use the oldest produce first.

Preserving Herbs

The few evergreen herbs, such as thyme and bay, can be picked and used the whole year round, but to enjoy most other herbs throughout the year, you will need to preserve them in some way.

The traditional method of doing this is to dry them. Some herbs can also be frozen and this is usually a more successful option for chervil, parsley and chives, which do not dry well. The flavour of stored herbs diminishes after a few months, so only keep small amounts.

Freezing herbs

A simple way to freeze herbs is to chop them and put them into ice-cube trays. Top up with water and freeze. They can be removed from the trays once frozen, and packed in polythene bags or boxes. Use the frozen blocks to flavour soups, sauces and stews; just stir them into the mixture as it is cooking.

Another way to freeze herbs (suitable also for basil, tarragon and mint) is merely to wash and drain them dry before popping the sprigs into polythene bags. They will become limp as they thaw so are not suitable for garnishes. Instead, crumble them into the dish they are to flavour while they are still frozen. Herbs frozen in this way will keep only for about three months in the freezer before becoming discoloured.

Drying herbs

If you are planning to dry herbs, be careful about when you pick them. All are best picked on a warm, sunny day in the morning after the dew has lifted. Pick them just before the flowering season; after this the leaves – which contain the flavour – toughen.

Choose only perfect specimens, with undamaged leaves. Discard any leaves that are withered or dead. You can dry herbs in a warm oven, spread out on wire racks or trays. Turn off the oven after an hour, but leave the herbs inside until it is cool.

Store dried herbs in a cool place, out of direct sunlight and use as required. Remember their flavour is more concentrated than that of fresh herbs as the water content has been evaporated, just leaving their

Dry sprigs of herbs in small bunches to see you through winter. Only dry a little of each, as they will not keep for more than a few months.

essential oils. When substituting dried herbs for fresh in a recipe, use a third, or half as much.

AIR-DRYING HERBS

1 Tie herbs in small bunches. Dip them for a few seconds in boiling water and then refresh them quickly under the cold tap. This helps to clean them and to retain their colour, but it is not essential. Shake off excess water and dab them on kitchen paper to get them as dry as possible.

2 Hang the bunches in a warm, dry place out of direct sunlight for around three days. Or spread them on a wire rack and leave in a warm cupboard for up to five days.

3 When the herbs are quite crisp and brittle to the touch, they are dry. Either crumble them with your fingers or crush them with a rolling pin, discarding any tough stalks. If you want a finer powder, pass them through a sieve. Store the crumbled herbs in air-tight jars and keep them in a cool, dark place.

Preserving Fruit

The only fruits which can be kept raw for longer than a month are the later varieties of apple. All other fruits must be preserved if you cannot eat them fresh from the tree or bush.

The most common ways to preserve fruit are freezing and bottling. Pickling, jam and jelly-making are other methods useful for using up a glut of fruit. A few fruits may also be dried.

DRYING

This method is particularly suitable for apricots, peaches and plums, but apples, pears and grapes may be dried too.

The principle of drying fruits is much the same as that for drying vegetables (*see* page 208), although it is particularly important not to let the temperature of the oven rise above 50°C (120°F) or Gas Mark 0 –¼ for at least the first hour, otherwise the skins will either harden or burst apart.

You can also dry fruits at normal air temperature. Prepare the fruits as for oven drying then spread them on wire racks or thread onto lengths of dowel and leave in a warm, dry place, such as an airing cupboard until shrivelled and dry.

Using dried fruits

You can use dried fruits just as they are or snack on them like fruity crisps, but for cooking they are often brought back to a more moist state. Soak the fruit in water, with sugar added if you like, until the pieces are soft and ready to use.

BEST METHODS FOR STORING FRUIT

The most successful and usual method of preserving or storing fruit is given in the chart below.

FRUIT	METHOD OF STORING OR PRESERVING
Apple	Store later varieties wrapped in oiled paper in boxes; otherwise freeze or dry
Apricot	Can be kept for up to a month in wooden trays in a cool, airy place, providing they were only just ripe when picked. Otherwise, freeze, bottle, pickle or make jam
Blackberry	Freeze, bottle, pickle or make jam
Blackcurrant	Freeze, bottle, make jam or jelly
Blueberry	Freeze
Crab apple	Pickle, make jam or jelly
Cherry	Freeze, bottle or make jam
Red and white currant	Freeze, bottle or make jelly
Damson	Freeze, bottle, pickle or make jam
Gooseberry	Freeze, bottle or make jam
Grape	Dry or make jelly or wine (*see* page 230)
Loganberry	Freeze, bottle or make jam
Melon	Freeze
Mulberry	Freeze, bottle or make jam
Peach and nectarine	Freeze, bottle or make jam
Pear	Freeze, bottle, dry or make jam
Plum and gage	Freeze, bottle, dry or make jam
Quince	Make jelly
Raspberry	Freeze, bottle or make jam
Rhubarb	Freeze or bottle
Strawberry	Freeze, bottle or make jam

Apricots, peaches and plums

Choose the largest varieties possible and select fruit that is unblemished, ripe, but firm. Wash the fruit if necessary, then halve it and remove the stones. Cover wire trays (which will fit in the oven) with muslin and lay the fruit out on these, in single layers, not touching. Place in an oven heated to the temperature recommended opposite and leave until the skins start to shrivel then raise the temperature very slightly.

Plums can be frozen, bottled, dried or used to make jam. Cut them in half and remove the stone before preserving them.

Thread apple rings onto a length of wooden dowel and hang it somewhere warm and dry until the fruit is ready.

OVEN-DRYING FRUIT

Commercially dried fruit is often prepared using varieties specially developed to retain their colour when dried. Don't despair if your own efforts look less than perfect – they will still taste delicious. You can follow these steps for drying root and tuber vegetables, too. Blanch vegetables, except for tomatoes, sweet peppers, okra, mushrooms, beetroot and onions, before drying and remove the stalks of mushrooms.

1 Start with only good quality, firm, blemish-free fruit that is just ripe. Peel, core and slice as necessary, cutting very thin and even slices.

2 For fruits that discolour, such as apples and pears, dip the slices in a weak solution of lemon juice: 6 tablespoons of lemon juice to 1 pint (500ml) of water.

3 Lie the slices on a wire rack over a foil-lined baking sheet, making sure that they do not touch. Arrange halved fruits cut-side down. Put the oven on its lowest setting, put the fruit in and leave the door slightly ajar.

4 Dry for the times given in the table (right), turning half way through and swapping the position of trays in the oven. The food is ready when it is dry and leathery.

5 Leave to cool completely before storing. Pack slices in air-tight containers, layered between parchment paper, and store in a cool cupboard or larder.

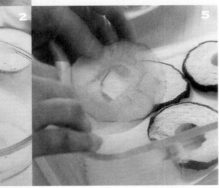

OVEN-DRYING TIMES FOR FRUIT

With your oven on its lowest setting, dry sliced and prepared fruits (and vegetables) as follows

FRUIT	TIME
Apple rings	6–8 hours
Apricots, halved and pitted	36–48 hours
Bananas, peeled and halved lengthwise	10–16 hours
Berries, left whole	12–18 hours
Cherries, pitted	18–24 hours
Herbs, tied in bundles	12–16 hours
Peaches, peeled, halved and pitted	36–48 hours
Peaches, sliced	12–16 hours
Pears, peeled, halved and cored	36–48 hours
Pineapple, cored and cut into 5mm (¼in) rings	36–48 hours
Plums, halved	18–24 hours
Vegetables, 5mm (¼in) slices	2 hours
Vegetables, 10mm (½in) slices	7–8 hours

These fruits are dry when no moisture comes out of them and the skin does not break when you squeeze them gently.

Apples

The best way to dry these is in rings. Choose crisp, sweet apples; peel and core them, then slice them into 5mm (¼in) rings. As you cut these, put them into some lightly salted water or a lemon juice solution to help prevent discoloration. Pat the apple rings dry on sheets of kitchen paper, then thread them onto thin wooden rods or canes. Hang these in the oven heated to the temperature given on page 221. They should dry in about six hours, by which time they will feel leathery and look dry and shrivelled on the outside. Spread them out on a wire tray and leave for a good 12 hours to dry.

Pears

Choose ripe, but firm fruit and peel and quarter them or cut into slices. Cut out the cores and drop the quarters into lightly salted water or lemon juice to help prevent discoloration. Spread out on muslin-covered wire trays and put these in the oven heated to the temperature given on page 221. They will take about the same amount of time as the apple rings to dry.

Grapes

The seedless variety are the best for drying and should be dried when they are just ripe. Wash them and pat them dry on sheets of kitchen paper. Spread out individually on muslin-covered wire trays and put in an oven heated to the temperature given on page 221. The grapes are dried when the skins are shrivelled and do not burst when you squeeze them gently.

FREEZING

Nearly all fruit freezes well, although different methods suit different types of fruit. For all methods, choose ripe, but not over-ripe fruits, which are not bruised or blemished in any way. Fruit is best frozen within a couple of hours of being picked.

Think about how the frozen fruit is likely to be used, too. If it is to be eaten whole in its straight, unfrozen state, it is best to open-freeze it, although this is the most time-consuming method. Fruit which is to be used in cooked pies or crumbles may be sugar-frozen, and if it is intended for mousses, fools and other similar dishes it is best to freeze it as a purée.

All frozen fruit must be thawed before using it in any way, although soft fruits which are to be used raw in a dessert can be thawed to a chilled state. The exception to this rule is if the frozen fruit is to be stewed; in this instance it can be heated gently from frozen.

Open-freezing

This is most suitable for soft fruits, such as strawberries, raspberries and blackberries. As with vegetables that are open-frozen, each fruit remains separate, so that as much as is wanted at any one time can be taken from the freezer bag. Wash the fruit only if absolutely necessary (the drier the fruit, the better the frozen results), hull it, then place each fruit separately on a tray; they should not touch one another. Freeze until the fruit is firm, pack it in freezer bags, seal it and then label it before returning it to the freezer. When thawed, the fruits will be considerably softer than if fresh, but will still retain their shape.

Golden rules for freezing

If you are freezing more than 1kg (2lb) of fruit at once, turn your freezer thermostat to 'fast freeze'. Always make sure that food is completely cold before putting it into the freezer.

Pack food tightly into rigid containers, trying not to leave any gaps. If there is room left in the container and you have no more food to freeze, fill the space with crumpled paper. Remember to leave a 2cm (1in) expansion gap for liquids. Sauces and purées can be stored in plastic bags, but to avoid awkward shapes, put the bags into boxes before filling and freezing them, then lift them out and seal once the contents are solid.

Sugar-freezing

This method is also suitable for soft fruits, but the fruit will be very mushy when thawed and is best used in cooked puddings. Wash the fruit if necessary, hull it, then either roll each fruit in caster sugar, or put them in a dish, sprinkle with sugar (add as much as you like according to taste), and stir gently when the sugar has dissolved.

Pack the fruit into rigid containers, seal, label and freeze. Another way of sugar-freezing is to layer fruit and sugar in alternating layers in rigid freezer-proof containers.

Freezing in syrup

This is suitable for stoned fruits and those which tend to be less juicy, such as apples and pears. They can be frozen in a heavy or light syrup, according to taste, what you want to use the fruit for and the type of fruit. Soft fruits are best frozen in a heavy syrup, while the more delicately flavoured fruit, such as pears or melons, are better in a light syrup.

For heavy syrups, dissolve 450g (1lb) of sugar in each 575ml (1 pint) of water; for a lighter syrup, halve the amount of sugar. When the syrup has completely cooled, pour it over the prepared fruit, packed into a rigid container. Make sure the fruit is submerged in the liquid before putting on the lid, by placing a piece of crumpled greaseproof paper on top of it.

It is a good idea to poach most stoned fruits – apricots, peaches and plums – before freezing, or else the skins are likely to become tough during the freezing process. They need only a few minutes simmering in a heavy syrup. When they have cooled completely in the syrup, they can be frozen in the normal way.

Freezing in a purée

Puréed fruit is useful for all sorts of cold mousses, soufflés, ice creams and sauces. It is also a good way to freeze fruit which is slightly over-ripe or imperfect (although all bruised or damaged parts should be discarded as they could affect the taste).

Soft fruits, such as raspberries, strawberries and blackberries, can be pushed through a sieve and frozen immediately. Sugar can be added before freezing, or after

thawing and before use.

Other, more robust fruits – gooseberries, blackcurrants, apples, apricots and others – must be lightly cooked before they can be liquidised or sieved, or the results will not be smooth. The purée must be quite cold before freezing.

FREEZING FRUIT

FRUIT	METHOD OF FREEZING
Apple	Sugar-freeze; poached in light syrup, or as a purée. If sugar-freezing or freezing in a light syrup, apple slices can be prevented from discolouring by dropping them into a bowl of water and lemon juice and adding lemon juice to the syrup.
Apricot	Sugar-freeze; poached in heavy syrup, or as a purée.
Blackberry	Open-freeze; sugar-freeze, or as a purée. They can also be frozen in a heavy syrup if wanted for pies or crumbles.
Blueberry	Open-freeze; sugar-freeze, or in a light syrup.
Blackcurrant	Open-freeze; sugar-freeze, or as a purée.
Cherry	Open-freeze; sugar-freeze, or in a light syrup. Choose red varieties and pit them before freezing.
Damson	Open-freeze; poached in a light syrup, or as a purée.
Gooseberry	All methods are suitable; choose according to the use for which they are required.
Melon	Cut flesh into cubes or balls and cover in a light syrup.
Loganberry	All methods are suitable; choose according to the use for which they are required.
Mulberry	All methods are suitable; choose according to the use for which they are required.
Peach and nectarine	Sugar-freeze, or poached in heavy syrup.
Pear	In light syrup (treat as for apples to prevent discoloration).
Plum and gage	Sugar-freeze; poached in heavy syrup, or as a purée.
Raspberry	All methods are suitable; choose according to the use for which they are required.
Rhubarb	Open-freeze (but the cut pieces should be blanched for one to two minutes first); in heavy syrup or as a purée.
Strawberry	All methods are suitable; choose according to the use for which they are required.

To make the most efficient use of your freezer space and your plastic boxes, freeze sauces and purées in bags contained within boxes. Pour in the liquid, freeze it and then lift out the bag with its frozen 'brick', seal it and stack it with your other frozen produce.

Bottling Fruit

Most fruit can be bottled, and it makes an invaluable standby for winter puddings. The bottles or jars should be made of thick glass with either a screw top or a secure, clip-on lid.

In both cases the bottles or jars should also have a thick rubber ring that fits round the top of the jar and ensures a truly air-tight seal. If air is allowed into the inside of the jar, the fruit will quickly ferment.

First, check your bottles

When planning to bottle fruit, check the bottles carefully first to ensure none have chips around the ring. If they do, the seal will not be air-tight. Make sure the lids are in good condition too – that glass is not chipped or cracked, metal is not bent or rusty, and that any spring clips are strong.

Test them before use to ensure that the seal is air-tight by filling the jars with water, putting on the rubber ring and the lid and then standing the bottles upside-down on a table. If there is any sign of leaking after five minutes or so, the bottles should not be used. Wash those you do intend to use in hot water just before filling them with the fruit but do not dry the inside, or you will spread germs, even with the cleanest tea towel. Instead leave them to drain turned upside-down.

Choosing the fruit

Use only perfect, unblemished fruit and grade it according to size so that fruit of a similar size is bottled together. Prepare it according to its type; apples and pears should be peeled, cored and sliced or

---

BOTTLING FRUIT

1 Prepare the fruit as required (*see* below) peeling, coring or cutting as necessary. Blanch peaches and apricots first to make it easier to remove their skins.

2 Pack the fruit evenly into the bottles, using the handle of a wooden spoon to push down and position the firmer fruits, such as apricots, if necessary.

3 Fill the jars with the firm fruits and then pour in the syrup, jerk the bottles sharply to release any air bubbles and top up with more syrup. When bottling soft fruits, it is better to fill the jars a quarter at a time, alternating fruit and syrup until the jar is full. This gives a better distribution of fruit and syrup.

4 Tighten the lids, and if they are screw tops, undo them a quarter turn – this prevents the bottles bursting during the sterilisation process which follows (spring clips are designed to avoid any danger of this happening).

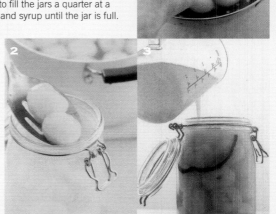

---

quartered (put them into cold, lightly salted water or lemon juice solution as you prepare them to prevent discoloration); apricots and peaches should be skinned, halved and stoned; cherries, plums and damsons can be bottled whole, or plums may be halved and stoned if you prefer – wash them all first.

Rhubarb should be cut into small chunks, and will pack better into the jars if it is steeped in hot sugar syrup overnight. All soft fruit such as blackcurrants, raspberries, loganberries and strawberries should be bottled whole, with the minimum of handling. Some people say that the flavour of bottled strawberries is

better if they are soaked overnight in syrup and their colour can be improved by adding a few drops of edible red colouring to the syrup.

Making a sugar syrup

Fruit is usually bottled in a sugar syrup, and although there is no reason why it cannot be bottled in plain water, the flavour will not be as good. Make a syrup with about 225g (8oz) of granulated sugar to 575ml (1 pint) of water – vary the strength according to the fruit and your taste. You can add flavourings to the syrup if you wish, such as vanilla pods or wintery spices, such as cinnamon or star anise.

PROCESSING TIMES FOR BOTTLING FRUIT

HOT WATER BATH METHOD

2 minutes
Apple slices, blackberries, blackcurrants, gooseberries, loganberries, mulberries, raspberries, rhubarb, strawberries (unsoaked)

10 minutes
Apricots, cherries, damsons, whole plums

20 minutes
Peaches, halved plums, strawberries (soaked)

40 minutes
Pears

OVEN METHOD

30–40 minutes
Apple slices, blackberries, blackcurrants, gooseberries, rhubarb

40–50 minutes
Apricots (whole), cherries, damsons, loganberries, mulberries, raspberries, strawberries (unsoaked)

50–60 minutes
Apricots (halved), plums (whole), strawberries (soaked)

60–70 minutes
Peaches, pears, plums (halved)

STERILISING BOTTLES

Bottled fruit must be sterilised to prevent the growth of organisms and bacteria which would otherwise spoil it.

There are many ways of sterilising bottles, but two of the simplest are described here.

Hot water bath, quick method

Pack the fruit into 1kg (2lb) jars and fill them with hot syrup, before securing the tops. Put them into a deep pan or any other large pan in which there is a false bottom (a fish kettle is ideal if you do not have a special sterilising pan); if the pan does not have a false bottom, you can improvise by using a wire grill or placing thickly folded newspaper, cardboard or a towel in the bottom.

The bottles must not touch one another – separate them with pads of folded newspaper. Pour warm water (just above body temperature) into the pan to cover the bottles and put the lid on. Bring it up to simmering point – 88°C (190°F) – in about 30 minutes and simmer. Remove the bottles using bottling tongs (or tip some water out of the pan and hold the jars with an oven cloth) and tighten the metal screw tops. Leave the bottles overnight to cool before testing the seal.

Oven method, wet pack

Pack the fruit into 1kg (2lb) jars and add boiling syrup to about 1cm (½in) from the tops. Dip the glass lids and the rubber bands in boiling water and put them on the jars, but do not screw on the metal tops or do up the clips. Stand the jars on a piece of cardboard or some thickly folded newspaper in the centre of and oven heated to 150°C (300°F) or Gas Mark 2. Make sure there is at least 5cm (2in) between the bottles at all points, then leave them for the times given below. Remove them one by one, preferably onto a wooden surface and either fasten the clips or screw on the metal tops. Test the seal the next day.

Testing the seal

Between 12 and 24 hours after processing the fruit, you can test it to see that the seal is correct. Unscrew the metal top, or release the clip, and pick up the bottle by the glass top only. (Put your hand underneath the bottle to catch it, just in case.) If the top remains in place, the seal is perfect. Label the bottles and store them in a cool, fairly dark place.

If the lid comes off, the seal is not good enough. Check the jar to see if there is a crack round the top and check the rubber band to make sure it has not perished. The fruit can be re-processed, but it is better used immediately.

Bottling fruit in alcohol

Prepare the fruit and pack it into clean, sterilised jars, layering it with sugar as you go, then fill the jars with your alcohol, shaking to remove any air bubbles and topping up again once more. You can use any alcohol that is more than 40 per cent proof, either using it on its own or combined with a sugar syrup to make a richer liquid.

Seal the jars and store them somewhere cool, dark and dry for at least two months – but the longer, the better. To help the sugar to dissolve, shake the jars every few days for the first month.

Cherries in brandy make a traditonal and always well-received gift. Choose your own combinations of fruit and spirit, adding other flavours if you like.

Making Jams and Jellies

This is another way of preserving fruit, although it changes the nature of the fruit even more than bottling does. Jam isn't as useful for making puddings and desserts as bottled fruit, but nevertheless, it is still a popular way of using a crop.

Jam is made by boiling fruit and water together until it will thicken when it cools into a jelly-like preserve. This is called the setting point. The set comes from pectin – a natural substance contained in fruit, which once released, reacts with the sugar. Some fruits are rich in pectin, such as apples, red and blackcurrants, damsons and gooseberries; others are poor, such as cherries, rhubarb, pears and strawberries. In between these are a number of fruits – apricots, blackberries, plums, loganberries and raspberries – which have a medium pectin content. This means that unless additional pectin is added to the fruit, the jam will be less firm than that made with pectin-rich fruits.

Choosing your fruit

Even though fruit for jam-making is to be cooked to a pulp, only good-quality, unblemished, fresh, just-ripe fruit should be used. Over-ripe fruit tends to lose its pectin and damaged or bruised fruit could affect the taste of the jam. Hull, wash and drain soft fruit such as raspberries and strawberries; peel, core and slice apples and pears; strip berries from the stem and halve apricots and plums, remove the stones and cut the flesh into quarters.

BASIC TECHNIQUES FOR JAM-MAKING

Whatever your choice of fruits, the method of jam-making is the same. Experiment with combinations of fruits and flavours – mixed summer berries or something more unusual, such as gooseberry and ginger.

The fruit should be cooked in a large pan (*see* page 212) over a gentle heat, adding water if necessary to stop the fruit sticking. Most soft fruits, such as raspberries and strawberries do not need any additional water, but the individual recipes will state this. Do not cover the pan during the cooking.

MAKING JAM

1 Sort through your fruits and discard any that are over-ripe, damaged or blemished. Prepare as necessary, by chopping, peeling, coring or stoning.

2 Put the fruit in your jam pan with a little water if necessary and start to heat it. Remove from the heat to add the sugar, then return to the hob and heat it gently, stirring, until the sugar has dissolved.

3 Bring to the boil and boil rapidly, without stirring, until the jam reaches setting point (*see* page 228). This usually takes between 10 and 15 minutes, depending on the quantity you are making.

4 Let the jam cool a little, remove any scum from the surface and leave the jam to sit for another 10 minutes until it is cool enough to handle safely.

5 Spoon the jam into warm, sterilised jars (a funnel and ladle make this job much easier and less likely to burn your hands), top with waxed discs and seal and label the jars.

When you make your own jams and jellies, you can try delicious combinations that you cannot get in the shops, such as pear and raspberry.

Sugar is usually added after the fruit has cooked down into a pulp and reduced in volume. Use granulated or preserving sugar, which dissolves quickly, and use the exact amount stated in the recipe. This will vary according to the pectin present in the fruit, so be sure to follow the recipe exactly, rather than adding more or less to suit your taste. If you add too much or too little sugar, the jam will not set properly and the flavour will also be impaired. It is a good idea to warm the sugar in a gentle oven before adding it to the fruit, and make sure it is thoroughly dissolved before bringing the jam back to the boil.

If you need to add pectin, you can buy it in bottles in most large supermarkets in late summer and autumn – peak season for making jam. You will also find jam sugar and preserving sugar, though ordinary granulated sugar is fine to use.

Finishing and bottling

When it reaches setting point, let the jam stand for a few minutes and then skim the scum off the surface, using a slotted metal spoon. A knob of butter stirred into the jam will remove all final traces of scum, and the jam can then be poured into warm, clean jars which have been left to dry.

Fill the jars to the rim and place a waxed circle of paper on top (these are sold specially for jam-making). Wet a cellophane cover (also sold for jam-making), stretch it over the top of the jar and secure it with a rubber band round the top of the jar. Providing the jam is still hot and the cellophane was wetted first, it will give an air-tight seal. Label the jars with the contents and the date of making and store in a dry, cool place until wanted.

Testing for setting point

The jam should be kept boiling until it reaches setting point. This can be determined by temperature if you have a special jam or sugar thermometer: setting point is 104°C (220°F). Alternatively, use one of the following simple tests.

Flake test

Take out a spoonful of jam, using a wooden spoon. Hold it for a minute to cool it, then tip the wooden spoon sideways; if the jam drops off the edge of the spoon in large flakes, setting point has been reached.

Saucer test

Put a little of the jam onto a cold

Keep a saucer in the fridge while you are cooking your jam, ready to test for the jam's setting point. If a skin wrinkles on the jam when you push it gently, it is ready.

saucer and let it cool. If the surface of the jam forms a skin which wrinkles as you push it gently with your fingers, the setting point has been reached.

Jam can be ladled straight into wide-necked jars, but remember that it will be very hot indeed and if you spill any while holding the jar steady, you will burn your hand. A jam funnel, with a wide neck to let pieces of fruit through, will save both time and accidents.

MAKING JELLIES

Fruit jelly often uses the same basic ingredients as jam, but the result is a smooth, clear preserve.

To achieve this, the fruit is placed into a jelly bag after it has been cooked, and allowed to drip slowly into a bowl or basin overnight, or for as long as 24 hours. It is important to let this process happen slowly. If you are impatient and squeeze or prod the bag too vigorously, particles of pulp will also come through, and the jelly will be cloudy. You can buy jelly-straining bags with their own stands or improvise with a square of muslin tied onto the legs of an upturned chair.

The liquid is then boiled with a precise amount of sugar, according to the volume of the juice, until setting point is reached. As only the liquid from the fruit is used, similar quantities of fruit make considerably less jelly than jam.

MARMALADE

If you are lucky enough to grow citrus plants that produce enough fruit, you can make your own marmalade.

Even if you cannot produce your own fruit, once you become proficient at making jams and jellies, you may like to try something different and make a batch of marmalade using shop-bought fruit.

The main difference between making jam and marmalade is that marmalade incorporates pieces of chopped peel, and this must be cooked separately first, to release the pectin and tenderise the skin.

MAKING MARMALADE

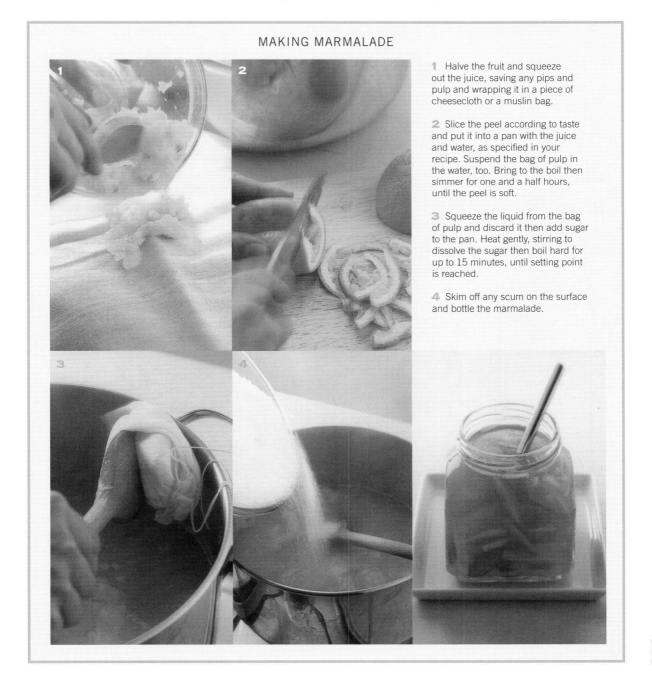

1 Halve the fruit and squeeze out the juice, saving any pips and pulp and wrapping it in a piece of cheesecloth or a muslin bag.

2 Slice the peel according to taste and put it into a pan with the juice and water, as specified in your recipe. Suspend the bag of pulp in the water, too. Bring to the boil then simmer for one and a half hours, until the peel is soft.

3 Squeeze the liquid from the bag of pulp and discard it then add sugar to the pan. Heat gently, stirring to dissolve the sugar then boil hard for up to 15 minutes, until setting point is reached.

4 Skim off any scum on the surface and bottle the marmalade.

Making Wine and Cider

Making your own wine and cider is an excellent way of using some of the produce you have grown or collected. You don't need a grapevine, but can make wine from a wide variety of ingredients to suit your own tastes.

Berries, fruit, flowers, vegetables and herbs can all be used to make wine, although some flowers must be avoided as they are poisonous, and not all vegetables make very palatable wine. Flowers that are worth experimenting with include rose petals, elderflower, mayflower, dandelion, coltsfoot, cowslip, primrose, gorse and meadowsweet. The main vegetables to avoid are pumpkin, marrow, potato, lettuce, tomatoes and turnips, although all vegetable wines tend to be an acquired taste.

Find your own blends

Amateur home wine-making is an experimental hobby: tastes are very individual and weights and measures are rarely critical. The steps to follow are the same whatever the ingredient you use and, as you get more confident you will find you need to turn to the recipe books less and less, following your own instincts and being inspired by the ingredients you have to hand, instead.

It is always a good idea to make small quantities of wine each time – about 4.5 litres (1 gallon) is a sensible amount. If it proves undrinkable, it is not such a terrible waste when you have to tip it away.

Cleanliness and patience are key

The two most important aspects of wine-making are absolute cleanliness and considerable patience. All the equipment (*see* below) should be sterilised before use, otherwise you run the risk of attracting vinegar fly or allowing bacteria to grow in the developing wine. Both will give the wine a strong vinegary taste, rendering it quite useless for drinking.

Sterilising is an easy process and all home wine-making suppliers sell various sterilising solutions which carry clear instructions for use. It is a good idea to sterilise equipment when you have finished using it, before putting it away, and then

Demijohns and air locks are essential pieces of equipment for making wine and you will probably need several of each. You can save old wine bottles to reuse or buy them at wine-making suppliers, together with new corks.

again when you are ready to use it the next time. After sterilisation, rinse the equipment in cold water and leave it to drain, rather than drying it on a cloth.

Patience is extremely important. If you do not leave your wine for long enough to mature (at least six months before bottling) it will not be worth all the effort. In many instances it improves still further if left for longer. If you make small quantities of wine frequently, you will soon find that you always have some fully-matured wine ready to drink, so you do not need to be impatient with the more recently-made vintage.

BASIC INGREDIENTS

Besides the chief fruit, vegetable, flower, berry or herb in your wine, you will need the following ingredients. Anything not readily available from your cupboards or the supermarket can be purchased online, at a chemist or a home-wine-making supplier.

Water According to each individual recipe. Some ingredients will need more additional water than others.

Sugar It is this which determines the alcohol content of the wine as well as the sweet or dry taste. Sweet or dry wine can be made from any ingredients, the deciding factor being the amount of sugar added.

Many recipes, old-fashioned ones in particular, tend to produce wine that is rather sweet, so if your taste is for a drier wine, you may find you need to reduce the amount of sugar considerably. As a guide, 250g of sugar per litre of liquid (2½lb of sugar per gallon) produces a dry wine; 300g of sugar per litre (3lb of sugar per gallon) produces

a medium wine and 350g of sugar per litre (3½lb of sugar per gallon) produces a sweet wine, although this should be slightly adjusted according to the natural sweetness of the chief ingredient. Use ordinary granulated sugar.

Yeast This brings about the fermentation process that turns the liquid into wine. Various types of yeast are available, although some will produce better results than others. Ordinary brewers' yeast can be used, but it is better to use a special wine yeast, some of which are sold in sachets already containing the essential nutrient (*see* below).

In addition, there are numbers of particular yeasts produced in the various wine-growing districts of the world. Experiment with the various kinds to find those you like best.

Nutrient Yeast is a living organism and needs feeding if it is to grow and do its work. The nutrient it needs to do this job of fermenting the wine is commercially available and the quantity to be added to the wine will be clearly stated on the bottle.

Acid The yeast needs acid conditions to bring about good fermentation. Most home-made wines need acid added to them, usually in the form of citric acid. Follow individual recipes for how much to add – it will depend on the natural acidity of the ingredients. Some need only the juice of one or two lemons.

Tannin This is a substance found in the skins of fruit, particularly those of red fruit. It gives wine its characteristic 'bite'. Wines made from red fruit and berries – such as

elderberries, damsons, plums and sloes – will not need extra tannin; most other wines, even white wines, will benefit from the addition of grape tannin, which you can buy from wine-making suppliers, although if you prefer, you could add some strong, cold tea instead.

Pectin-destroying enzymes These should be added to wines made from fruit that is particularly high in pectin (such as apples, black- and redcurrants, damsons and gooseberries), which can make the wine rather cloudy.

Campden tablets These can be used for sterilising equipment and they are also added to the wine at a certain stage in the making (*see* below) to kill off any lingering bacteria.

ESSENTIAL EQUIPMENT

Making wine requires some specialist equipment and it is very difficult to muddle through with everyday items, trying to improvise and compromise. Fortunately, you can often find much of what you need for sale second hand.

It is a good idea to keep things simple when you first start, in case you don't wish to carry on beyond the first sip of your first bottle. Even so, you will need to purchase some key items. If you enjoy wine-making, you can always buy more specialist equipment as you go on.

At the very least, you will need some demijohns, a hydrometer (for testing the sugar levels and, therefore, the strength of your wine), plenty of empty wine bottles and new corks, a funnel, airlock, siphon tube and corking machine.

HOW TO MAKE WINE

The basic procedure for wine-making is the same whatever sort of wine you are producing. Always choose top-grade, unblemished ingredients that are fresh and ripe.

Start by boiling or steeping your vegetables or fruits (right); flowers should be stripped from the plant, placed in a container and bruised with a wooden spoon before boiling water is added to them. They, too, are left to steep for a few days.

Some recipes stipulate adding sugar and a campden tablet at this stage (with apples, a campden tablet helps to prevent the fruit discolouring or beginning to oxidise). This is to extract the maximum amount of flavour from the ingredients, but stirring the mixture each day will also help. Be guided by common sense: strawberries turn mushy very quickly and release all their flavour to the liquid within a couple of days; harder fruit or berries will need longer.

Preparing the yeast

Get the yeast working in a starter bottle before adding it to the wine. Put the yeast into a small bottle with some fruit juice, sugar and nutrient, plug the top with a piece of cotton wool and leave it in a warm place. Some types of yeast will begin to activate within a few hours; most take a couple of days.

Racking and bottling the wine

Ferment the wine in a demijohn (right) until the air lock has stopped bubbling. Shake the jar, then leave it for another couple of days – but no longer. The next stage is to filter the liquid into a clean, sterilised jar, leaving the sediment at the bottom of the old jar. This process is known

MAKING WINE

1 Wash and peel the vegetables or fruit you are using for the wine, and then chop into small pieces. Simmer vegetables in water until tender or steep fruit in a large container of boiling water, cover and leave until the fruit is thoroughly mushy.

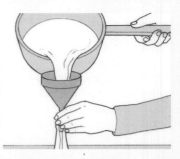

2 Yeast can be added at this stage of the process. It is mixed with fruit juice, sugar and nutrient in a small bottle of its own and added to the wine after a few days.

3 When the ingredients have steeped, strain the liquid through a sieve and a piece of muslin. Add the yeast, sugar, nutrient and other ingredients if you have not done so already.

4 Strain this liquid, known as the 'must' through a piece of muslin in a plastic funnel into a sterilised fermentation jar or demijohn.

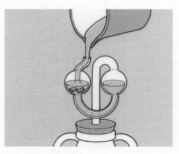

5 Carefully fit an airlock into the top of the demijohn. Half-fill it with distilled water, to which is added a quarter of a campden tablet. Keep the wine at around 21°C (70°F) – too hot and the wine will spoil, too cold and fermentation will slow down or stop.

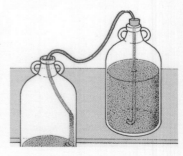

6 When fermentation has ceased (the airlock stops bubbling), rack the wine by siphoning the liquid into a clean demijohn and seal it firmly with a bung. Do this at least twice more to remove all sediment before finally siphoning it into bottles, corking and labelling.

as racking. Place the clean jar at a lower level and siphon off the wine from the old jar through a tube.

Taste the wine at this stage, for if it is too sharp or dry, you could add some concentrated syrup or sugar dissolved in water. In any event, top up the jar with water and add a campden tablet to ensure that no bacteria is allowed to get to work. This jar should then be fitted with an air-tight rubber bung and stored preferably in a place where the temperature is about 21°C (70°F).

The wine should be left for at least six months before it is bottled. If, during this time, a heavy sediment forms at the bottom of the jar, it should be racked again. It does not matter how many times you rack the wine – and it is a good idea to do so at least two or three times. The more you do, the better the wine is likely to be, as it helps to reduce any risk of the sediment at the bottom of the jar tainting the wine.

Bottling

The final process is to pour the wine into sterilised bottles. The corks, too, should be soaked in a sterilising liquid. If you soak them for 24 hours in cold, boiled water, they will also soften, which makes them easier to drive into the bottles.

The wine should be filtered and then poured into the bottles so that it comes to a level about 2cm (¾in) below the cork. Drive the cork into the bottle, then label the wine with the name and date of bottling. Wine should always be stored on its side, so the cork is kept moist. If it is allowed to dry out, bacteria is able to enter the bottle and the wine will turn vinegary. No wine should be drunk for at least one month after bottling, and it is advisable to leave it much longer if you can.

MAKING CIDER

If you have a surfeit of apples and have made enough apple wine, you can turn the remainder into cider. Pears can be made into perry.

In both cases, it is only the juice of the fruit that is used – no yeast, water or sugar (unless you want to speed the fermentation or produce a very sweet cider). The best cider will be made from a mixture of sweet and more sour-tasting apples, and you will get the greatest amount of juice if you let them soften a little first. This does not mean leaving them to rot; if you have many heavily bruised apples, the cider will not have a good taste.

Crushing your apples is the first stage in making cider. You can do this by hand with a mallet or in a proper cider press.

The apples need crushing. If you find you enjoy your cider and the process of making it, and have a lot of apples to spare, it may be worth investing in a cider press; these are expensive pieces of equipment, but it is possible to make your own.

An alternative is to hit the apples hard with a wooden mallet, wrap the pulp in muslin or calico and press it to extract the juice. Another method is to liquidise the apples or put them through a food-processor then press them through muslin in the same way. You can even push the wrapped-up pulp through a mangle.

After that the juice can be poured into a clean, sterilised demijohn or earthenware jar. Lay an inverted saucer over the top and leave the juice to ferment. If you want to speed the process, you can add yeast in the way you would in wine-making, but this is not necessary.

Rack the cider (*see* page 232) after fermentation has finished, and only bottle it when it has stopped giving off gas. Like wine, it will improve if left in the bottle for some months before drinking.

When bubbles have stopped escaping through the air lock, the cider is ready for bottling, but let it rest for a while before you drink it.

FLAVOURED GIN AND OTHER ALCOHOL

Sloe gin is a countryside favourite, traditionally steeped through the winter to be ready in time for Christmas, but you can use other spirits and fruits to make your own liqueurs.

You don't need good quality alcohol to make sloe or damson gins, but flavoured vodkas will taste smoother if you start with a moderately good base spirit. Citrus vodkas are popular, but you can infuse either spirit with any flavours you like or have available, such as blackberries, damsons, raspberry, apple or cherry. Slice your fruits if they have skins, so that the flesh is exposed. Sloes and damsons should be pricked with a pin to break the skin, although you can also put the fruits in the freezer to split them.

For flavouring vodka, remove any rind, seeds or pips, put the fruit in a large jar or other sealable container

Sloe gin is a potent and warming liqueur, best taken in small measures, but also makes a fruity contribution to cocktails.

Home-made wines and spirits make great presents and are fun to share with guests. Try making something unique with your own particular blend of flavours.

and add the vodka until the fruit is all submerged. Steep the vodka for about two weeks, shaking every couple of days, then strain through a jelly bag or coffee filter paper and bottle. Allow the vodka to rest for up to four weeks before drinking.

Sloe and damson gin
These gins are more like a liqueur than a spirit, as they include a quantity of sugar and are allowed to steep for several months. Prick the skins of the sloes or damsons and put them in a demijohn or several large bottles until they are half full. Add the same weight of sugar and top up with the gin.

Shake the bottles every day for the first week and then every week for the next two or more months. The longer you leave it before straining and bottling, the better the flavour of the gin.

You can use the steeped fruits in pies or sauces, although they will have taken on some of the alcohol.

Goats' Milk

Goats' milk can be made into all the dairy products – cream, butter, yoghurt and various cheeses – most usually associated with cows' milk, but cheese is usually the most successful.

Most people find it impractical to make cream and butter from goats' milk because of the amount of milk needed (plus the quantity of whey left as residue), and the sophisticated, expensive equipment that must be used. Four and a half litres (1 gallon) of milk, for example, makes only about 450 to 900ml (¾ to 1½ pints) of cream, which is essential to make good quality butter. It is hardly worth doing so unless you can use 4.5 litres (1 gallon) of cream at a time and for this you would need at least four goats in prime milking condition – too many for the average household. Never mix milk from different days, as this will give the milk a very 'goaty' taste.

MAKING YOGHURT AND CHEESE

The most successful by-products from goats' milk for the small goat-keeper to make are yoghurt and soft cheeses.

To make yoghurt, first pasteurise the milk. Heat it to at least 72°C (162°F) and maintain this temperature for 15 seconds, before cooling it quickly to a temperature below 12°C (55°F). Alternatively, heat it gently to a temperature between 60° to 76°C (140° to 170°F), maintain this for 30 minutes and then quickly cool it to 12°C (55°F) or less.

After this a yoghurt culture must be added; special goat cultures are available and they will carry instructions for use. Alternatively, use shop-bought plain live yoghurt. Just add between a quarter- and a half-carton of plain yoghurt to 575ml

Soft goats' cheese is a simple and delicious way to enjoy your goats' milk and it will stay fresh for longer than the milk itself.

MAKING GOATS' CHEESE

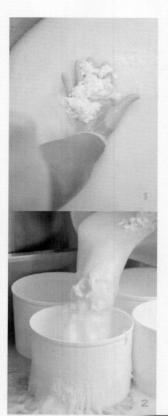

There are three easy ways of making soft cheese:

1 Allow the milk to sour naturally by letting it stand in a fairly warm place for 36–48 hours. Then wrap it in thick cheesecloth and let it drip into a bowl. After another 36–48 hours, you will be left with the cheese in the cloth and a bowl of whey beneath. You can also do this using yoghurt you have made, but it will need to drip for about two days and has a rather sour taste. Try mixing it with garlic or chopped herbs.

2 You can also strain the cheese through perforated moulds and then tip out the cheese, ready-formed into neat rounds.

3 In this method, rennet is added to the milk. Rennet is obtainable from health shops and chemists, but make sure it is cheese-making rennet, not that suitable only for making junket. The rennet is likely to come with instructions for use, but the procedure is to warm the milk to about 32°C (90°F), add the rennet, let the mixture stand for about 30 minutes and then put it through the cheesecloth. It will be ready much quicker than the other two cheeses and has a very mild taste. As it is the quickest cheese to make, the milk has less chance to assume a goaty taste. Shape the cheese into rolls or roundels, if you wish.

(1 pint) of milk, then leave it covered in a warm place. An airing cupboard is not really warm enough, but you could use a thermos flask placed in warm water or a special yoghurt-making machine.

Leave the yoghurt for up to about eight hours, then put it in the fridge. It will thicken as it cools but goats' milk yoghurt generally has a thinner consistency than shop-bought yoghurt or that made with cows' milk. You can use the yoghurt you make as the culture for more yoghurt for about a week. After that, it will begin to go off.

Goats' cheese

Both soft and hard cheeses can be made from goats' milk, but soft cheeses are more suitable for most home production and can be made without any special equipment that you do not already have at home.

The problem with making a lot of cheese is that you can end up with a great deal of whey, which does not have much use. You could use it to try to make a sort of mysost, or Norwegian whey cheese. This is a thick-textured, light-brown cheese, that has a very distinctive, caramel-like taste. Strain the whey into a clean pan and bring it to the boil, stirring constantly. Skim off and retain the thick matter that comes to the surface and coagulates, then continue boiling and stirring the mixture. When it has reduced in volume by about three-quarters, return the coagulated matter to the pan and boil it some more, stirring vigorously. When the cheese has thickened and is a light-brown colour, take it from the heat, but continue beating it until it is cool and too thick to stir any more. Pour it into a greased container and leave it to cool completely and set.

Preserving Meat and Fish

If you kill a chicken, it will probably only be one at a time and you can eat it straight away, but if you slaughter a pig or catch a good haul of fish, you will need to preserve the results in some way to eat them over a longer period.

Freezing is the simplest, safest and most effective way to keep produce fresh. For a large animal, the abattoir may also joint and cut up the carcass for you, or you could ask a local butcher to do it, perhaps in return for taking a cut or two.

Smoking and curing are other methods of preserving meat and fish and with the right equipment, you can do this at home. However, they will not preserve it for long, and are best considered as ways of adding flavour, rather than longevity.

Preparing fish

If you plan to freeze any fish you catch, put them into ice as soon as you catch them, keeping them in a cool box at the water's edge. When you get home, gut them, clean them and scale them as soon as possible.

Dip each fish in very cold, salted water and allow it to drain well before wrapping in waxed paper and tin foil and freezing. Rub individual fillets with olive oil to prevent them from drying out, then wrap separately or interleaved between sheets of waxed paper. Fish will keep for six months in the freezer.

To scale fish, cover all nearby surfaces with newspaper – the scales will fly everywhere. Use a blunt knife to scrape away the scales, working

Home Smoking

Fish and meat can both be smoked, a process that adds a delicious flavour, even though it is no longer considered a reliable preservation method. If you have an open fire, you can smoke small quantities at a time in the chimney, but a better solution is to turn an old wooden barrel or crate into a smoker (or you can buy smokers ready to use). You need some space at the bottom for the sawdust, which creates the smoke, and racks or rods above this for suspending the meat or fish. Finally, there need to be some holes in the side and top for the smoke to escape.

The temperature should not be high enough to cook the flesh, so allow the flames to die down until the fire is just smouldering smokily.

The wood you use will affect the flavour you achieve. Pine is not recommended, as it will impart a hint of cleaning product to your food. Better choices are oak or wood from fruit trees.

If you can keep the fire at a consistently low heat, 10–12 hours should be long enough for smoking

You can smoke whole fish, fillets or steaks of meaty fish, such as salmon. If you catch herring when fishing at sea, you could smoke your own kippers.

fish; bacon or hams will need a whole day or more, depending on their size and how strong you want the flavour. If you need to keep taking the produce out while the fire burns too brightly, you will need to allow considerably longer – keep count of the hours that the food is actually in the smoker and work up to the total it needs.

from the tail towards the head of the fish. Take care not to tear the skin by holding your knife at the wrong angle or by pressing too hard. Rinse the fish under cold, running water to wash away any loose scales that are clinging to the skin

To gut a round fish, insert a sharp knife into the belly of the fish at the vent and split it up to the head. Scrape out the intestines and other

innards, taking care not to damage the flesh. Cut off the tail, head and fins and open out the fish, pressing it flat on a board, with the skin-side uppermost. Press hard along the backbone to break and loosen it, then turn the fish over and gently and carefully ease the backbone and side bones away from the flesh with a knife. Check for stray bones that remain and remove them.

WATER AND ENERGY CONSERVATION

The Self-Sufficient Home
Conserving Energy
Keeping the Heat in
Solar Power
Alternative Energy Sources
Saving and Recycling Water

The Self-Sufficient Home

Being truly self-sufficient for your domestic water and energy supplies as well as your food is likely to be an impossible dream unless you have your own clear stream, and even then it is not practical for most households. But you can get a long way towards this ideal of self-sufficiency by reducing your reliance on mains power and water to the absolute minimum.

For many people, the driving force behind growing your own fruit and vegetables and keeping your own livestock for meat is very often a desire to minimise your own impact on the planet, cutting down on unnecessary food miles, energy wasted by large corporations in producing, packaging and selling food, the widespread spraying of chemicals onto commercially produced crops and more.

Trying your best to reduce your own waste that goes into the dustbin, recycling, composting, conserving energy and water and maybe even generating some of your own power all go hand in hand with these aims and the ideal of self-sufficiency.

Packaging on shop-bought goods contributes in a large way to the problem of landfill. You can help by growing your own food, so that you buy less in the shops, but also by choosing products that are not over-packaged in plastic.

Tackling waste

The ultimate goal of the most enthusiastic self-sufficient homeowners is to throw nothing away, using only things that can themselves be reused or recycled or that are packaged in recyclable materials.

This is unlikley to be practical in most cases, but whatever you can do to reduce the contents of your dustbin will help to relieve the pressure on landfill rubbish dumps and minimise the harmful gases and waste created there as the rubbish rots.

Try to support shops and choose products that use as little non-recyclable packaging as possible. Read the labels: even some plastic-feeling materials can now be composted. And always think before you buy, to be sure that you really do need what you have picked out. Also try to support local suppliers and manufacturers, to minimise unnecessary food miles.

Saving energy in the home

Switching off lights when you leave a room and turning off any radios or televisions that are left playing to an empty room – these are obvious, but nonetheless effective ways to reduce your energy consumption. Read the tips on the following pages to find out other simple ways to cut down on the gas and electricity you use without even realising.

If you are lucky enough to have a large area of sustainable woodland on your property, it is worth considering converting your heating and cooking appliances to run on solid fuel, supplied from your own trees. Burning wood may be considered polluting, but as long as you plant trees to replace those you burn it is actually less damaging to the environment than the process required to produce electricity by commercial power generators or the gas or other fuel extracted from natural gas or oil wells.

Being water wise

In Britain, where tap water is drinkable, every drop of water that we use has been processed and cleaned to a high standard, even if we are only using it to flush the toilet or water the plants. This is an expensive process, but also a wasteful one, using a great deal of energy and resources.

There are many ways to reduce your household water consumption (*see* pages 247-8) and the volume of water you flush away each year, relieving pressure on the water treatment works as well as saving yourself money. Always try to collect as much rainwater as you can. Not only is it free, but it is actually far better for your plants than watering them with highly chlorinated and treated tap water. Consider reusing your grey water, too, that is water used in the house for washing – this will not be drinkable, but is often perfectly good for watering plants.

Conserving Energy

Follow these simple tips in and around the home to reduce your energy use and help to conserve precious resources. You could be surprised at how much money you can save, too.

Get into the habit of always switching electrical appliances off properly. Consistently leaving your television on stand-by, rather than switching it off at the set can add up to as much as 10 per cent of your electricity bill total. Of course, switching something on and off when it is a

If you have sustainable woodland on your property burning wood is a better choice for heating than using gas or electricity.

frequently-used appliance is likely to be irritating and something you won't stick to, but make it a household policy to switch off around the house at the end of each day.

The same goes for lights. There is no excuse for leaving lights burning in an empty room, except in a handful of cases for security. Only put the lights on when you really need to. Don't automatically switch on all the lights in a room if a single table lamp is sufficient and try to avoid children getting into the habit of needing a light on to get to sleep.

Low-energy options

Incandescent light bulbs are being phased out within Europe and being replaced by low-energy compact fluorescent lights. If you still have old-style bulbs in your house or in outbuildings around your property it is worth replacing them. The new energy-saving bulbs last on average between six and 15 times longer than a traditional incandescent bulb and use 80 per cent less energy to run. Most will pay for themselves within a year and last far longer than that. Replacing a 100W standard bulb with the equivalent 20W low-energy CFL (compact fluorescent light) can save you between £10 and £15 a year in electricity.

Don't heat empty spaces

Just as it makes no sense to light a room with no-one in it, you can also conserve energy by not heating rooms in your house that are not used regularly, such as spare bedrooms. Turn off the radiator and close the door until you are expecting visitors. Check the room regularly and air it so that it does not get musty or damp. It will soon warm up again when you need to use it.

ENERGY-WISE HEATING

Heating your home accounts for more than one third of most energy bills; add on the cost of heating the water, and it comes to around two thirds of the total. In warmer climates, you may save money on heating, but are likely to spend at least as much on cooling your home with air conditioning instead.

The boiler is the heart of any heating system, so make sure that it is as efficient as possible. Have it serviced once a year. If your boiler needs replacing, choose a condensing boiler. These are expensive to buy, but are so much more efficient than the alternatives that they will pay for themselves, and more.

Controlling the heat

Make sure that your central heating controls are as advanced as possible. Fit radiators with individual thermostatic valves, that switch on and off according to the temperature in the room. This is a far more efficient method than switching all the radiators on and off according to a single whole-house thermostat.

If the temperature in the room with the main thermostat rises enough to switch the heating off, but you find that it is still cold in the room you are using, you will probably turn up the heating to the entire house to compensate. With TRVs, (thermostatic radiator valves) you can set the temperature for each room independently: warmer in a living room, where you are likely to sit still, for example, than in a kitchen, where the cooker and general activity will add to the heat.

The most sophisticated programmers allow you to set different target temperatures according to the day of the week and time of day.

Turn it down

Turning your thermostat down by just one degree can save you as much as 10 per cent of your heating bill, and you are unlikely even to notice. Lower the temperature on your hot-water thermostat a fraction, too.

CHOOSING AND USING WHITE GOODS

Always seek out energy-saving appliances when you need a replacement. All are now rated according to their energy-efficiency, with the best rating being A++.

It is just as important to make sure that you are buying an appliance that is appropriate for your needs as it is to follow the manufacturer's energy ratings. A high-rated washing machine is no good for a large family if it is also a small one – running a large-capacity, B-rated machine every couple of days is probably still more efficient than a A++ rated machine that is too small for your requirements and needs to be used every day.

If you intend to freeze a lot of your produce to see you through the winter, consider investing in a chest freezer, but be realistic about how big it needs to be. Keeping a half-empty freezer cold takes a lot of energy; far better to have a smaller freezer that is well-stocked and, therefore, more efficient.

Where you keep your freezer will also affect its efficiency. If it is in the house, where the temperature remains fairly constant it should run at its maximum efficiency, but in an outbuilding the temperature might fluctuate more. Make sure that it does not get too hot in summer in an uninsulated or metal-roofed shed, as it will have to work much harder in these conditions to keep your food cold. In a kitchen, avoid putting your fridge or freezer next to the oven or a radiator, for the same reason.

Washing clothes at a lower temperature can make a noticeable energy saving without compromising on cleaning.

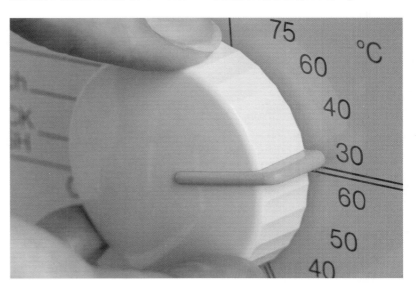

Keeping the Heat in

If your home is not well insulated and sealed against draughts, your precious heating will simply escape to warm the air outside.

Good household insulation is vital to keep in your heating, but will also help to keep your home cool in hot weather, saving energy that would otherwise be spent on air conditioning or fans. Most people assume that insulating the home means doing the 'big ticket' jobs, like upgrading the loft insulation or installing cavity wall insulation. These are, of course, the jobs that will save you the most if your house does not currently have either, but there are many small things you can do that can also have a noticeable effect.

Stop the small gaps
Using well-fitting curtains and closing them can make a big difference, particularly in rooms with old, draughty windows. This is especially true in cold weather, when the temperatures outside are considerably lower than those in the house. Buy heavy-weight curtains, that fit close to the wall and install a pelmet at the top.

Inspect your front and back doors, too. Fit escutcheon plates to any mortise lock key holes, with holes that go right through to the outside, and install a letterbox cover flap to seal that against draughts.

Fitting draught excluders
Gaps around doors and windows are as bad as leaving the door or window open. Install well-fitting draught excluders all round the house and you could reduce the heat lost from your property by as much as 25 per cent in the coldest months.

Keeping water warm
Make sure that hot-water pipes are lagged – split foam tubes that slip onto the pipes are quick to fit, easy and effective, but you can also use felt or wool bandage-type insulation, wrapping it round and round the pipes in overlapping turns. Pay particular attention to bends in the pipe and valves that break the pipe run to make sure that the whole length of pipe is insulated.

Look at your hot-water tank, too, and make sure that it is well insulated. The best type is a modern cylinder with hard insulation sprayed onto the tank itself – it will feel solid if you tap it. If you still have an old, uninsulated tank, wrap it in a lagging jacket and make sure that it is securely fixed.

Making big improvements
If your loft insulation does not meet the current Building Regulations minimum requirements of 270mm thick, it is worth upgrading by adding an extra layer of blanket insulation across the whole loft if you can.

Check your loft to make sure that it is adequately insulated. Warm air will rise up and out of a poorly-insulated roof.

You may be able to get a grant towards the cost, either from your power supply company or your local council. Even so, this does not have to be an expensive job and will certainly help to make big savings in the long term. Hot air rises, and it will soon leak out of a poorly-insulated roof.

Installing cavity wall insulation also qualifies for a grant in many areas. Solid walls are much harder to insulate effectively without compromising on the size of the room by fitting battens to the wall on the inside and a dummy wall on top of that to create an internal air gap.

Double glazing
Good glass makes a big difference to the temperature inside your house. The best double glazing will retain heat well, but also reflect heat on sunny days, helping to keep rooms cool inside. This is called low-emissivity glass and the best low-emissivity double-glazed units are filled with argon gas to improve the insulation even more.

Solar Power

How much use you can make of solar power depends on where you live and the climate. In the United Kingdom, domestic solar panels are seldom able to generate enough electricity to replace your mains supply, certainly not consistently throughout the year, but solar-powered hot water systems are more viable.

For generating electricity, you will need photovoltaic (PV) solar panels. With new developments, these are getting more efficient all the time and you no longer need to cover an entire roof elevation with panels to generate enough electricity to power an appliance. Nonetheless, they are

Solar panels work best when they are installed at an angle of around 60 degrees, to catch the maximum benefit from the rays of the sun.

very expensive to buy and install and are extremely unlikely to be able to generate enough electricity for you to disconnect your property from the National Grid.

The most modern systems do work even on overcast days, though, and if you make an effort to cut down drastically on the electricity you use unnecessarily in the house, generating your own electricity might soon become a more feasible option.

Is it worth it?

Before you take the plunge and invest in some solar panels, you must do your homework. Consider how much electricity your household uses, what the likely peak output is for the system you have in mind – remember that you will only achieve peak output in peak conditions – and calculate how long the payback time is likely to be. For maximum efficiency, panels should be mounted facing south – they are usually fitted on a south-facing elevation of your

Planning permission

You may need planning permission to install a bank of solar panels on the roof of your house. Check with your local planning authority before you do the work.

roof – but they work on daylight, not necessarily direct sunlight, so they will also generate power on even a north-facing slope, but not as much.

Power without cables

Photovoltaic solar panels are an excellent choice for powering lights in barns, sheds and outbuildings that are not connected to the house's electricity supply, and this can make shutting the hens in, early morning milkings, and evening rounds of your livestock an easier task. You can even power fans or heaters for a greenhouse from a solar panel or

pumps for watering or extracting water from a stream or pond for other use.

Make sure that the panels are situated in a bright, unshadowed place where they can work most efficiently. You can also link up batteries to store energy for times when the solar panels are not producing enough power, but be sure to include a controller to prevent the batteries from overcharging.

If you want to install a system like this it is a good idea to discuss your requirements with an expert, first. They will help you to estimate how much power you are likely to need, how large your batteries should be and how best to set up your miniature stand-alone circuit. The Energy Saving Trust is a good place to start. Alternatively, you can buy simple kits for DIY installation and these are usually good enough to provide power for seven hours of light a day throughout the year.

HEATING HOT WATER

Solar thermal systems very simply use the heat of the sun to heat water for domestic use and they are very effective. As long as the sun shines, you should have plenty of hot water in your tank.

Just like photovoltaic panels, solar thermal units for heating water are usually mounted on the roof of a house. Water pipes zigzag over a panel backed with a black, heat-absorbing plate and this is all encased in a glass-topped, insulated box to minimise heat loss. Different systems are available, with differing degrees of sophistication and insulation. The more you pay, the greater the efficiency of the system; try to calculate how long it will take to pay for itself in heating savings and which is the most financially viable choice for you.

Whichever type of panel you choose, the water that flows through

the pipes is not the actual water you will be using in the house, but is a closed system of water pipes that then flow through the house's hot-water cylinder, warming the water inside, just as the electric element of an immersion heater does. It is a good idea to retain an electric immersion heater as a back-up (you cannot switch the sun back on if you suddenly run out of hot water in the evening), but in most cases, it should be possible to heat all or most of your hot water in this way, even in winter.

Just as with solar power panels, these are a good option for providing hot water in outbuildings, such as a dairy, where it would be difficult or prohibitively expensive to link up with the main house's hot-water system.

The more panels you have, the more power you will generate. Try to calculate how much power you need and install the necessary area of solar panels to match it.

Alternative Energy Sources

Depending on where you live, you may have even more options for generating some or all of your own electricity from the wind or nearby water in a stream.

Commercial wind farms undoubtedly have a big impact on the countryside and divide people into those who appreciate their value in terms of energy conservation and others who see them as eyesores. On a domestic scale, though, if you live in a suitable situation, a single, fairly small wind turbine can make a big impact on your electricity bill.

Wind turbines are still quite new in domestic settings, and are more likely to be effective in rural areas, where there are not so many buildings to disrupt the wind. Use batteries to store energy created on a windy day.

In built-up areas, air turbulence around buildings makes turbines inefficient and they are rarely successful investments. But in a rural setting, where you have more space between buildings they can be a viable option. The wind turbine itself should be mounted around 9m (30ft) higher than any obstacle within 100m (100 yards).

Roof-top models with small wingspans can generate fairly small amounts of electricity, but stand-alone models, up to 15m (45ft)

Selling your power

In some cases you may find that you can generate more power than you actually need and can sell some of the excess back to the National Grid. This will help to speed up the payback time of your investment in the generating equipment. But to do this, you will also need to have installed 'grid synchronisation' equipment and made arrangements with your supplier. Make enquiries with your power supply company to find out whether this is feasible before you make any additional purchases.

across, mounted on masts or stands will be more effective. Just like solar panels, the energy generated on windy days can be stored in batteries for use when the wind has dropped.

The British Wind Energy Association keeps records of wind speeds around the country and this will help you to decide whether or not a wind turbine is likely to be a reliabel source of power where you live. It is vital to check with your local planning authority, too, to make sure that you will not contravene any restrictions. Planning permission will not be granted if you are too close to power lines, an airport or air strip, roads, railways or a listed building, or if any of several other factors apply to your proposal.

If it is feasible for your particular plot, it is a good idea to combine your solar panels and wind turbines into a 'dual-fuel' generating system. This will reduce the possibility of you finding yourself without power at any time. If the wind is not blowing, you can draw from the solar panels.

Energy from water

Few people are lucky enough to have a running stream passing through their property, but if you are one of the fortunate ones and your stream is sufficiently fast-flowing, you may be able to harness the power of the water with a water turbine. Just like an old-fashioned water wheel, the moving current makes the wheel spin and a generator attached to the wheel makes electricity as it turns.

You must obtain permission from the Environment Agency and, depending on the system you propose to use, you may also need an abstraction licence – some schemes require you to divert water from the main stream and use this 'bypass' as your energy plant.

Saving and Recycling Water

Conserving water is not just about cutting your water bill. The energy used to cleanse water for the mains supply is a huge drain on resources and climate changes mean that even the water itself is in short supply at times.

In a fruit and vegetable plot, there are many things you can do to minimise the amount of clean, household water you need to use. Chief among these is to collect as much rainwater as possible and save it for watering the plants.

Position water butts or large water tanks at as many rain downpipes as you can. Don't forget outbuildings and sheds with pitched roofs. You can also link several butts in a series

if you have room, as one water butt will fill up surpisingly quickly when it rains, and empty fast, too, when you start to use the water.

Make sure that tanks have a secure lid or are covered with strong wire mesh that is not easy to dislodge. This is essential to avoid the risk of children or animals falling in and drowning.

Using the stored water

Most water butts come with a tap for filling a watering can. Watering by hand in this way is ideal, as you also have chance to check your crops for ripeness or signs of disease as you go, but it may not be the most efficient use of your time, particularly at busy times of year. Rather than

Collected rainwater is perfect for watering plants: it is slightly warm and full of nutrients, rather than chemicals.

going back to using the outside tap at times like this, you can buy submersible water butt pumps. These run on electricity, so you will need a power source nearby, but you can attach your hosepipe to the pump and use it to water the beds with collected rainwater.

Underground tanks

If you are doing any major construction work or digging up old ground as part of setting up your plot, it may be worth considering installing a large, underground rainwater tank. This will enable you to store far more water than you could in a collection of water butts and the water can be pumped up to a tap for use.

GREY WATER

It is a more complicated system to install, but 'grey water' – that used for washing in basins, baths and showers – can also be treated and reused in the garden for watering your plants.

You can also collect water from dishwashing and clothes washing, although it is likely to require more treatment before it can be reused.

With some plumbing adjustments inside the house, these drains can be diverted into a tank, preferably a large underground tank, since you will collect a lot of water in this way. The water must be treated, usually with a combination of filters and biological cleansers, before use, so you must take expert advice before you embark upon a scheme of this type. You will also need power to drive the necessary pumps for moving water through the treatment process and pumping it to the surface for use.

BEING WATER-WISE

There are also ways inside the house to cut down on the amount of water you use every day.

Flushing the toilet accounts for around one third of the water used in most households. If you have old WCs with large tanks, each flush will be using far more water than is really needed. You can put water-saving devices inside the cistern to reduce the volume of water stored for each flush – even a housebrick will do the job. And try not to flush the toilet after each use unless you have to.

When the time comes to renew your toilet, look for one with a compact, slimline cistern and a dual-flush option, that allows you to choose between a half and full flush.

Washing and waste

Think about the water you are using while you wash. Turn off the tap while you brush your teeth or shampoo your hair in the shower, then turn it back on to rinse. Take showers rather than daily baths, although remember that a five-minute power shower can use as much water as a soak in the bath.

Fitting water-saving showerheads can help to reduce your usage and don't overfill basins and baths or leave them running unattended. If you run too much hot water, you will then need to add more cold water before you can use it.

Dripping taps are an obvious source of waste, so always fix drips promptly. If you need to replace a tap, consider a water-saving mixer tap instead. Even standard mixer taps are usually more economical, as they provide a balanced flow to the temperature you want, but some lever-operated taps offer a low-flow

Stopping leaks

A leaking underground pipe left unnoticed will waste many gallons of water. If you have a water meter, get to know your normal usage and keep an eye on the reading from time to time to make sure that it is not giving an unusually high reading that could indicate a leak.

Another way to check is to turn off all the water-using appliances in the house, take a meter reading, wait for an hour and then take another. The reading should be the same, unless water is seeping out through a damaged pipe.

Look out, too, for new boggy patches around your plot or garden or a drop in the pressure from taps. If you think you may have a leak, contact your water supply company, who will inspect the pipe with a camera to find the crack, if there is one. If the leak is within your property's boundary, fixing it is your responsibility and should be done as soon as possible.

A water-saving flush allows you to choose between a half and full flush, and uses less water than a conventional flushing system.

setting that you must override with a harder push to get a full jet of water.

Choosing appliances

Modern washing machines and dishwashers are far more economical in their water usage than they used to be, and the most efficient can wash an entire load in less water than you would use when washing by hand. The least efficient dishwashers are likely to use around twice as much water as hand washing a load of dishes.

Whatever machine you have, always wait until it is full before switching it on, to avoid wasting water on a part-load and then needing to use it again later on. If your machine has an economy setting, use it, and only buy appliances that are an appropriate size for your family's needs. Don't buy a family-sized dishwasher just for the few occasions when you have a houseful of visitors if, for most of the year, there are only two people living in your house.

Take showers, rather than baths, to use less water and fit aerating showerheads to be even more efficient.

WASTE WATER AND DRAINAGE

You can help to relieve the pressure on mains drainage systems by diverting your waste water or excess rainwater into soakaways or septic tanks and may be able to make yourself self-sufficient and cut off from the mains drains.

Many rural properties feed waste water into a septic tank, as it is not economical to run drainage pipes in remote areas. These are large tanks and also incorporate a wide area of drainage bed, so they are disruptive to install, but could be an option if you are digging up ground for another reason. Septic tanks need regular maintenance and emptying, so ensure that there is access for a lorry to get to the site where you are planning to put it.

Soakaways will dispose of rainwater run-off that cannot otherwise be stored in tanks or water butts. They are not used for dirty household water. You can make your own or buy kits of parts, these comprise a large, deep hole filled with rubble and other freely-draining material. The water in a downpipe is fed into the soakaway and gradually seeps into the surrounding soil, slowly enough not to flood it in heavy rain.

Over time, soakaways become clogged with debris and need to be cleared and replaced nearby or with fresh drainage material.

WATER AND ENERGY CONSERVATION • WATER

INDEX

Picture Credits

We would like to thank the following for the use of their pictures reproduced in this book:

Alamy
162 tl © David Page, r © Image Source, 169 br © Rachel Husband,180 © Chad Ehlers, 207 © Gary K Smith, 233 © Eric Warren, 248 © Justin Kase z06z

Alison Candlin 52, 113

GAP Photos
12 John Glover, 21, 29 t Clive Nichols, 34 br Jenny Lilly, 35 John Glover, 38 br Michael Howes, 45 Frederic Didillon, 61 tl Mark Winwood, tr Rice/Buckland, 63 t Juliette Wade, c Sarah Cuttle, b Fiona Lea, 98 tr Juliette Wade, c Michael Howes, 100 tr Tommy Tonsberg, c Jonathan Buckley, 104 c Friedrich Strauss, 111 tr Rice/Buckland, br Howard Rice, 114 bl Friedrich Strauss, 133 tr Mark Bolton

Garden Picture Library
60 Michael Howes (Ansell Howes Assoc), 112 cr Juliette H Wade (Espalier Media Ltd), 133 bl Photos Lamontagne, 135 cr Michael Howes (Ansell Howes Assoc), 208 Geoff Kidd

Getty
2-3 Roger Charity, 26 Alan Buckingham, 33 t Mike Harrington, 72 Alan Buckingham

iStockPhoto
4, 5, 6, 10-11, 18, 20 t, 22 tl, 24 t, 31, 33 b, 34 bl, 36, 37, 38 bl, 39, 42, 43, 44, 46-47, 49, 51, 53, 55, 56-57, 58, 68 t, 73, 74, 75 tl, 79, 81, 82, 83, 86 t, 87, 88 br, 89, 91, 92, 93, 101, 102, 103, 105, 110, 118, 119, 121, 122, 123, 124, 126, 128, 129, 131, 134, 136 l, 139 t (x3), 154, 155, 158, 159, 163, 164 r, 165 r, 167 tr, 168, 169 t, 170, 171, 172, 173, 174, 175, 176, 177, 178-179, 181, 182 b, 184 bl, 188 br, 189 b, 192, 196, 197, 199, 201, 202, 203, 230, 237

Shutterstock
5 b, tc, 7, 13, 14, 15, 19, 20 b, 28 tl, 30, 41, 48, 67, 108-109, 140-141, 142, 143, 145, 146, 147, 152-153, 161, 166, 167 bl, 182 t, 183, 185, 186, 187, 188 t, 190-191, 193 bl, 194 bl, 195, 209, 218, 238-239, 240, 241, 242, 243, 244, 244-245, 246, 247, 249, 250, 253, 254, 256

StockFood
5 bc, 132, 165 tl, 204-205, 206, 210, 214, 215, 217, 219 tr, 221 t, 223, 225, 228, 234, 235, 236

Louise Turpin 29 b, 40, 200

Decorative chapter opener and running head artworks by Louise Turpin.

Front cover Clockwise from top left: Getty/Foodcollection, Getty/Lee Avison, Getty/FhF Greenmedia, Getty/Matt Armendariz, Getty/Rachel Weil, Getty/Frank Greenaway, Getty/Dorling Kindersley. Centre: iStockPhoto
Spine iStockPhoto
Back cover (all Getty) l Chris Whitehead, r Judd Pilossof, b Roger Charity
Back cover flap Alison Candlin

All other photographs and illustrations are the copyright of Quarto and Quantum Publishing. While every effort has been made to credit contributors, the publisher would like to apologise should there have been any omissions or errors – and would be pleased to make the appropriate correction for future editions of the book.

Some of the material used in this book originally appeared in *Practical Self Sufficiency*, and *Perfect Preserves*, published by Quarto Publishing plc and Quintet Publishing Ltd.

Author and editor Alison Candlin
Art Editor Louise Turpin